Knowledge Management Dynamics in a Transformative Environment

Edited by Muhammad Mohiuddin,
Elahe Hosseini, Mohammad Osman Gani
and Slimane Ed-Dafali

Published in London, United Kingdom

Knowledge Management Dynamics in a Transformative Environment
http://dx.doi.org/10.5772/intechopen.1005548
Edited by Muhammad Mohiuddin, Elahe Hosseini, Mohammad Osman Gani and Slimane Ed-Dafali

Contributors
Albena Vutsova, Biao Zhao, Denver Naidoo, Fei Song, Foziah Gazzawe, Gour C. Saha, Ikechi Agbugba, Jiangmeng Li, Lelethu Mdoda, Martina Arabadzhieva, Mohammad Ghaffari Feyzabadi, Mukesh Singh, Mzuyanda Christian, Samane Sadeghian, Sarika Singh, Weiqiang Jin

First published in London, United Kingdom, 2026 by IntechOpen
IntechOpen is the global imprint of INTECHOPEN LIMITED, registered in England and Wales, registration number: 11086078, 167-169 Great Portland Street, London, W1W 5PF, United Kingdom

For EU product safety concerns: IN TECH d.o.o., Prolaz Marije Krucifikse Kozulić 3, 51000 Rijeka, Croatia, info@intechopen.com or visit our website at intechopen.com.

British Library Cataloguing-in-Publication Data
A catalogue record for this book is available from the British Library

Knowledge Management Dynamics in a Transformative Environment
Edited by Muhammad Mohiuddin, Elahe Hosseini, Mohammad Osman Gani and Slimane Ed-Dafali
p. cm.
Print ISBN 978-1-83634-494-0
Online ISBN 978-1-83634-493-3
eBook (PDF) ISBN 978-1-83634-495-7

Meet the editors

Dr. Muhammad Mohiuddin is an Associate Professor of International Business at Laval University, Quebec, Canada. He has taught at Thompson Rivers University, Canada; University of Paris-Est, France; Osnabrück University of Applied Science, Germany; and Shanghai Institute of Technology and Tianjin University of Technology, China. He has published research in *Research Policy, Applied Economics, Review of Economic Philosophy, Strategic Change, International Journal of Logistics Research and Applications, Sustainability, Journal of Environmental Management, Journal of Global Information Management, Journal of Cleaner Production, M@N@GEMENT*, and more. He is a member of the board of directors of the Canadian Council on Small Business and Entrepreneurship (CCSBE). He is also the co-managing editor of Transnational Corporations Review.

Elahe Hosseini received her Ph.D. in organizational behavior and human resource management at Yazd University. She is a lecturer at Yazd University and Shiraz University in Iran. Her research interests include employee voice, human resource management, and social and entrepreneurial activities that foster entrepreneurship in developing countries. She has also published in several international journals and has participated in conferences in several countries. Her doctoral thesis examines the employee voice in knowledge-based companies in Iran. She serves as an editor or an editorial board member for several distinguished journals, including the *Iranian Journal of Management Studies* and the *International Journal of Management and Enterprise Development*. She also serves as a reviewer for a series of distinguished international journals, including *Sustainability Journal, Journal of Transnational Corporations Review*, and *Sage Open*.

Mohammad Osman Gani is a postdoctoral fellow at the University of British Columbia, Okanagan, Canada. He has completed his Ph.D. and MSc from Hiroshima University, Japan. His research interests are leadership, e-commerce, digital marketing, supply chain management, and tourism. He has published several journal articles in different peer-reviewed international journals. He has published several books, book chapters, and case studies on emerging fields in management, marketing, and technology.

Dr. Slimane Ed-Dafali is an Associate Professor of Management (HDR) at the National School of Commerce and Management (ENCG) at Chouaib Doukkali University, Morocco, where he conducts teaching and research. His current research is focused on entrepreneurial finance, innovation, knowledge management strategy, family business, and corporate governance. He has contributed to different research projects with various scholars and universities. He has conducted applied research for institutional associations, including the Moroccan Private Equity Association (AMIC). He is also a member of the International Academic Association of Governance (AAIG) and the Family Business Center. Dr. Ed-Dafali also serves as a referee for several international journals.

Contents

Preface

This Edited Volume is a collection of reviewed and relevant research chapters on developments in the field of knowledge management. The book includes scholarly contributions from various authors and is edited by a group of experts in Information and Knowledge Engineering. Each contribution comes as a separate chapter complete in itself but directly related to the book's topics and objectives.

The book includes the following chapters:

1. Integrating Ontology in Information Science and AI: Evolution, Applications, and Future Directions

2. Perspective Chapter: Cross-Level Unbiased Prior Knowledge-Guided Deep Representation Learning

3. Leveraging Mobile Applications to Boost Smallholder Farmers' Productivity in the Eastern Cape, South Africa: Effects on Sustainable Food Security

4. Unlocking Collective Wisdom: The Power of Knowledge Sharing in Modern Organizations

5. Cross-Domain Knowledge Transfer in Large Models: Transforming Knowledge Management Dynamics

6. Knowledge Sharing: Theoretical Lenses and Practical Implications

7. Environmental Challenges in SMEs through KM Prism

The target audience comprises scholars and specialists in the field.

IntechOpen

Chapter 1

Integrating Ontology in Information Science and AI: Evolution, Applications, and Future Directions

Foziah Gazzawe

Abstract

Ontology is often interchanged with metaphysics and is the study of existence. Ontology has evolved and is used in many industries, including artificial intelligence (AI); however, there is inadequate information on how it is applicable in information science. The goal of this paper is to explore ontology and show how it is applied in information science and its integration with AI. The methodology for this paper is qualitative methods, using a systematic review of documents from online databases. The researcher assessed a total of 160 documents, and after the removal of duplicates and irrelevant sources, only 19 were found to meet the requirements through a systematic review. They show an overview of ontology, how it has been used in information science and AI, its development, advantages, and disadvantages. The results show how technology, particularly AI, has influenced ontology adoption in information science. In the future, more experts are needed to ensure that computers process human commands without being destructive, highlighting the importance of ontology in creating intelligent, context-aware AI systems.

Keywords: ontology, ontology integration, ontology in information science, ontological modeling, ontological knowledge representation

1. Introduction

Ontology has revolutionized information science, and we must credit all the philosophers who helped develop this field. This paper aims to understand ontology in information science, from the beginning to how it is applicable in information science today. It will focus on the different areas in which ontology applies to information science, with examples. Furthermore, it will describe the pros and cons of ontology in information science and how it is applied to understand different concepts. Again, it will evaluate how different forms of ontology is applicable and how they are implemented. A different form of ontology expressions will be discussed to conclude the paper.

2. Research gap and problem

Most of the literature has looked at ontology in general use and fails to show how it is directly associated with information science. Also, the advancement in Artificial intelligence and machine learning that uses big data and metadata could have a challenge to how the ontology is implemented, and the literature provides little information on how this could be solved in order to have informed decision-making. For instance, knowledge-based systems need to give accurate output based on shared heuristics, as advancements are being made for more intelligent systems. Trends in research in information science are changing every day due to technological influence. Search engines based on keywords are unable to retrieve information through semantic matching. As a result, users apply a lot of effort and need to have background knowledge in interpreting the information. Therefore, these problems can be solved by the semantic web, which uses OWL and RDF.

3. Literature review

3.1 Emergence of ontology

Ontology is concerned with what is existence and how we categorize things. One school of thought holds that all things in the universe are intrinsically linked. However, many think there are distinct types of physical objects worldwide. The **Figure 1** will present the conceptual framework of the main components of ontology. It can be studied as the groundwork for learning how people see and investigate the environment. Gideon Harvey, one of the earliest authors to coin the term "Ontology," developed philosophical principles in 1663 [1]. A later classification by Christian Wolf placed ontology as a branch of metaphysics. But Martin Heidegger's idea of

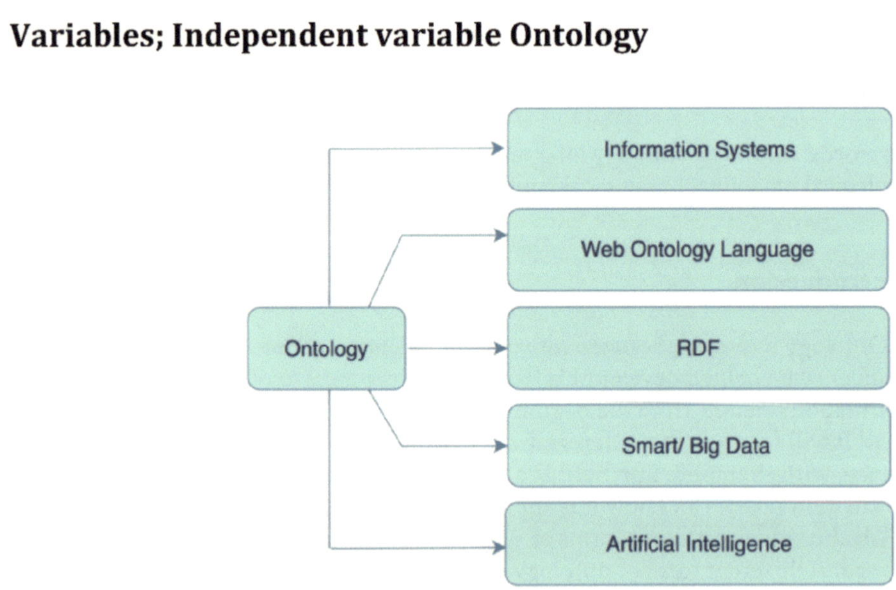

Figure 1.
Main components of ontology.

ontological difference ultimately shaped the field. By asking thoughtful questions, Socrates helped his audience understand they knew relatively little about the topics under discussion. According to Plato, there is a sharp divide between the ideal and material worlds. Most things, he saw, were vulnerable to the passage of time and rotted or expired. In the perfect world, concepts, and classes were organized, while entities and instances were filed away separately.

Aristotle believed that metaphysics was the original philosophy and classified various aspects of the natural world into distinct groups. He referred to logic as a toolkit for the scientific method. He was interested in learning more about communication. The major categories he had developed allowed him to differentiate between individuals based on their substance, amount, activity, or affection [2]. It eventually became the norm for highly advanced technology. Porphyry of Tyros (234–305 AD) intended to further what Aristotle had accomplished and attempted to simplify portions of his writing so that novices could understand it. Genes, species, differences, property, or accidents were the primary classifications [3].

3.2 Ontology development

There are numerous reasons why ontologies are developed, these include sharing of common knowledge of information structure among software agents or people; enabling domain knowledge reuse; making domain assumptions explicit; separation of operation knowledge from domain knowledge; and domain knowledge analysis [4].

Ontology was established to answer questions regarding what exactly exists in the world and whether or not it is real. The philosophers developed their own unique theories and conceptions to better understand the world around them. The reason is that philosophers attempt to comprehend the fundamental nature of everything in the universe [5]. The development of ontology led to an increase in the amount of study that was done, as well as made philosophers more open-minded about the fact that there is more than one method to examine how things exist. Ontology is a term utilized in the scientific community to define the nature of things and the methodology behind determining what is real. Ontology was developed to frame things in basic logic to ensure that all individuals understand. Our knowledge influences any intelligence projects as humans regarding the meaning and how to link them to answer specific questions or make decisions. If we key in the right data to the computer, it processes what we want in the semantic web. The idea came from connecting documents from the web. The resource description framework presents inputs in subject, predicate, and object. It uses identifiers to add more information to different items and is the core of linked open data. When exporting data as RDF, the identifiers remain constant when an individual wants to translate into another language [6]. Once the identifiers are merged, it is easy to connect information with other databases. Information in different places is published in different formats and is linked to finding more information about a specific subject.

Web ontology language is based on RDF and is the standard for ontology development. The main components in the language are the classes, properties, individuals, or restrictions. It helps to break down the components and establish their relationships. The OWL model must include all the data about different projects and any restrictions [7]. Including key information in the model is important to ensure that the system recognizes and prioritizes it. For instance, if all the stakeholders are included, and the budget for the project is 3 million, then it will be easier to prioritize as the system will recognize that the budget is high. If a double entry or similar leader is doing different roles, the language must be modified to ensure that it recognizes that the entry was not an error [4].

When OWL and RDF are integrated, they create smart data. The computer understands the data and can identify any errors in multiple documents [8]. When a company needs to investigate a specific issue and go through many documents, the two models can be used to make the process easier and faster as the computer can recognize the commands. The system recognizes what the user wants and needs and analyzes all data sources to identify the gaps that could help solve a problem. Information science has benefited from the two models as they allow data from different sources to be linked and provide the appropriate information influencing decision-making [4].

3.3 Ontology application areas

Ontology applies in research, education, and sociology. In sociology, it helps to understand the current social facts and investigate if more are yet to be discovered. It analyzes whether ideas are social constructs or objective reality. As sociology aims to understand society, ontology helps to evaluate the nature, dynamics, and characteristics of different social groups [9]. In education, it describes how students' education and exposure influence their worldview. Students need to understand that they shape their world, and it affects how they see the world. They need to get education on different facts based on alternative ontology. In place of having complex arguments, they need to understand that there is no right way to view the world and use it as a learning opportunity [10]. In research, it helps to ensure that researchers are certain of the nature of the different issues that they are investigating. It helps define the truth claims about the reality of a specific issue. It makes it easier for the researcher to decide the validity of their claims [11]. It also guides how they deal with conflicting ideas about the existence of things in the world.

3.4 Information science and ontology

The first thing ontology studies in information science are how distinct ontologies are generated. It investigates the proper means of portraying reality. It studies the validity of ontologies and how they may be utilized to develop ontologies for information systems. Ontology is used to understand how to develop concepts and how they are interrelated. In artificial intelligence, ontology implies that ideas that exist can be represented. It also ensures that all meanings are defined, understood, can be interpreted accurately, and can be shared [12]. Information science has many data sets that are related and interconnected, and it influences the quality and their corresponding data.

Ontology studies the various ways in which they can be represented in computer science. By utilizing concepts like classes, relations, and characteristics as an example. Classes can have relationships with one another and can have subclasses that share that relationship [13]. A further component of ontology is the individuals or instances that compose it. They are the fundamental building blocks of ontology and can be either real or hypothetical. Information systems illustrate how theoretical concepts are grounded in concrete occurrences and qualities [14]. Thus, with the aid of logic, information systems permit individuals to represent knowledge. It provides direction on how to infer implicit knowledge from different ontology types and domains, illuminating the interconnections between data sets in the information sciences [15].

3.5 Advantages of using ontology in IT

Using ontology helps to identify patterns, make predictions, and generate insights that would otherwise be difficult without it [15]. It is also effective in making sense of large quantities of data when searching for accurate information on relationships between different classes or objects. Ontology ensures that we use specific models to find information that will help us understand the domain [16]. Domain sharing is faster and better, allowing software applications to work together without crashing. It guides the appropriate data strategies that will be used in looking for information about different theories. Using ontology increases the opportunities for accessing quality data used in entity analysis [17]. Information systems can use, reuse and replicate the information they get from the data collected. It applies to many industries, including healthcare, finance, education, and automotive. There is easier collection of data and accuracy in the data collected, and there is a greater speed in accessing data in the information system.

3.6 Disadvantages of using ontology in IT

Applying ontology in information technology and system can be challenging since it requires users to maintain a line of reasoning. The information systems can be difficult to alter since the data used could be more flexible. A complex information system may make it challenging for researchers to make sense of their data if they are working with a large amount of it [18]. If individuals who understand ontology use it for malicious reasons, it could be used to commit crimes or create conflict in different industries. Ontology also requires knowledge and skills to navigate and ensure that the computers have the right information to give the best results.

3.7 Methods of relationships for various concepts

It is useful to simplify the ideas so anyone may grasp them. Models of knowledge in various forms are captured by ontology. Then, people from different backgrounds will use the models to find answers to some really deep questions about the world. Classes and relations are the two primary building blocks of any ontology [19]. Classes stand in for concrete ideas, whereas connections reveal how those classes are related to one another. In information science, algorithms simplify connections and provide consumers with easier access to relevant data [20]. In ontology, one can find one-of-a-kind connections that emerge from incorporating material concepts into either the internal or external spheres. It is crucial to identify their constituent classes and determine whether or not they may function as standalone elements. It shows philosophers what they can build upon in terms of the metaphysical parts and how they come together. What theories are useful for deducing the interdependencies between classes, relationships can also be affected by this.

3.8 Different types and forms of ontology

Information science has many data sets, and ontology makes it easier to understand the data and allows them to be understood by people. It helps to understand the relation of components that form the data sets. Once we understand the data sets, we can understand the relationships between different subjects in different locations. Companies that adopt big data depend on ontology to ensure they have systems they understand or can act upon. It helps to categorize data based on its source and size while providing storage for complex relationships in the most efficient ways possible.

It has become necessary in artificial intelligence to identify relationships among different entities. The goal is to design a data structure that allows interpretation and understanding of machine learning. It also provides a powerful analysis of data mining, predictive analytics, and other machine-learning techniques. Ontology in information science enhances how we automate data for decision-making and reasoning with limited human interaction [21]. It is applicable in software development and provides a standardized way of organizing and classifying data. It allows them to understand their data and make sense of it easily.

Top-level ontology is general across all domain authorities as they represent general concepts. Aristotle came up with the Tree of Knowledge, where he tried to distinguish several categories within the world. Time, space, and events are independent of a specific domain. John Sowa came up with K.R. Ontology, where classes were organized in a lattice. All classes in the structure are interconnected and have a top and bottom element. According to Albert North Whitehead, it has about 27 concepts that come from process philosophy.

Domain ontology is focused on specific domains and defines fundamental concepts from generic domains [22]. The terms defined in the top-level ontology are further specified, such as the specific subject types. Task ontology describes fundamental concepts based on the tasks, such as the lifecycle of anything. It is a further subdivision of top-level and domain ontology. Application ontology is an integration of task and domain technology fit together. They are focused on a specific task and are a specialization of task and domain technology. Information science uses these concepts to automate how domains are grouped, and they help to present the required information.

Ontology could also be categorized based on the level of semantic expressivity. It begins with controlled vocabulary and ends with complex logic, such as disjunctiveness or inversiveness. It mostly applies to philosophy as they try to understand the world's reality. Controlled vocabulary lists terms that can be used to describe other things. The next level is the glossary, where scientists informally describe terms with natural language help. The next level is thesauri, describing terms based on synonyms and homonyms. It is followed by taxonomy, where there is a hierarchal taxonomy. It is mostly implemented in science and healthcare, which helps to understand the facts about the different classes in the hierarchy. Finally, it is integrated with technology and helps define the data sets that form information systems [23].

4. Methodology

This research used a systematic review of previous journals from online sources. The focus was on information regarding ontology as a whole then narrowing down to ontology in information science. The researcher used several online repositories of journals such as ResearchGate, Elsevier, Wiley, and Sage. A more detailed illustration of the search strategy is shown below (**Figure 2**).

The selection criteria were also based on articles published within 10 years, that is, not later than 2013 (2013–2023). Further, sorting was done to analyze documents that were written in English and those that allowed full access to the whole content. We searched the online database using the following keywords: Ontology development, ontologies in information sciences, ontology in information systems, ontologies

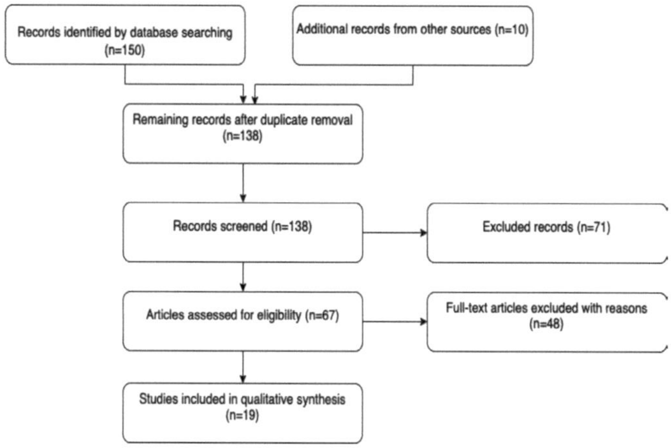

Figure 2.
Summary of the research strategy used.

and information systems, and ontologies information system development. There were no restrictions on the positioning of the noun phrases and keywords. Duplicate documents were eliminated the remaining documents were assessed for relevance by reading the abstract and conclusion. However, in some cases where the information in the abstract and the conclusion were insufficient, we examined the whole document to obtain relevant information regarding the topic. Out of the 67 relevant studies, 19 studies were found to be eligible to be included in the systematic review. The entire content of all the 19 articles was perused through to identify relevant content. By doing so, gaps were identified to guide our study and future recommendations.

5. Results and findings

The outcomes demonstrate that philosophers have employed ontology in their quest to make sense of the world. It is been refined and implemented in numerous fields, including academia, training, and social science. However, research shows that it has been successfully adopted in the field of information science. Different languages demonstrate how people can communicate their needs to computers in a way that can be understood and implemented to yield optimal results in a variety of fields. Computers are now able to process large amounts of data and provide accurate results, improving the efficiency of many fields, including law enforcement and medicine.

Finding the connections between the various ideas has been made easier as a result of its application. Today, businesses can use big data to classify information and make educated decisions based on a variety of ontologies. There are systems that process the data in order to give the correct findings, and the visuals help to show the relationships or establish the gaps in the data. To get a better grasp on existence, we need to embrace technology so that we can be certain that we have the best possible systems to assist us in going beyond what we can see and what we already know. It is possible that this will be the next best thing that will revolutionize a variety of industries and provide solutions to some of the world's most complex problems.

There are several methodologies used in the development of information systems. These methodologies include Rapid Application Development, Waterfall

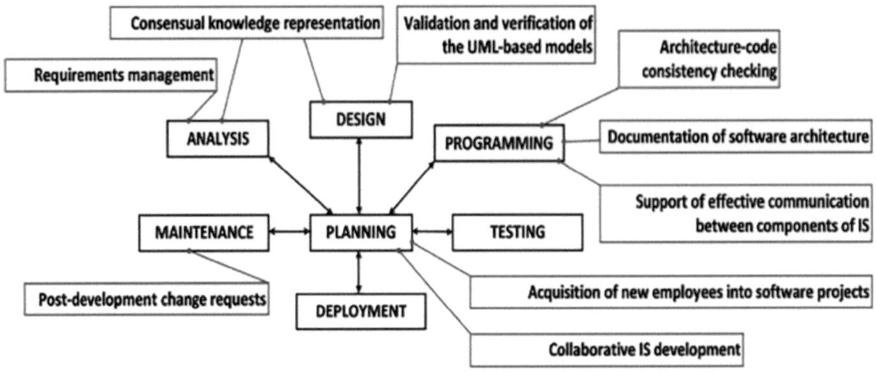

Figure 3.
The contribution of ontology in SDLC.

method, Agile methodology, and Rational Unified Process. However, the Systems Development Life Cycle is the most used methodology for the development of information systems. It is from the phases of this methodology that other methodologies were developed. The phases of SDLC to which ontologies can be beneficial include analysis, design, programming, testing, deployment, and maintenance. The **Figure 3** summarizes the contribution of ontologies to various stages of the Systems Development Life Cycle.

6. Conclusion and future recommendation

In conclusion, ontology has allowed individuals to share their knowledge with computers and process data that helps make more effective decisions. This concept has been built from the philosophical domain of explaining the existence of things and how they relate to each other. This document has widely explained the development of ontology and how it has been widely applied in information science, for instance, the sharing of domains and the reuse of information-by-information systems in making informed decisions. However, ontology also has disadvantages when it comes to metadata and complexity in information systems. There is still a wider gap that needs to be explored in the future for this field to be well understood and effective in solving problems. Individuals need to fully understand and expand their knowledge in implementing ontology due to technological diversity and robustness.

Author details

Foziah Gazzawe
College of Computer Science and Information Systems, Umm Al-Qura University, Makkah, Saudi Arabia

*Address all correspondence to: fhgazzawe@uqu.edu.sa

References

[1] Qanwal S, Haq N, Karim S. Ontology of self: AThematic analysis of Coelho's philosophical style in the alchemist. Pakistan Journal of Social Sciences. 2022;**42**(2):507-522

[2] Anderson RL. Transcendental idealism as formal idealism. European Journal of Philosophy. 2022;**3**(3):899-923

[3] Datta S. Aristotelian essence and it's critical approach. Journal of Indian Council of Philosophical Research. 2020;**37**(3):451-470

[4] Husáková M, Bureš V. Formal ontologies in information systems development: A systematic review. Information. 2020;**11**(2):66. DOI: 10.3390/info11020066

[5] Zyphur MJ, Pierides DC. Statistics and probability have always been value-laden: An historical ontology of quantitative research methods. Journal of Business Ethics. 2020;**167**(1):1-18

[6] Van Assche D, Delva T, Haesendonck G, Heyvaert P, De Meester B, Dimou A. Declarative RDF graph generation from heterogeneous (semi-) structured data: A systematic literature review. Journal of Web Semantics. 2022;**75**:100753

[7] El Idrissi B, Baïna S, Mamouny A, Elmaallam M. RDF/OWL storage and management in relational database management systems: A comparative study. Journal of King Saud University, Computer and Information Sciences. 2021;**34**(9):7604-7620

[8] Liao CH, Wu YF, King GH. Research on learning owl ontology from relational database. Journal of Physics: Conference Series. 2019;**1176**(2):022031

[9] Rotolo M. Culture beneath discourse: An ontology of cognitive cultural entities. American Journal of Cultural Sociology. 2021

[10] Stancin K, Poscic P, Jaksic D. Ontologies in education—State of the art. Education and Information Technologies. 2020;**25**(6):5301-5320

[11] Jusoh S, Awajan A, Obeid N. The use of ontology in clinical information extraction. Journal of Physics: Conference Series. 2020, May;**1529**(5):052083

[12] Chu SC, Xue X, Pan JS, Wu X. Optimizing ontology alignment in vector space. Journal of Internet Technology. 2020;**21**(1):15-22

[13] Nasution MKM. Ontology. Journal of Physics: Conference Series. 2018;**1116**(2):022030

[14] Farooqi N, Gawich M, Khozium MO. An automated approach for medical ontology maintenance system. Life Science Journal. 2020;**17**(11):23-31

[15] Thị Anh Lê P, Phước Cường N. Ontology based semantic information search. Journal of Science, Educational Science. 2015;**60**(7A):21-29. DOI: 10.18173/2354-1075.2015-0049

[16] Tianxing M, Zhukova N, Vodyaho A, Aung TT. A meta-mining ontology framework for data processing. International Journal of Embedded and Real-Time Communication Systems (IJERTCS). 2021;**12**(2):37-56

[17] Norris E, Hastings J, Marques MM, Mutlu ANF, Zink S, Michie S. Why and how to engage expert stakeholders in ontology development: Insights from

social and behavioural sciences. Journal of Biomedical Semantics. 2021;**12**(1):1-8

[18] Ahmad IS, Bakar AA, Yaakub MR. A review of feature selection in sentiment analysis using information gain and domain specific ontology. International Journal of Advanced Computer Research. 2019;**9**(44):283-292

[19] Chen L, Lu D, Zhu M, Muzammal M, Samuel OW, Huang G, et al. OMDP: An ontology-based model for diagnosis and treatment of diabetes patients in remote healthcare systems. International Journal of Distributed Sensor Networks. 2019;**15**(5):1550147719847112

[20] Kersloot MG, van Putten FJ, Abu-Hanna A, Cornet R, Arts DL. Natural language processing algorithms for mapping clinical text fragments onto ontology concepts: A systematic review and recommendations for future studies. Journal of Biomedical Semantics. 2020;**11**(1):1-21

[21] Leshcheva I, Begler A. A method of semi-automated ontology population from multiple semi-structured data sources. Journal of Information Science. 2022;**48**(2):223-236

[22] Lubani M, Noah SAM, Mahmud R. Ontology population: Approaches and design aspects. Journal of Information Science. 2019;**45**(4):502-515

[23] Poole W. Seventeenth-century 'double writing'schemes, and a 1676 letter in the phonetic script and real character of John Wilkins. Notes and Records: The Royal Society Journal of the History of Science. 2018;**72**(1):7-23

Chapter 2

Perspective Chapter: Cross-Level Unbiased Prior Knowledge-Guided Deep Representation Learning

Jiangmeng Li and Fei Song

Abstract

The great success of deep representation learning largely depends on the large amount of data available for model training. However, labeling data that satisfies the assumption of independent and identical distribution brings unaffordable workloads, resulting in the connectionism-based data-driven learning paradigm encountering a development bottleneck. The essential reason is that the traditional deep representation learning paradigm aims to enable the model to perform supervised training on a specific data domain, so the model can only obtain the domain-biased discriminative information, and the insufficient supervised data directly incurs the model not to obtain sufficient discriminative information. To remedy such a deficiency, researchers focus on introducing unbiased prior knowledge to guide the training of deep representation learning models, to improve the model's unbiased discriminative representation ability, thereby enhancing the performance of deep learning models on discriminative tasks.

Keywords: unbiased prior knowledge, representation learning, self-supervised learning, knowledge graph, causality

1. Introduction

With the increasing development of machine computing performance, deep learning methods based on connectionism have attracted the attention of more and more researchers. This method aims to establish a deep artificial neural network model by simulating the neural network system of the human brain, learning from the data, and ultimately completing the corresponding prediction task. After training with the large amounts of data, such deep learning models are able to match or exceed human capabilities on specific tasks. In view of the powerful data fitting capabilities, deep representation learning has developed from research focusing on basic theory to general technology research for tasks related to daily life and industry. Such methods can solve many practical problems with high quality, but there are still many challenges. As Moore's Law gradually becomes inapplicable to the development of today's machine computing speed [1], the development of data-driven deep representation learning paradigm has encountered a bottleneck, since although the research on neural network architecture search has left a significant mark in the development history of deep representation learning, such as ResNet [2], SENet [3] and other neural network architectures [4, 5], it is difficult for researchers in this classic research direction to efficiently explore the network architectures that significantly improve model performance.

Therefore, deep representation learning researchers began to explore how to improve the performance of the model under the premise of limited computing performance. A very intuitive idea is to input large-scale annotation data into the model to enhance the model's capabilities [6]. But there is a key problem with this approach: In some specific scenarios in the real world, the workload of labeling these large-scale training data is very huge. Particularly for some specific annotation tasks, such as satellite radar target detection, fine-grained classification of biological images, and medical image processing, the annotation can only be completed by experts with rich experience. When the annotated training data is insufficient, deep representation learning models are often prone to over-fitting problems; that is, the trained model only has good performance on the training dataset, but performs weakly on the test dataset. In addition, deep representation learning methods also require that training data and test data satisfy the premise assumption of independent and identical distribution. However, due to the complexity of real-world scenarios, biases in the data collection process, and the fact that training data and test data come from different data sources, the phenomenon of data covariate shift will occur. For example, training and test data collected for the same object may come from cameras at different angles or from different background environments. This covariate shift in data directly leads to the problem of insufficient generalization of deep representation learning models. Therefore, using large-scale annotated datasets to train deep representation learning models cannot enable the model to generalize to obtain excellent performance on various heterogeneous datasets. The essential reason behind this phenomenon is that the traditional deep representation learning paradigm requires supervised training of the model on a specific data domain, so that the model can obtain biased discriminative information about the data domain. When the supervision data is sparse, the model cannot obtain sufficient discriminative information. In addition, the deep representation learning model based on this training paradigm has a natural problem of weak generalization.

To solve the above problems, researchers focus on using unbiased prior knowledge to guide the training of deep representation learning models, thereby improving the model's unbiased discriminative representation capabilities, thereby enhancing the discriminability and generalization of deep learning models on downstream tasks. The unbiased prior knowledge-guided deep representation learning paradigm aims to utilize human unbiased prior knowledge to guide the deep representation learning model to efficiently mine useful information from data during training. The unbiasedness of knowledge specifically refers to the fact that this type of knowledge does not depend on a single data domain (such as a specific dataset) and should be universal in multiple or even all data domains. The *a priori* nature of knowledge refers to the existence before this type of knowledge is empirical induction on a single specific data domain. In the field of representation learning, prior knowledge represents the external knowledge available to the model before it is trained on a specific dataset. Therefore, compared with the traditional data-driven deep representation learning algorithms, using prior knowledge to guide the training of deep representation learning models can effectively alleviate the model's over-reliance on machine computing power and large amounts of data annotation information, and weaken training data and test data. The impact of issues such as covariate offset on model performance makes the trained model have better generalization and discriminability. Due to the high abstraction and versatility of unbiased prior knowledge, it can often consistently and efficiently improve the ability of deep representation learning models to mine discriminative information from data. Even under the conditions of limited machine computing performance and training data volume, this learning paradigm can still effectively improve the generalization and discriminability of the model on downstream tasks.

According to the order of the representation learning process, deep representation learning guided by unbiased prior knowledge can be divided into three levels: task-level, feature-level, and interpretability-level. Specifically, deep representation learning guided by task-level unbiased prior knowledge focuses on using human unbiased prior knowledge as task hypotheses to construct the auxiliary learning tasks, thereby guiding the deep representation learning model to obtain discriminative information from the data. In the field of representation learning, this learning method is called self-supervised representation learning. This representation learning method aims to learn effective feature representations from unlabeled data by designing appropriate self-supervised tasks, for example, contrastive learning [7–9]. The most intuitive way to implement deep representation learning guided by unbiased prior knowledge at the feature-level is to obtain the corresponding knowledge features from the human knowledge base and guide the model for training. A representative research is to obtain features from the knowledge graph composed of unbiased prior knowledge and then assist the model to obtain discriminative information from the training data, for example, the knowledge graph-based methods [10–12]. The research content within the interpretability-level is relatively extensive, mainly re-examining deep representation learning methods from a theoretical perspective, finding an interpretable theoretical basis that supports the effectiveness of the method, and optimizing and improving representation learning methods under its guidance. It is worth noting that these theoretical frameworks are composed of human unbiased prior knowledge, such as the causality theory [13].

This chapter takes deep representation learning guided by unbiased prior knowledge as the research topic. This learning paradigm aims to rationally utilize unbiased prior knowledge during the training process to guide the deep representation learning model to mine discriminative information from the limited data, thereby improving the model's predictive performance on downstream tasks. Although research in this field has achieved a series of results, there are still some challenges that need to be overcome. For example, there are the challenges of low sample efficiency within the task-level, the challenge of the lack of knowledge introduction roadmap within the feature-level, and the challenge of insufficient guidance of representation learning theory within the interpretability-level. Focusing on the above challenges, we have conducted in-depth research on deep representation learning algorithms guided by unbiased prior knowledge. In general, deep representation learning guided by unbiased prior knowledge can effectively learn a high-quality representation that is discriminative, generalizable, and robust, and this representation has great potential for practical applications in the real world. Therefore, the research topic of deep representation learning algorithms guided by unbiased prior knowledge has important research significance and practical value.

2. Related work

The goal of deep representation learning guided by unbiased prior knowledge is to use rich human unbiased prior knowledge to promote the deep representation learning model to obtain discriminative, generalized, and robust features under the conditions of limited training data and machine computing performance, thereby enhancing the model's prediction on downstream tasks. Deep representation learning guided by unbiased prior knowledge can be divided into three levels: task-level, feature-level, and interpretability-level. The similarity between them is that they all introduce unbiased prior knowledge as guidance in the training process. The difference is that the periods and approaches of introducing the unbiased prior knowledge in the representation learning process are different. This chapter explores representative research on deep representation learning guided by unbiased prior knowledge at different levels and has made important progress in solving problems in the corresponding fields. In the following, we conduct research on deep representation learning guided by unbiased prior knowledge from three representative research directions: self-supervised representation learning within the task-level, representation learning based on knowledge graphs within the feature-level, and representation learning guided by theory within the interpretability-level.

2.1 Self-supervised representation learning within the task-level

Self-supervised representation learning methods have achieved remarkable success in the field of representation learning without manual annotation. This type of method helps deep representation learning models to obtain discriminative information from unlabeled data by constructing auxiliary self-supervised tasks based on unbiased prior knowledge as task hypotheses. Generally, self-supervised representation learning methods focus on promoting the model to learn crucial information from the data through discriminant-oriented self-supervised tasks constructed based on unbiased prior knowledge. For example, for classification tasks, features obtained from data of the same category should also be clustered in the hidden layer space. Contrastive learning, as the outstanding discriminative self-supervised representation learning method, achieves state-of-the-art performance on a variety of downstream tasks [14–22]. Concretely, Deep InfoMax [23] aims to enhance representation learning by maximizing mutual information between the input and output of the encoder. CPC [24] adopts noise contrastive estimation [25] as a contrastive loss function to train models, achieving this objective through the use of Kullback-Leibler divergence [26] to maximize mutual information across multiple views. CMC [7] and AMDIM [27] focus on applying contrastive learning to multi-view datasets. SimCLR [8] and MoCo [9, 28] improve contrastive learning by leveraging large batches or memory banks, increasing the diversity of negative sample features to boost model performance. To sample informative negative samples, DebiasedCL [29] and HardCL [30] design sampling strategies by using unlabeled positive sample learning methods [31, 32]. Inspired by previous work [33], the researchers provided a theoretical framework based on information theory for discriminative self-supervised representation learning [34], and proposed a method based on the information bottleneck theory to improve the performance of contrastive learning. However, these methods rely on a large number of negative samples to learn valuable feature representations, thereby avoiding training collapse. SimSiam [35] and BYOL [36] propose non-negative sample comparative learning by using Siamese networks and stop-gradient, and this method can effectively avoid the model degradation problem during the training process. SSL-HSIC [37] provides a unified framework for contrastive learning methods without negative examples based on the Hilbert-Schmidt independence criterion [38]. In the evaluation of downstream tasks, discriminative self-supervised representation learning methods based on contrastive learning have achieved consistent and impressive results.

2.2 Representation learning based on knowledge graphs within the feature-level

The knowledge graph is a knowledge data structure constructed by an inductive understanding of unbiased prior knowledge. Therefore, the knowledge graph can be regarded as a database of human knowledge. Relying on the features obtained from the information of the knowledge graph to enhance the performance of the deep representation learning model is the implementation roadmap of the representation learning method based on the knowledge graph within the feature-level. Knowledge graph is a new generation of knowledge base used to describe facts about real-world entities and their relationships. The emergence of knowledge graphs is inseparable from the development of the semantic web. According to the definition of triples in the semantic web [39], the knowledge graph is a set of RDF triples in the form (s, p, o), that is, (subject, predicate, object), where s and o are entities, and p is a predicate or relationship. When the entities of these triples are viewed as nodes and relationships as edges, a directed multi-relationship graph is formed. In recent years, knowledge graphs have attracted great attention from academia and industry. Knowledge graphs include general domain knowledge graphs, such as WordNet [40], YAGO [41], DBPedia [42], Freebase [43], WikiData [44], NELL [45], CN-dbpedia [46], ConceptNet [47], and domain-specific knowledge graphs, such as Open PHACTS [48], Watson [49], AMiner [50]. They have been widely used in many research fields, such as information retrieval, question answering, and recommendation systems [51]. In addition, many commercial knowledge graphs have also been developed as products, such as Google KG [52]. They can provide more efficient and powerful services to the company's products. Representative deep representation learning methods based on knowledge graphs include ConvE [53], ConvKB [54], CapsE [55], and KG-BERT [56]. These methods use neural networks to learn parameters such as weights and biases, organize the parameters into network layers with nonlinear activation functions, and identify potentially the important patterns from the input data in the knowledge graph.

2.3 Representation learning guided by theory within the interpretability-level

In the long-term process of human exploration of nature, researchers have summarized a lot of theoretical knowledge to explain observations of the physical world. The theoretical knowledge gradually precipitates into systematic theoretical frameworks, and these theoretical frameworks often have strong generalization and robustness. The representation learning method under the introduction of theory within the interpretability-level aims to use the theoretical framework formed by humans to guide the training process of deep representation learning. In recent years, the exploration of deep representation learning methods under the guidance of causal inference theory has made important achievements. Causal inference [13, 57] has been widely used in various fields such as statistics, economics, and computer science. In the field of computer vision, causal inference leverages the deconfounding methods [58, 59] and counterfactual inference methods [13, 57] to eliminate the pseudo correlation between various variables in representation learning, thereby improving the performance of the model on downstream tasks, since eliminating confounding factors improves the estimates of the true causal effects between variables. CaaM [60] introduces the causal attention module into unsupervised methods, thereby learning causal features. CIRL [61] builds a structural causal model to formalize the domain generation problem and separate causal factors and non-causal factors in the input data, thereby learning domain-independent representations. D&R [62] introduces causal inference in the few-shot object detection task and builds the corresponding structural causal model, to understand the intrinsic paradigm behind the learning method of applying knowledge distillation. Under the guidance of structural causal models, deep representation learning methods can effectively improve the prediction of the model.

3. Task-level deep representation learning guided by unbiased prior knowledge

As the most representative research in deep representation learning guided by unbiased prior knowledge at the task-level, self-supervised representation learning has achieved remarkable success in the field of unsupervised representation learning. In the research on self-supervised representation learning, the unbiased nature of knowledge is reflected in the fact that the self-supervised tasks proposed by this learning method are based on human knowledge and are not limited to a specific data domain; the priori nature of knowledge is reflected in the fact that the knowledge of constructing self-supervised tasks exists *before* the empirical induction on a single specific data domain. Self-supervised representation learning methods have a wide range of uses in practical applications, and the key lies in how to design appropriate self-supervised representation learning objectives. In addition, judging from recent progress, unsupervised methods can achieve better performance than supervised methods by introducing self-supervised contrastive learning tasks [14, 23, 24, 27, 63]. This also proves the development potential and practical application value of self-supervised representation learning. Therefore, this chapter will focus on the low sample efficiency problem of self-supervised contrastive learning within the task-level, progressively study the causes of this problem, and then provide corresponding solutions.

3.1 Problem analysis

Contrastive learning methods have achieved empirical success in computer vision [64, 65]. Under the setting of self-supervised learning (SSL), recent researches demonstrate the superiority of contrastive methods [7, 23, 29, 30]. These methods extract features by comparing various representations of an image in a hidden space, for instance, images after the jitter process, the cropped images, and other random augmented images. In the conventional contrastive learning framework, two views of the *same* image are treated as a positive pair, while views from *different* images are treated as a negative pair. The contrastive loss [24, 25] encourages the model to bring positive pairs closer and separate negative pairs in the feature space.

However, this learning paradigm suffers from the need for a large number of pairs to contrast, for example, large batch size or memory bank size, because many pairs are not informative to the model; that is, in hidden space, positive pairs are already very close, while negative pairs are far apart, contributing little to optimization. Contrastive learning methods require a large number of pairs to acquire informative pairs, and thus, the advanced data augmentations [8, 27] are imposed, for example, jittering, random cropping, color channel separation, and so on. The large memory banks [7, 9] are also crucial for improving performance on downstream tasks. Recent works in contrastive learning largely depend on carefully selecting informative negative pairs [29, 30], supported by the sufficient informative positive pairs. However, when the number of pairs is limited, contrastive loss can lead to feature collapse [36, 66], where the model outputs identical features for all images.

To address this issue, we propose an efficient self-supervised contrastive approach designed to learn both discriminative and anti-collapsing features under constraints such as small batch sizes and lightweight neural networks. While prior work has focused on aggressive *data* augmentations, the informativeness of features derived from such augmented data is challenging to quantify, as deep neural networks generate features in a mapping-agnostic manner. Instead, our method directly incorporates augmentations at the *feature* level, demonstrating that well-designed feature augmentations can significantly enhance optimization.

3.2 Methodology

Our objective is to learn representations capturing the shared information across multiple views using self-supervised contrastive learning in an effectively and efficiently manner. Formally, we define the input multi-view dataset as $X = \{X_1, X_2, \ldots, X_N\}$, where N is the total number of samples. Each X_i is composed of M views of a given sample, with $i \in \{1, \ldots, N\}$. For each sample X_i, we represent x_i as a random variable corresponding to views sampled from the distribution $x_i \sim \mathcal{P}(X_i)$. Additionally, x_i^j refers to the j-th view of the i-th sample, where $j \in \{1, \ldots, M\}$.

3.2.1 The preliminary of contrastive learning

According to the basics of contrastive learning [7, 8], the core principle of contrastive learning is to learn embeddings that increase the similarity between views of the same sample while distinguishing views of different samples in the latent space. For a multi-view dataset X, pairs of views from the same sample $\left\{x_i^j, x_i^{j'}\right\}$, where $j, j' \in \{1, \ldots, M\}$, are defined as *positives*, while pairs from different samples $\left\{x_i^j, x_{i'}^{j'}\right\}$, where $i \neq i'$, are considered *negatives*.

To implement contrastive learning, each input x_i^j is passed through a view-specific encoder $f_{\theta_j}(\cdot)$ to generate a representation h_i^j. This representation is then transformed into a feature vector z_i^j using a projection head $g_{\vartheta_j}(\cdot)$, where θ_j and ϑ_j represent the parameters of the encoder and the projection head, respectively. To evaluate the similarity between features $\left\{z_i^j, z_{i'}^{j'}\right\}$, where $i \neq i'$, a discriminative function $d(\cdot)$ is used. Both the encoder $f_{\theta_j}(\cdot)$ and the projection head $g_{\vartheta_j}(\cdot)$ are optimized using a contrastive loss [24], which is expressed as:

$$\mathcal{L} = -\mathop{\mathbb{E}}_{X_S}\left[\log \frac{d(\{z^+\})}{d(\{z^+\}) + \sum_{k=1}^{K} d(\{z^-\}_k)}\right]. \tag{1}$$

Here, $X_S = \{\{z^+\}, \{z^-\}_1, \{z^-\}_2, \ldots, \{z^-\}_k\}$ represents a set of *pairs* randomly selected from X, consisting of one positive pair $\{z^+\}$ and K negative pairs $\{z^-\}_k$, where $k \in \{1, \ldots, K\}$. This setup is necessary because the contrastive loss function processes only *one* positive pair per iteration. During testing, the projection head $g_{\vartheta_j}(\cdot)$ is removed, and the representation h_i^j is directly utilized for downstream tasks.

3.2.2 Meta feature augmentation with regularization of margin injection

Recent contrastive learning methods often rely on complex data augmentations to enhance the informativeness of views. However, this unguided approach usually requires a large amount of training data, such as large batch sizes or memory banks, to be effective. To address this, we propose a meta feature augmentation (FeAug) method that generates informative augmented features by adjusting its network parameters based on the encoder's performance (*via* gradient feedback). An overview of the FeAug architecture is illustrated in **Figure 1**.

To achieve this, we introduce a group of Meta Augmentation Generators (MAGs), denoted as $a_\omega(\cdot) = \{a_{\omega_1}(\cdot), \dots, a_{\omega_M}(\cdot)\}$, corresponding to all M views, with $\omega = \{\omega_1, \dots, \omega_M\}$ as their parameters. For simplicity, we define f_θ and g_ϑ as the collections of view-specific encoders and projection heads, respectively, where $\theta = \{\theta_1, \dots, \theta_M\}$ and $\vartheta = \{\vartheta_1, \dots, \vartheta_M\}$. During training, the encoders $f_\theta(\cdot)$, projection heads $g_\vartheta(\cdot)$, and MAGs $a_\omega(\cdot)$ (parameterized by ω) are jointly optimized. Following the meta learning framework [67, 68], we first train $f_\theta(\cdot)$ and $g_\vartheta(\cdot)$ using self-supervised contrastive loss. Then, MAGs $a_\omega(\cdot)$ are updated by calculating their gradients based on the performance of $f_\theta(\cdot)$ and $g_\vartheta(\cdot)$. This performance is measured *via* the gradients of $f_\theta(\cdot)$ and

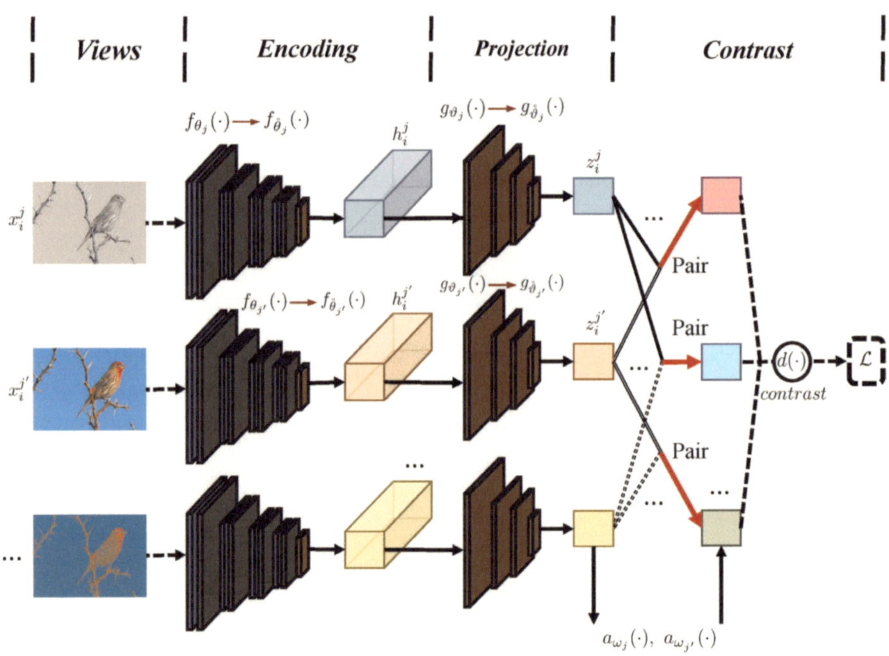

Figure 1.
The architecture of FeAug consists of two main components: the data encoding process and the meta feature augmentation process. During training, the process begins by fixing $a_{\omega_j}(\cdot)$ and $a_{\omega_{j'}}(\cdot)$, while optimizing $f_{\theta_j}(\cdot)$, $g_{\vartheta_j}(\cdot)$, $f_{\theta_{j'}}(\cdot)$, and $g_{\vartheta_{j'}}(\cdot)$ with the loss function $\mathcal{L}$. Subsequently, the encoders and projection heads are frozen, and $a_{\omega_j}(\cdot)$ and $a_{\omega_{j'}}(\cdot)$ are updated in a meta learning fashion. This iterative training cycle continues until the model converges.

$g_\vartheta(\cdot)$ when the contrastive loss is back-propagated. The encoders, projection heads, and MAGs are trained iteratively until convergence.

Specifically, the training process begins by updating the parameters θ and ϑ of the encoders and projection heads using the standard contrastive loss. Next, the parameters ω of the MAGs $a_\omega(\cdot)$ are updated using a meta learning strategy. This encourages the augmented features to contain more informative content, enabling the encoders $f_\theta(\cdot)$ to better leverage both the original and augmented features for contrastive tasks. As a result, the encoders' ability to extract discriminative information improves on the same training data. The meta updating objective for adjusting ω is formalized as follows:

$$\arg\min_{\omega} \mathcal{L}\left(\left\{g_{\mathring{\vartheta}}\left(f_{\mathring{\theta}}(\tilde{X})\right), a_\omega\left(g_{\mathring{\vartheta}}\left(f_{\mathring{\theta}}(\tilde{X})\right)\right)\right\}\right), \tag{2}$$

where $\tilde{X}$ represents a minibatch drawn from the training dataset X. The set $\left\{g_{\mathring{\vartheta}}\left(f_{\mathring{\theta}}(\tilde{X})\right), a_\omega\left(g_{\mathring{\vartheta}}\left(f_{\mathring{\theta}}(\tilde{X})\right)\right)\right\}$ includes both the original features and the augmented meta features. The parameters $\mathring{\theta}$ and $\mathring{\vartheta}$ correspond to the encoders and projection heads, respectively, and are updated through a single step of gradient back-propagation.

$$\mathring{\theta} = \theta - \ell \cdot \nabla_\theta \mathcal{L}\left(\left\{g_\vartheta\left(f_\theta(\tilde{X})\right), a_\omega\left(g_\vartheta\left(f_\theta(\tilde{X})\right)\right)\right\}\right). \tag{3}$$

The parameter $\mathring{\vartheta}$ is derived consistently, with ℓ serving as the shared learning rate for both θ and ϑ. The core idea of the meta-updating objective leverages the second-derivative technique [67–69] to train $a_\omega(\cdot)$. Specifically, the Hessian matrix, representing the second derivative of the combined parameter set $\{\theta, \vartheta\}$, is used to update ω. This update is computed by retaining the computational graph of $\{\theta, \vartheta\}$ and taking the derivative with respect to ω.

In practice, a significant challenge arises when the original features lack sufficient informativeness. This limitation makes it difficult to produce large gradients through contrastive learning with uninformative features. Consequently, the meta-augmented features (MAGs) generated by $a_\omega(\cdot)$ tend to collapse, resulting in augmented features that closely resemble the original ones. The root cause of this collapse is attributed to the small gradient changes in the encoder and projection heads, $g_\vartheta\left(f_\theta(\cdot)\right)$, which reduces the update step size for $a_\omega(\cdot)$. This, in turn, causes the optimization process of $a_\omega(\cdot)$ to stagnate in a local optimum, failing to produce the augmented features with additional useful information.

To address this issue, a margin is introduced to encourage $a_\omega(\cdot)$ to generate more diverse and informative augmented features. This margin acts as a regularization term in the meta-updating objective, pushing the augmented features beyond simple replication of the original features. Without this margin, MAGs are prone to generating collapsed features, as observed in practice. The approach to inject this margin into $a_\omega(\cdot)$ is formally defined as follows:

$$\begin{aligned} \sigma^+ &= \min\left[\min\left(\left\{d\left(\{z^+\}_{k^+}\right)\right\}\right), \max\left(\left\{d\left(\{z^-\}_{k^-}\right)\right\}\right)\right] \\ \sigma^- &= \max\left[\min\left(\left\{d\left(\{z^+\}_{k^+}\right)\right\}\right), \max\left(\left\{d\left(\{z^-\}_{k^-}\right)\right\}\right)\right] \end{aligned} \tag{4}$$

where $\left\{d\left(\{z^+\}_{k^+}\right)\right\}$ is a set of the outputs (similarities) of positives computed by the discriminating function $d(\cdot)$, and $k^+ \in \{1, \dots, K^+\}$ where K^+ represents the number of positives in a minibatch. $\left\{d\left(\{z^-\}_{k^-}\right)\right\}$ is a set of the discriminating outputs of negatives, and $k^- \in \{1, \ldots, K^-\}$ where K^- represents the number of negatives. Note that only original features are used in Eq. (4). We call the formulated margin generation approach as *"Large,"* and we also propose two more approaches, called *"Medium"* and *"Small."* The margins are injected between the original features and augmented features by adding regularization term in the meta updating objective, which can be formalized as:

$$\mathcal{R}_\sigma = \frac{1}{\hat{K}^+}\sum_{\hat{k}^+=1}^{\hat{K}^+}\left[d\left(\{\hat{z}^+\}_{\hat{k}^+}\right) - \sigma^+\right]_+ + \frac{1}{\hat{K}^-}\sum_{\hat{k}^-=1}^{\hat{K}^-}\left[\sigma^- - d(\{\hat{z}^-\}_{\hat{k}^-})\right]_+ \tag{5}$$

where $\{\hat{z}^+\}_{\hat{k}^+}$ represents a set of positive pairs, each consisting of one *original* feature and one *augmented* feature, with $\hat{K}^+$ denoting the total number of such positive pairs. Similarly, $\{\hat{z}^-\}_{\hat{k}^-}$ refers to a set of negatives, where each pair also includes one *original* feature and one *augmented* feature, with $\hat{K}^-$ being the total number of negative pairs. The function $[\cdot]_+$, defined as $[a]_+ = \max(a, 0)$, acts as a cut-off-at-zero operation.

This regularization is incorporated into the update rule for ω as follows:

$$\omega \leftarrow \omega - \ell' \cdot \nabla_\omega \mathcal{L}\left(\left\{g_{\mathring{\vartheta}}\left(f_{\mathring{\theta}}(\tilde{X})\right), a_\omega\left(g_{\mathring{\vartheta}}\left(f_{\mathring{\theta}}(\tilde{X})\right)\right)\right\}\right) + \alpha \cdot \mathcal{R}_\sigma \tag{6}$$

where ℓ' represents the learning rate for ω, and α is a hyperparameter controlling the influence of the margin-injected regularization term. The regularization term $\mathcal{R}_\sigma$ ensures that the meta-augmented features (MAGs) are more informative by encouraging them to differ significantly from the original features.

In practice, applying margin-injected regularization leads to more concentrated feature representations. For instance, features corresponding to the same image become more similar, while the gap between features of different images increases. This demonstrates that the generated augmented features not only avoid collapse but also help the encoders learn more diverse and non-collapsed feature representations.

3.2.3 Model objective

Concretely, we adopt margin-injected meta feature augmentation in the contrastive learning paradigm to achieve desired discriminative multi-view representations, and the proposed $\mathcal{L}$ is incorporated to replace the conventional contrastive loss $\mathcal{L}$. The formal definition of our proposed method is

$$\mathcal{L} = \mathcal{L}^{ori} + \delta \cdot \mathcal{L}^{aug} \tag{7}$$

where $\mathcal{L}^{ori}$ represents the loss *NOT* including the meta augmented features, and $\mathcal{L}^{aug}$ represents the loss including such features. Both $\mathcal{L}^{ori}$ and $\mathcal{L}^{aug}$ are derived by following the optimization-driven unified contrast principle [70]. δ is a coefficient that controls the balance between them. It is important to highlight that the margin-injected regularization term, $\mathcal{R}_\sigma$, is exclusively applied during the meta-training phase of the MAGs, that is, for $a_\omega(\cdot)$. During the standard training process of the encoders and projection heads, $\mathcal{R}_\sigma$ is not utilized. The purpose of $\mathcal{R}_\sigma$ is to ensure that the augmented features remain informative, enabling the encoder to learn discriminative and effective representations more efficiently.

3.3 Experimental exploration

We evaluate our FeAug on well-known datasets, including Tiny ImageNet [71], STL-10 [72], CIFAR10 [71], and CIFAR100 [71]. The benchmark methods for comparison include BiGAN [73], NAT [74], DIM [23], SwAV [14], SimCLR [8], CMC [7], MoCo [9], BYOL [36], Barlow Twins (BT) [66], DACL [20], LooC [21], DCL [29], and HardCL [30]. To ensure fair and efficient comparisons under the limited training inputs, we set a uniform batch size of 64. We use a backbone network comprising five convolutional layers from AlexNet [75] (referred to as "conv") and an additional two fully connected layers ("fc"). None of the backbone encoders are pre-trained, and we adopt identical data augmentation strategies and memory banks as used in CMC [7].

For evaluation, we conduct 20 independent trials, using the average performance over the last 20 epochs as the final result for each trial. Additionally, we report 95% confidence intervals for our results, while results without confidence intervals are drawn from published sources. Our comparisons include a fully-supervised baseline (similar to AlexNet [75]) and state-of-the-art unsupervised methods. **Table 1** presents the results across the four datasets, with the final two rows showing our method's performance. As shown in the table, FeAug outperforms all prior methods on these datasets. Furthermore, compared to the fully-supervised baseline trained end-to-end (without fine-tuning), FeAug demonstrates notable improvements in most downstream tasks, highlighting its effectiveness in modeling discriminative information, especially when supervision is limited (e.g., with small training datasets).

Model	STL-10		CIFAR10		CIFAR100		Tiny ImageNet	
	conv	fc	conv	fc	conv	fc	conv	fc
FS	**68.70**		**75.39**		**42.27**		**36.60**	
BiGAN	71.53	67.18	62.57	62.74	37.59	33.34	24.38	20.21
NAT	64.32	61.43	56.19	51.29	29.18	24.57	13.70	11.62
DIM	72.86	70.85	73.25	73.62	48.13	45.92	33.54	36.88
SwAV	70.32±0.4	71.40±0.3	68.32±0.2	65.20±0.3	44.37±0.3	40.85±0.3	39.56±0.2	38.87±0.3
SimCLR	75.57±0.3	77.15±0.3	80.58±0.2	80.07±0.2	50.03±0.2	49.82±0.3	36.24±0.2	39.83±0.1
CMC	83.03	85.06	81.31±0.2	83.28±0.2	58.13±0.2	56.72±0.3	41.58±0.1	40.11±0.2
MoCo	77.50±0.2	79.73±0.3	76.37±0.3	79.30±0.2	51.04±0.2	52.31±0.2	35.90±0.2	41.37±0.2
BYOL	81.73±0.3	81.57±0.2	77.18±0.2	80.01±0.2	53.64±0.2	53.78±0.2	41.59±0.2	41.90±0.1
BT	80.97±0.3	81.43±0.3	76.63±0.3	78.49±0.2	52.80±0.2	52.95±0.2	39.81±0.3	40.34±0.2
DACL	80.34±0.2	80.01±0.3	81.92±0.2	80.87±0.2	52.66±0.2	52.08±0.3	40.61±0.2	41.26±0.1
LooC	81.92±0.2	82.60±0.2	83.79±0.2	82.05±0.2	54.25±0.2	54.09±0.2	42.04±0.1	41.93±0.2
DCL	83.79±0.3	84.20±0.2	82.17±0.2	83.72±0.2	58.48±0.2	57.16±0.2	41.64±0.2	41.36±0.1
HardCL	83.16±0.3	85.15±0.2	83.04±0.2	86.22±0.2	58.97±0.3	59.13±0.2	42.89±0.2	42.01±0.2
FeAug	**85.41±0.3**	**85.62±0.2**	**87.87±0.2**	**88.12±0.2**	**59.97±0.3**	**61.06±0.2**	**44.51±0.2**	**45.36±0.2**

FS is the fully-supervised model.

Table 1.
Experiments with benchmark methods and the proposed FeAug. conv and fc are treated as backbones in the experiments. The bold entries represent the best-performing results for each dataset and model architecture.

While DACL and LooC aim to improve contrastive learning through *data* augmentation, FeAug takes a different approach by enhancing contrastive learning *via feature* augmentation. This approach is straightforward yet powerful, as contrastive learning operates directly on features, whereas image augmentations require an additional encoding step to translate into features. Our experimental results confirm that FeAug achieves superior performance on benchmark datasets, further validating its effectiveness.

4. Feature-level deep representation learning guided by unbiased prior knowledge

An intuitive method to achieve deep representation learning guided by unbiased prior knowledge within the feature-level is to obtain the corresponding knowledge features from the human knowledge base, and then use these features to guide the training of the deep representation learning model. Since the knowledge graph is a graph-structured knowledge base built using human knowledge, it can be used as a knowledge base of unbiased prior knowledge. Relying on features obtained from knowledge graphs to enhance the performance of deep representation learning models is the implementation roadmap of deep representation learning methods based on knowledge graphs at the feature-level. In the research on representation learning based on knowledge graphs, the unbiased nature of knowledge is reflected in the fact that the knowledge graphs are based on human knowledge and are universal in multiple or even all data domains; the priori nature of knowledge is reflected in the fact that the knowledge graph exists before model training and experience induction on a single specific data domain. This chapter introduces the deep representation learning method based on feature-level unbiased prior knowledge, obtains features from the general unbiased prior knowledge base, and guides the training of the deep representation learning model.

4.1 Problem analysis

Large-scale self-supervised vision-language pre-training approaches, such as CLIP [76] and ALIGN [77], have emerged as efficient alternatives to traditional supervised visual representation learning. These methods utilize modality-specific encoders to jointly learn image and text representations by aligning paired image-text data through contrastive loss during pre-training. Leveraging extensive datasets, these models acquire a wide range of visual concepts, resulting in representations that demonstrate strong generalization capabilities and adaptability to diverse downstream tasks.

The zero-shot generalization ability of vision-language models is highly dependent on the textual input format, as highlighted in Ref. [78]. Providing the text encoder with plain category labels (e.g., class names) often leads to suboptimal performance. To address this, recent studies have introduced prompt-based methods to enhance textual inputs [78–80]. During inference, classification weights—derived from textual label features—are generated by inputting prompts describing candidate categories into the text encoder. These label features are then compared with image features produced by the image encoder to perform classification.

However, using fixed prompt templates poses challenges, as their effectiveness varies across tasks. For instance, Zhou et al. [78] demonstrated that the prompt "a photo of a [Y]" achieves an accuracy of 60.86% on the Flowers102 dataset [81], while a more specific prompt "a flower photo of a [Y]" improves accuracy to 65.81%. Conversely, on the Caltech101 dataset [82], the simpler prompt "a [Y]" yields better accuracy (82.68%) compared to "a photo of [Y]" (80.81%). These findings illustrate that prompt performance is task-dependent and not universally optimal.

To overcome these limitations, recent research [11, 12, 78, 83, 84] has explored learning prompts from the limited labeled data, such as in few-shot scenarios. Typically, these methods optimize learnable prompts based on empirical risk, though the semantic significance of learned prompts and their mechanisms remain unclear. We hypothesize that explicitly incorporating the semantic information of text labels is crucial for enhancing pre-trained models, especially in few-shot contexts. Supporting this hypothesis, experimental comparisons reveal that both semantic prompts and extended semantic prompts improve CLIP's performance. However, the additional improvement achieved by longer prompts is limited, suggesting that performance gains are driven by the inclusion of meaningful semantic content rather than simply increasing prompt length.

4.2 Preliminaries

4.2.1 Vision-language pre-training

CLIP [76] presents a framework for learning semantic representations from a large volume of image-text pairs.

Architecture. CLIP comprises two encoders: an image encoder, implemented using ResNet [2] or ViT [85], and a text encoder, built using a Transformer [86]. The image encoder extracts high-dimensional visual features, while the text encoder processes word sequences into textual representations.

Training. Text inputs are tokenized using byte pair encoding [87], converted to 512-dimensional vectors, and processed by the text encoder. The input sequence length is capped at 77 tokens. Images are encoded into an embedding space by the image encoder. CLIP is trained on a massive dataset of 400 million image-text pairs, aligning the embedding spaces of the two modalities using contrastive loss [8]. This enables the model to generalize effectively to downstream tasks.

Inference. CLIP performs zero-shot image classification by evaluating the similarity between image features and label features generated by the text encoder. For a given image $\boldsymbol{x}$, the image encoder $f^I(\cdot)$ produces features $\boldsymbol{h}$, while the text encoder $f^T(\cdot)$ generates label features $\{\boldsymbol{l}_i\}_{i=1}^K$ from prompts $\{\boldsymbol{p}_i\}_{i=1}^K$, formatted as "a photo of a [Y]," where K is the number of categories and [Y] represents a class label. The prediction probability is calculated as:

$$\mathcal{P}(y = i|\boldsymbol{h}) = \frac{\exp\left(\frac{<\boldsymbol{l}_i, \boldsymbol{h}>}{\tau}\right)}{\sum_{j=1}^K \exp\left(\frac{<\boldsymbol{l}_j, \boldsymbol{h}>}{\tau}\right)}. \tag{8}$$

where y denotes the semantically correct category for $\boldsymbol{x}$, τ is a temperature parameter, and $\langle\cdot,\cdot\rangle$ denotes cosine similarity. Unlike conventional classifiers limited to closed-set concepts, CLIP's zero-shot paradigm enables classification across open-set categories by leveraging textual descriptions.

4.2.2 Graph representation learning

Graph definition: A graph $\mathbf{G} = (\boldsymbol{V}, \boldsymbol{E})$ comprises nodes $\boldsymbol{V}$ and edges $\boldsymbol{E}$. For a graph dataset $\mathcal{G} = \{\mathbf{G}_i | i \in [1, N^G]\}$, sampled from the distribution $\mathcal{P}(\mathcal{G})$, where N^G denotes the number of graphs in the dataset, the goal is to learn an encoder $f^G(\cdot) : \mathcal{G} \to \mathbb{R}^{d^G}$, where d^G is the dimensionality of the graph embedding space.

Graph neural networks (GNNs): GNNs are commonly used for graph representation learning. Each node $\boldsymbol{v} \in \boldsymbol{V}_i$ is encoded into a feature vector $\boldsymbol{H}_{\boldsymbol{v}}$. At the k-th layer, the representation is updated as:

$$\boldsymbol{H}_{\boldsymbol{v}}^{(k+1)} = COMBINE^{(k)}\left(\boldsymbol{H}_{\boldsymbol{v}}^{(k)}, AGG^{(k)}\left(\boldsymbol{H}_{\boldsymbol{u}}^{(k)}, \forall \boldsymbol{u} \in \mathcal{N}(\boldsymbol{v})\right)\right), \tag{9}$$

where $\mathcal{N}(\boldsymbol{v})$ represents the neighbors of $\boldsymbol{v}$, and AGG and COMBINE are learnable functions. After multiple layers, a readout function aggregates node features $\{\boldsymbol{H}_{\boldsymbol{v}} | \boldsymbol{v} \in \boldsymbol{V}_i\}$ into a graph-level representation $\boldsymbol{g}_i$:

$$\boldsymbol{g}_i = READOUT\ (\boldsymbol{H}_{\boldsymbol{v}}, \boldsymbol{v} \in \boldsymbol{V}_i). \tag{10}$$

4.3 Methodology

Based on the experimental results presented in **Figure 2**, we derive the following key assumption regarding the use of prompts in pre-trained vision-language models:

> Assumption 4.1 (Semantic information in prompts). Incorporating *label-relevant semantic content* into prompts enhances the performance of pre-trained vision-language models in zero-shot inference tasks.

Building upon Assumption 4.1, we introduce a novel method, termed CapKP, designed to effectively integrate label-relevant semantic information into prompts.

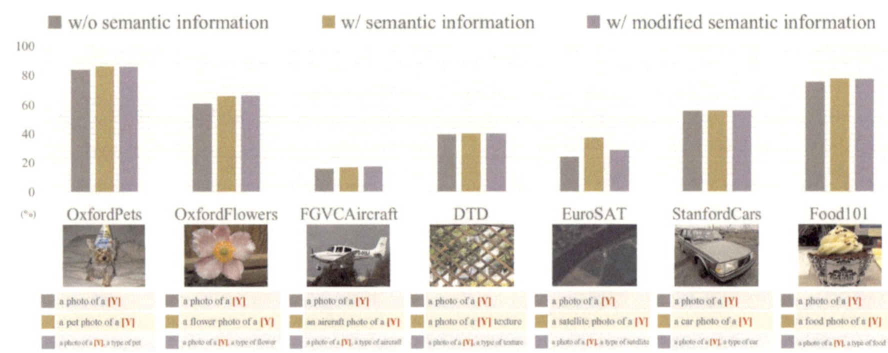

Figure 2.
Comparison of various prompt forms for CLIP is conducted through zero-shot inference experiments, with the results displayed in a histogram. The bars in gray represent prompts lacking semantic information, as used in the original CLIP. The brown bars indicate the prompts containing simple, coarse-grained semantic information, while the purple bars correspond to prompts that use more words to describe similar semantic content. The results show that prompts with semantic information and longer semantic prompts both enhance CLIP's performance. However, the improvement from longer semantic prompts over simpler semantic prompts is minimal, indicating that the performance boost stems from the inclusion of meaningful semantic information rather than merely increasing the number of words in the prompt.

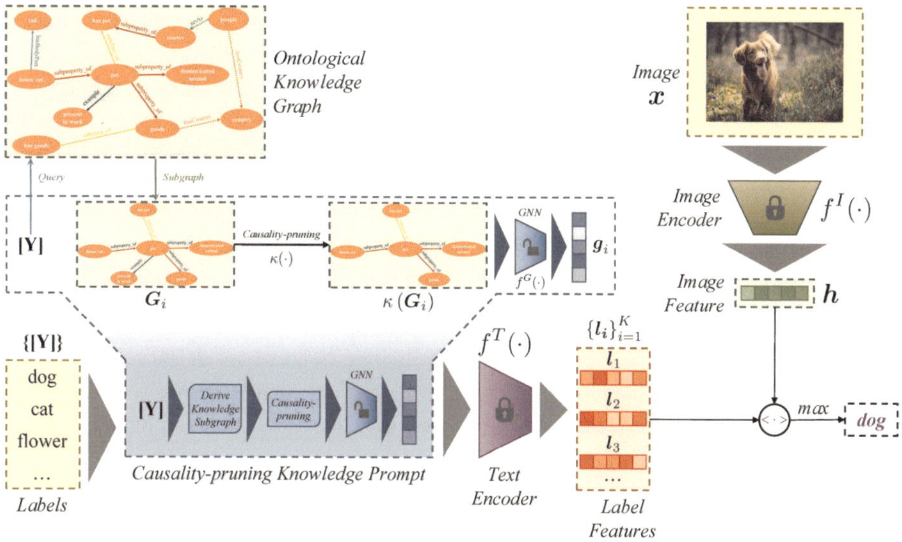

Figure 3.
The Causality-pruning Knowledge Prompt (CapKP) framework introduces a method for dynamically learning label-specific semantic prompts, moving away from the reliance on fixed prompt templates. This is achieved by incorporating refined knowledge derived from an external knowledge graph. The proposed CapKP method consists of two main components: (1) ontology-enhanced knowledge embedding, which employs the label token as a query to extract a label-relevant subgraph from an ontological knowledge graph; and (2) causality-pruned graph representation, which refines the representation by systematically removing edges and nodes deemed causally irrelevant, thereby improving the overall quality of the resulting graph structure.

The architecture of CapKP is depicted in **Figure 3**[1]. The CapKP framework is empowered by two core components: ontology-enhanced knowledge embedding and causality-pruned graph representation.

4.3.1 Learn prompts with sufficient knowledge

We replace the input of CLIP's text encoder, that is, the lower-cased byte pair encoding representation, with the learnable prompt, which is acquired by using the proposed CapKP.

Label-specific prompt. We generate the label-specific prompt set $\{\boldsymbol{p}_i\}_{i=1}^K$ by

$$\boldsymbol{p}_i = (\boldsymbol{\mu} + \lambda \cdot \varphi([\mathbf{Y}]_i)) \oplus b([\mathbf{Y}]_i), \tag{11}$$

where $\boldsymbol{\mu}$ represents a set of learnable feature vectors initialized randomly using Gaussian distributions. The function $\varphi(\cdot)$ corresponds to our proposed CapKP framework, and λ acts as a balancing coefficient to regulate the interaction between $\boldsymbol{\mu}$ and $\varphi(\cdot)$. The term $b([\mathbf{Y}]_i)$ refers to the lower-cased byte pair encoding (BPE) representation of the label $[\mathbf{Y}]_i$, while $\oplus$ denotes the concatenation operation. Importantly, the output of $\varphi(\cdot)$ produces a vector of the same dimensionality as $b([\mathbf{Y}]_i)$, such as 512 dimensions in the case of CLIP. After generating prompts $\{\boldsymbol{p}_i\}_{i=1}^K$, they are fed into

[1] We acknowledge the potential issue of notation reuse. Specifically, the "i" used in $\boldsymbol{G}_i$ and $\{\boldsymbol{l}_i\}_{i=1}^K$ represents two independent indexing variables, adopted here for simplicity.

the text encoder $f^T(\cdot)$, yielding classification weights $\{\boldsymbol{l}_i\}_{i=1}^K$. The prediction probability is then computed using Eq. (8).

Label-shared prompt. By analyzing the training data used for vision-language models, we observe that input texts often lack label-specific, discriminative semantic details. Instead, they frequently include semantic elements shared across multiple labels. For instance, in the descriptions "a [golden retriever] runs on the grass with its tail wagging" and "an [Alaskan] sits on a couch with a floppy tail," only generalized semantic information, such as "tail," is emphasized, while label-specific information is absent. This pattern is particularly prevalent in the context of fine-grained labels. Based on this observation, we propose the following extended assumption:

> Assumption 4.2 (Generalized semantic information in prompts). *Label-specific semantic information* may introduce redundancy for pre-trained vision-language models, whereas *generalized label-shared semantic information* plays a pivotal role in constructing effective prompts.

We thus propose a label-shared prompt form by

$$\boldsymbol{p}_i = \left(\boldsymbol{\mu} + \lambda \cdot \psi\left(\lfloor \left\{ \varphi\left([\mathbf{Y}]_j\right) \right\}_{j=1}^{K} \rceil \right)\right) \oplus b([\mathbf{Y}]_i), \tag{12}$$

where $\lfloor \cdot \rceil$ presents a cascade concatenation function, detailed by $\lfloor \left\{ \varphi\left([\mathbf{Y}]_j\right) \right\}_{j=1}^{K} \rceil = \varphi([\mathbf{Y}]_1) \oplus \varphi([\mathbf{Y}]_2) \oplus \ldots \oplus \varphi([\mathbf{Y}]_K)$, and $\psi(\cdot)$ presents a linear mapping function in CapKP.

4.3.2 Ontology-enhanced knowledge embedding

We propose to retrieve an ontological knowledge graph by treating an input label as the query and further capture the corresponding high-order knowledge representation through a GNN. Given an input label $[\mathbf{Y}]_i$, we start by locating the 1-hop label-relevant subgraph $\boldsymbol{G}_i$, which is performed by obtaining the knowledge graph entity with the largest semantic similarity to $[\mathbf{Y}]_i$ and retrieving all neighbor entities that are directly connected to it by an edge. We refine the extracted subgraph through causality-pruning, which eliminates redundant elements, and subsequently encode the pruned subgraph into a vector using the function $\varphi(\cdot)$ as defined in Eq. (11) and Eq. (12):

$$\varphi([\mathbf{Y}]_i) = \boldsymbol{g}_i = f^G(\kappa(\boldsymbol{G}_i)) \tag{13}$$

where $\kappa(\cdot)$ represents the proposed *causality-pruning* function, and $f^G(\cdot)$ is implemented using a graph neural network (GNN). To analyze the structural proximity among entities in the knowledge graph, we employ the aggregation function $AGG(\cdot)$ in the GNN, as suggested by [88]. Let $\boldsymbol{v}$ denote a node corresponding to a label-relevant entity, and $\boldsymbol{e}_{v,u}$ denote an edge representing a relation between entities $\boldsymbol{v}$ and $\boldsymbol{u}$. The aggregation function $\widehat{AGG}(\cdot)$ is defined as:

$$\widehat{AGG}(\boldsymbol{v}) = MLP\left(\boldsymbol{H}_v + \sum_{\boldsymbol{u} \in \tilde{\mathcal{N}}(\boldsymbol{v})} \frac{\exp\left(\left[\boldsymbol{H}_v, \boldsymbol{H}_{e_{v,u}}\right]\right)}{\sum_{\boldsymbol{u}' \in \tilde{\mathcal{N}}(\boldsymbol{v})} \exp\left(\left[\boldsymbol{H}_v, \boldsymbol{H}_{e_{v,u'}}\right]\right)} \boldsymbol{H}_u\right) \tag{14}$$

where *MLP* is a non-linear network, $\boldsymbol{H}$ represents the feature embedding of a node or an edge, $[\cdot,\cdot]$ denotes an inner-product operation, and $\tilde{\mathcal{N}}(\boldsymbol{v})$ is the set of neighboring nodes of $\boldsymbol{v}$ in the causality-pruned graph $\kappa(\boldsymbol{G}_i)$.

4.3.3 Causality-pruned graph representation

To formalize the concept behind causality-pruning, we redefine the notion of *Granger causality* [89] in the context of knowledge graphs:

> Definition 4.1 (Granger causality in knowledge graphs). Granger causality [89, 90] describes the causal relationship between variables where one variable influences another. In knowledge graphs, if variable χ, such as a specific *relation-type*, enables better prediction of another variable Υ (a higher score computed *via* a *graph rule*) when combined with all other available information Ω, as compared to predictions made without χ, we say that χ Granger-causes Υ [90].

Given a label-relevant subgraph $\boldsymbol{G}_i$ and a set of relation-types $\{\boldsymbol{r}_m\}_{m=1}^{N^R}$ from the retrieved ontological knowledge graph, our goal is to eliminate relation-types that are *decoupled* from predicting $\boldsymbol{G}_i$ based on Granger causality. To achieve this, we evaluate the individual causal effect of each relation-type $\boldsymbol{r}_m$ on the learned representation $\boldsymbol{l}_i$ of the knowledge subgraph $\boldsymbol{G}_i$, following the methodology of Refs. [91, 92].

Figure 4 illustrates the causality-pruned graph representation, where the *Graph Rule* is employed to quantitatively determine whether a specific relation-type satisfies Granger causality for predicting the graph. The graph rule indicates that the greater the change in loss before and after pruning, the higher the score of the candidate edge. Based on Definition 4.1 and the proposed *Graph Rule*, we quantify the causal contribution of a relation-type $\boldsymbol{r}_m$ to the output of the final text encoder $f^T(\cdot)$ by measuring its impact on reducing the joint model error, formulated as:

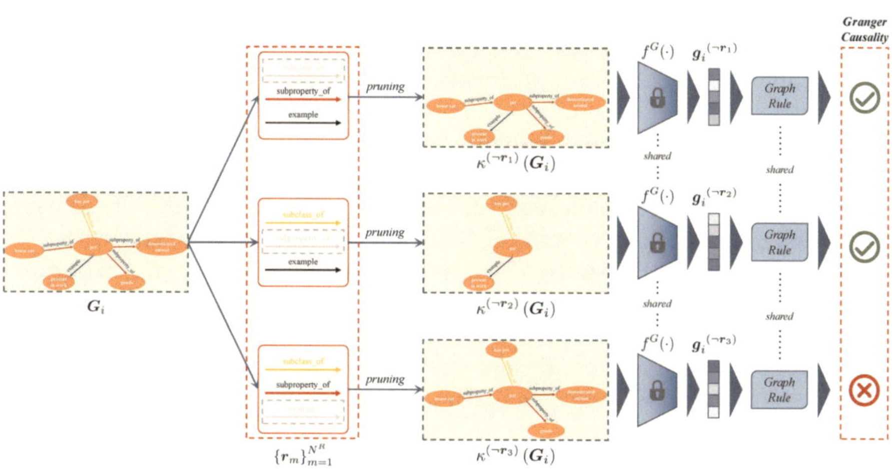

Figure 4.
An example of the rationale of causality-pruned graph representation. Following the first principle of Granger causality, we refine the derived knowledge subgraph $\boldsymbol{G}_i$ *by pruning the edges that are causally decoupled from the downstream task. We determine the Granger causality by iteratively removing the edges related to a relation-type* $\boldsymbol{r}_m$ *and then checking the oscillation of the result, which is computed by following a specific graph rule. Only causally related edges are kept and others are pruned. Note that the graph encoder* $f^G(\cdot)$ *is fixed throughout the process.*

$$\Delta_{\epsilon,r_m} = \epsilon_{\mathcal{K}^{(\neg r_m)}(G_i)} - \epsilon_{G_i} \tag{15}$$

where ϵ_{G_i} denotes the joint model error of the $f^G(\cdot)$ and $f^T(\cdot)$ when considering the computation graph, and $\epsilon_{\mathcal{K}^{(\neg r_m)}(G_i)}$ denotes the joint model error excluding the relation-type r_m. We determine the Granger causality between r_m and predicting the graph by

$$\begin{cases} r_m \quad \textit{Granger}-\textit{causes} \quad \Upsilon, & \Delta_{\epsilon,r_m} > 0 \\ r_m \quad \textit{NOT} \quad \textit{Granger}-\textit{causes} \quad \Upsilon, & \Delta_{\epsilon,r_m} \leq 0 \end{cases} \tag{16}$$

where Υ refers to the hypothesis that a specific relation-type contributes to the model's ability to predict the graph and enhances the textual representation $\boldsymbol{l}_i$, learned jointly by $f^G(\cdot)$ and $f^T(\cdot)$.

4.3.4 CapKP variants

The full version of our proposed approach is referred to as CapKP. To evaluate the impact of its individual components, we conduct an ablation study by removing the causality-pruning module, resulting in a variant called KP. Additionally, we investigate two types of prompts introduced in Section 4.3.1 and Section 4.3.1, where label-specific prompts and label-shared prompts are denoted as SPE and SHR, respectively.

4.4 Experimental exploration

Experiments are conducted on 11 publicly available image classification datasets: ImageNet [6], Caltech101 [82], StanfordCars [93], FGVC Aircraft [94], Flowers102 [81], OxfordPets [95], Food101 [96], SUN397 [97], UCF101 [98], DTD [99], and EuroSAT [100]. These datasets encompass a wide range of tasks, including general object classification, scene recognition, action recognition, fine-grained object categorization, texture classification, and satellite image recognition, providing a comprehensive evaluation benchmark.

Following the protocol of CLIP [76] and CoOp [78], we train our model on 1, 2, 4, 8, and 16 shots and evaluate its performance on the respective test sets. For each experimental setting, we report the average performance over three independent runs. Our approach is compared with two key baseline models: (1) CLIP [76], which employs manually designed prompts, using seven prompt templates as outlined in Ref. [76] for prompt ensembling; and (2) CoOp [78], which automatically generates prompts, where the optimal variants of CoOp are used for fair comparisons.

Experimental results across the 11 benchmark datasets are presented in **Figure 5**, with the top-left subfigure summarizing the average performance over three runs. CapKP consistently achieves superior results across various shot settings. As the number of shots increases, all evaluated methods exhibit improved performance, yet CapKP consistently outperforms the baseline methods.

5. Interpretability-level deep representation learning guided by unbiased prior knowledge

In the field of sciences, humans have summarized a lot of theoretical knowledge in the long process of exploring nature. The theoretical knowledge has been verified in

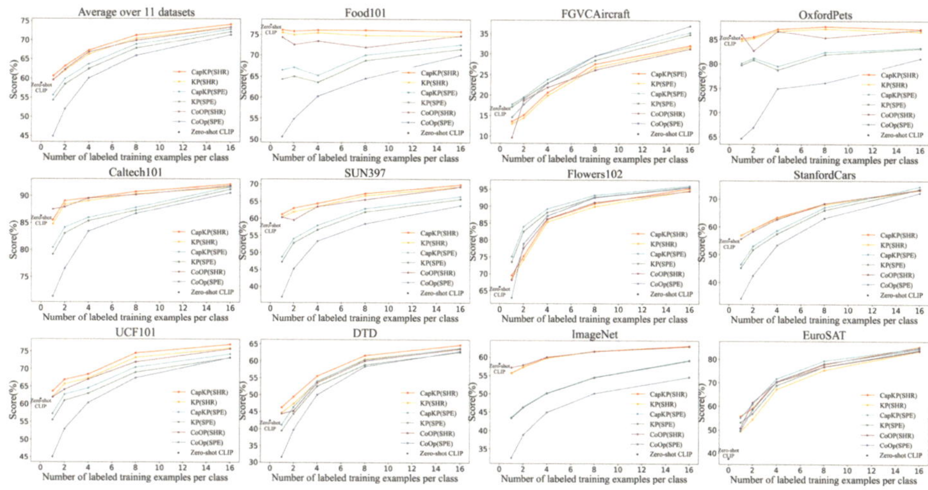

Figure 5.
Comparisons of few-shot learning on 11 datasets. CapKP consistently outperforms baselines within different shots.

practice and can explain the phenomena of the objective world observed by humans within a relatively broad theoretical boundary. With the gradual improvement of the theory, knowledge has accumulated into a systematic theoretical framework. These theoretical frameworks tend to be highly generalizable and robust. The deep representation learning under the guidance of interpretable-level theory studied in this chapter aims to use the theoretical framework formed by humans to guide the training process of deep representation learning. In representation learning research guided by theory, the unbiased nature of knowledge is reflected in the fact that the theoretical framework is based on human knowledge and is not limited to a specific data domain, such that the theoretical knowledge can be applied to a large number of data domains. The priori nature of knowledge is reflected in the fact that knowledge of these theoretical frameworks exists before empirical induction on a single specific data domain. In interpretable-level related research, a representative work is the deep representation learning method guided by the causal inference theory. In recent years, deep representation learning methods guided by causal inference theory have made important achievements in the fields of computer vision and natural language processing. Therefore, this chapter theoretically analyzes the current advanced deep representation learning methods from the perspective of causal inference, identifies the problems existing in these methods, and finally proposes corresponding improvements that can solve the raised problems. The above research findings will be elaborated below.

5.1 Problem formulation

5.1.1 The paradigm of contrastive learning

In this work, we focus on representation learning methods based on contrastive learning (CL). The primary objective of CL is to train a general-purpose feature extractor f, which maps samples from the original input space into a latent space, enabling the extraction of meaningful and intrinsic features.

Formally, we begin by randomly selecting a minibatch of training data, denoted as $X_{tr} = \{X_i\}_{i=1}^{N}$, where X_i represents the i-th sample, and N is the total number of samples in the minibatch. We perform stochastic data augmentation (e.g., random crop) to transform each sample X_i into two augmented views X_i^1 and X_i^2. Since there are N samples in X_{tr}, we finally obtain $2N$ augmented samples denoted as $X_{tr}^{aug} = \{X_i^1, X_i^2\}_{i=1}^{N}$. Then, we feed all training samples into the feature extractor f to get their feature representations, that is, $Z_i^j = f\left(X_i^j\right), i \in \{1, \dots, N\}, j \in \{1, 2\}$. The general objective of CL is formulated as:

$$L_{ct} = \sum_{i=1}^{N} \sum_{j=1}^{2} -\log \frac{\exp\left(\frac{\text{sim}\left(Z_i^j, Z_i^{3-j}\right)}{\tau}\right)}{\sum_{k=1,}^{N} \sum_{l=1, l \neq j}^{2} \exp\left(\frac{\text{sim}\left(Z_i^j, Z_k^l\right)}{\tau}\right)} \tag{17}$$

where τ represents the temperature hyper-parameter and $\text{sim}(u, v) = u^T v / \|u\| \|v\|$ denotes the dot product between l_2 normalized u and v (i.e., the cosine similarity). For a sample X_i^j randomly selected from the dataset X_{tr}^{aug}, CL regards it as the anchor, the pair $\left\{X_i^j, X_i^{3-j}\right\}$ as positive, the pairs $\left\{X_i^j, X_k^l\right\}_{k=1, k \neq i, l=1}^{k=N, l=2}$ as negatives. According to the defined objective (17), we compute the loss L_{ct} across all positive pairs.

5.1.2 Structural causal model

Minimizing the objective function (17) aims to bring the positive sample X_i^{3-j} closer to the anchor while pushing the negative samples X_k^l further away from the anchor. From this viewpoint, the anchor can be regarded as a label, implying that minimizing (17) is equivalent to predicting X_i^{3-j} as the label X_i^j. Accordingly, the structural causal model (SCM) implied in contrastive learning (CL) is depicted in **Figure 6**. In this SCM, nodes represent abstract data variables, and directed edges denote (functional) causal relationships, for example, the edge $X_i^{3-j} \rightarrow Y\left(X_i^{3-j}\right)$ signifies that X_i^{3-j} is the cause, and $Y\left(X_i^{3-j}\right)$ is the effect. In the following, we discuss the proposed SCM and the reasoning behind its construction in greater detail.

The causal link $X_i^{3-j} \rightarrow Y\left(X_i^{3-j}\right)$ indicates that X_i^{3-j} corresponds to its label $Y\left(X_i^{3-j}\right)$, where $Y\left(X_i^{3-j}\right)$ is defined as X_i^j, making the anchor equivalent to the label. Hence, $Y\left(X_i^{3-j}\right) = X_i^j$, assuming that X_i^{3-j} is similar to its anchor.

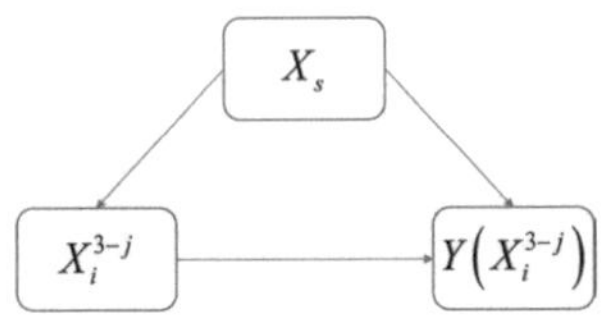

Figure 6.
The proposed SCM between semantic information X_s, positive sample X_i^{3-j}, and anchor (or label) $Y\left(X_i^{3-j}\right)$.

In the SCM, $X_i^{3-j} \leftarrow X_s \rightarrow Y\left(X_i^{3-j}\right)$, X_s represents semantic information and acts as the convolution kernel for the feature extractor f. The causal links $X_i^{3-j} \leftarrow X_s$ and $X_s \rightarrow Y\left(X_i^{3-j}\right)$ imply that the feature representations of X_i^{3-j} and $Y\left(X_i^{3-j}\right)$ in the latent space are extracted through f, where each feature channel corresponds to specific semantic information.

An effective contrastive learning model should capture the true causal relationship between X_i^{3-j} and $Y\left(X_i^{3-j}\right)$ and generalize well to unseen data. For instance, the label prediction $Y\left(X_i^{3-j}\right)$ should rely on foreground features rather than background information. However, in the proposed SCM, the increased likelihood of $Y\left(X_i^{3-j}\right)$ given X_i^{3-j} arises not only from the direct causal link $X_i^{3-j} \rightarrow Y\left(X_i^{3-j}\right)$ but also from the spurious path $X_s \rightarrow X_i^{3-j} \rightarrow Y\left(X_i^{3-j}\right)$. For example, background features in X_i^{3-j} might contribute useful context for anchor prediction. Therefore, to determine the true causal relationship between X_i^{3-j} and $Y\left(X_i^{3-j}\right)$, causal intervention $P\left(Y\left(X_i^{3-j}\right)|do\left(X_i^{3-j}\right)\right)$ must replace the observational distribution $P\left(Y\left(X_i^{3-j}\right)|X_i^{3-j}\right)$.

5.1.3 Performing the backdoor adjustment for causal intervention

To address the above issue, we first explain why feature extractors f trained by traditional contrastive learning approaches tend to capture background-dependent semantic features.

This issue arises partly due to the limited number of positive samples. As shown in objective 17, for a given anchor, only one positive sample exists, while there are $2N-2$ negative samples. Among these, some negative samples may be false negatives, sharing similar foreground information with the anchor. Due to the random sampling process, background similarity between false negatives and the anchor is typically lower than the foreground similarity. However, since positive pairs are derived from the same original image, their foreground and background are both similar. During optimization of 17, the shared foreground and background in positive pairs tend to jointly pull the positive sample closer to the anchor, especially when positive sample diversity is limited. Observations also reveal that false negatives with semantically equivalent information to the anchor [7] are pushed further away, reducing their foreground similarity but inadvertently amplifying the role of background similarity. Consequently, this process enhances the influence of background features, leading contrastive learning models to extract background-dependent semantics.

To mitigate this issue, we propose employing backdoor adjustment [13] to remove the interference from background-dependent semantics and achieve $P\left(Y\left(X_i^{3-j}\right)|do\left(X_i^{3-j}\right)\right)$.

Specifically, backdoor adjustment assumes the ability to observe and stratify the confounder. In the proposed SCM, the confounder is represented by X_s, which can be decomposed into distinct semantic features, denoted as $X_s = \left\{Z_s^i\right\}_{i=1}^n$, where each Z_s^i

represents a stratification of semantic features. Formally, the backdoor adjustment for the proposed SCM is expressed as:

$$P\left(Y\left(X_i^{3-j}\right)|do\left(X_i^{3-j}\right)\right) = \sum_{i=1}^{n} P\left(Y\left(X_i^{3-j}\right)|X_i^{3-j}, Z_s^i\right)P\left(Z_s^i\right) \tag{18}$$

where $P\left(Y\left(X_i^{3-j}\right)|do\left(X_i^{3-j}\right)\right)$ represents the true causality between $Y\left(X_i^{3-j}\right)$ and X_i^{3-j}.

5.2 Methodology

5.2.1 Introducing the semantic regularizer within meta learning

In this subsection, we detail the implementation of backdoor adjustment during the training process. As illustrated in Eq. (18), the first step involves defining the functional representations of Z_s^i.

Assume the output of the feature extractor f, denoted as Z_i^j, has dimensions $w \times h \times c$, where w and h represent the spatial width and height, and c indicates the number of feature channels. More specifically, Z_i^j can be expressed as $Z_i^j = \left[Z_{i,1}^j, \ldots, Z_{i,c}^j\right]$, where $Z_{i,r}^j \in \mathbb{R}^{w \times h}$ represents the feature map of the r-th channel, with $r \in \{1, \ldots, c\}$. For pre-trained CNN-based feature extractors, it is generally accepted that each channel encodes specific semantic information or visual concepts [101, 102]. However, a single channel may not be sufficient to fully capture a distinct visual concept. This challenge motivates us to define a weight vector for each semantic concept. Our approach assumes that each semantic concept corresponds to a subset of channels, where the weights for channels within the subset should be larger, while channels outside the subset receive smaller weights.

Let $a_t = [a_{1,t}, \ldots, a_{c,t}]^{\mathrm{T}}$ define the weight vector associated with a specific semantic concept. We then model the functional representations of Z_s^t as $Z_s^t = a_t$, with $P\left(Z_s^t\right) = \frac{1}{n}$, where n is the number of semantic concepts. Consequently, the functional implementation of $P\left(Y\left(X_i^{3-j}\right)|X_i^{3-j}, Z_s^t\right)$ is expressed as:

$$P\left(Y\left(X_i^{3-j}\right)|X_i^{3-j}, Z_s^t\right) = \frac{\exp\left(\frac{\mathrm{sim}\left(Z_i^j, a_t \odot Z_i^{3-j}\right)}{\tau}\right)}{\exp\left(\frac{\mathrm{sim}\left(Z_i^j, a_t \odot Z_i^{3-j}\right)}{\tau}\right) + \sum\limits_{\substack{k=1,\\ k\neq i}}^{N} \sum\limits_{\substack{l=1,\\ l\neq j}}^{2} \exp\left(\frac{\mathrm{sim}\left(Z_i^j, Z_k^l\right)}{\tau}\right)}, \tag{19}$$

where $a_t \odot Z_i^{3-j} = \left[a_{1,t} \cdot Z_{i,1}^{3-j}, \ldots, a_{c,t} \cdot Z_{i,c}^{3-j}\right]$. As a result, the overall backdoor adjustment is presented as:

$$P\left(Y\left(X_i^{3-j}\right)|do\left(X_i^{3-j}\right)\right) = \sum_{t=1}^{n} \frac{\exp\left(\frac{\text{sim}\left(Z_i^j, a_t \odot Z_i^{3-j}\right)}{\tau}\right) \times \frac{1}{n}}{\exp\left(\frac{\text{sim}\left(Z_i^j, a_t \odot Z_i^{3-j}\right)}{\tau}\right) + \sum_{k=1, k\neq i}^{N} \sum_{l=1, l\neq j}^{2} \exp\left(\frac{\text{sim}\left(Z_i^j, Z_k^l\right)}{\tau}\right)}. \tag{20}$$

The proposed meta semantic regularizer can be conceptualized as a learnable module f_{msr}, designed to produce a semantically relevant weight matrix A_s. This module is implemented using a convolutional neural network, where $A_s = [a_1, \ldots, a_n]$. Specifically, given an input sample X, we first apply a stochastic data augmentation module to generate two augmented samples, $\{X^1, X^2\}$. Subsequently, X is fed into the module f_{msr} to compute the weight matrix A_s, which is shared by both augmented samples $\{X^1, X^2\}$.

5.2.2 Model objectives

Here, we introduce the objective function for the proposed interventional contrastive learning framework with the meta semantic regularizer (MSR). The overall learning framework of MSR is depicted in **Figure 7**. MSR comprises three core components: the feature extractor f, the meta semantic regularizer f_{msr}, and the projective head f_{ph}. The meta semantic regularizer is jointly trained with the feature extractor in an iterative two-stage process during each epoch.

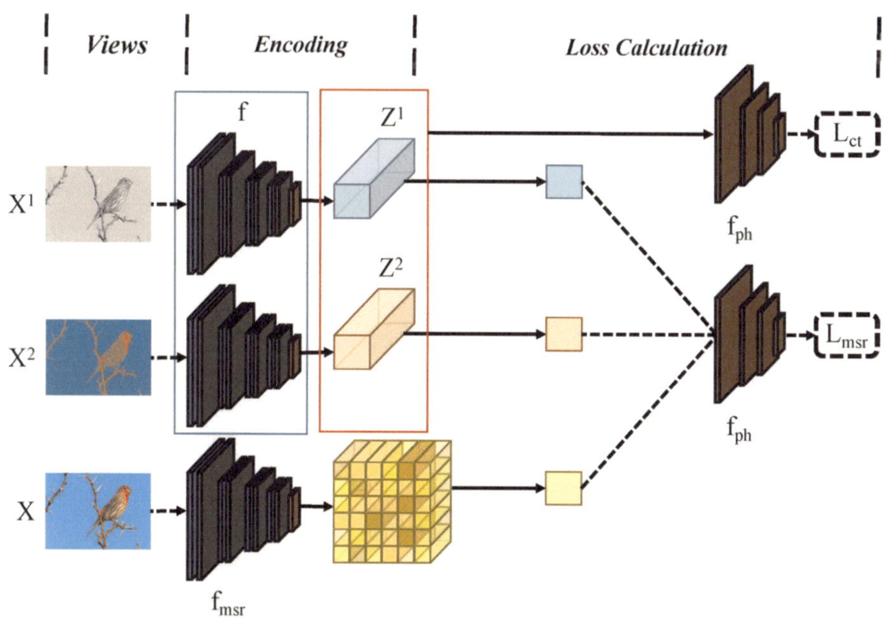

Figure 7.
The framework of the proposed MSR.

In the first stage, the feature extractor f and projective head f_{ph} are updated using the augmented training datasets X_{tr}^{aug} and the semantically relevant weight matrix A_s. In the second stage, the meta semantic regularizer f_{msr} is updated by computing gradients based on the contrastive loss. This alternating training process is repeated until the model converges.

During the first stage of each epoch, the parameters of f and f_{ph} are optimized by minimizing the objective function L_{to}, which is formulated as:

$$\min_{f, f_{ph}} L_{to} = L_{ct} + \lambda L_{msr}, \tag{21}$$

where L_{ct} is shown in the objective 17, λ is the hyper-parameter, and L_{msr} is presented as:

$$L_{msr} = \sum_{i=1}^{N} \sum_{j=1}^{2} - \log P\left(Y\left(X_i^{3-j}\right) | do\left(X_i^{3-j}\right)\right). \tag{22}$$

In the second stage of each epoch, we employ a meta-learning-based training strategy to optimize the parameters of f_{msr}. Specifically, the goal is to update f_{msr} such that the generated weight matrix enhances the performance of the primary contrastive learning task when f and f_{ph} are trained using this matrix. In other words, f_{msr} is encouraged to produce a weight matrix that maximizes the effectiveness of contrastive learning on the same training data.

To achieve this, we begin by updating the parameters of f and f_{ph} once using the learning rate α, as follows:

$$\begin{aligned} f^1 &= f - \alpha \nabla_f L_{to}, \\ f_{ph}^1 &= f_{ph} - \alpha \nabla_{f_{ph}} L_{to}, \end{aligned} \tag{23}$$

The aforementioned updating processes aim at learning the appropriate f and f_{ph}. Accordingly, f^1 and f_{ph}^1 can be treated as f_{msr}, since $\nabla_f L_{to}$ and $\nabla_{f_{ph}} L_{to}$ are related to f_{msr}. f_{msr} is updated by minimizing

$$\min_{f_{msr}} L_{ct}\left(f^1, f_{ph}^1\right) + \gamma L_{uni} \tag{24}$$

where γ is a hyperparameter, $L_{ct}\left(f^1, f_{ph}^1\right)$ denotes the contrastive loss L_{ct} computed using the parameters f^1 and f_{ph}^1, and L_{uni} represents the uniformity loss. The purpose of L_{uni} is to regulate the distribution of the elements in A_s, ensuring that it approximates a uniform distribution. This encourages the extracted visual semantics to be as diverse as possible. Using the Gaussian potential kernel [103–105], L_{uni} can be expressed as:

$$L_{uni} = \log \sum_{a_i, a_j \in A_s} G_t(a_i, a_j, t) \tag{25}$$

where $G_t(a_i, a_j, t) \triangleq \exp(2t \cdot a_i^{\mathrm{T}} a_j - 2t)$, where t is a fixed hyperparameter. It is worth noting that the average pairwise Gaussian potential has a strong connection to the uniform distribution; for further details, please refer to [105].

An important question arises: why does minimizing objective (24) enable f_{msr} to learn semantic information? Recall that only the semantic information shared between positive pairs can effectively align X_i^{3-j} and $Y\left(X_i^{3-j}\right)$, thus reducing the contrastive loss. According to the SCM, this shared semantic information includes both background-related and foreground-related features. The logic behind objective 24 is that minimizing the contrastive loss encourages f_{msr} to capture the shared semantic information. This process can also be viewed as enhancing the optimization of L_{ct} based on itself, akin to a "learning to learn" paradigm. This reasoning underpins why the method is referred to as a meta semantic regularizer.

5.3 Experimental exploration

We evaluate our MSR approach on several benchmark datasets, including Tiny ImageNet [71], STL-10 [72], CIFAR10 [71], and CIFAR100 [71], following the experimental setup of SimCLR [8]. **Table 2** presents the experimental results (linear evaluation and 5-NN classification) for the compared methods using a ResNet-18 feature extractor on small- and medium-sized datasets. We incorporate the Meta Semantic Regularizer into four models, resulting in four MSR-based variants: SimCLR+MSR, BYOL+MSR, LMCL+MSR, and ReSSL+MSR. The hyperparameters λ and γ are set as follows: for SimCLR+MSR, both are set to 1; for BYOL+MSR and LMCL+MSR, $\lambda = 0.1$ and $\gamma = 1$; and for ReSSL+MSR, $\lambda = 0.01$ and $\gamma = 1$.

From **Table 2**, it is evident that all MSR-enhanced models outperform their respective baselines. Notably, the best results are consistently observed for BYOL +MSR and LMCL+MSR, demonstrating the efficacy of the proposed MSR. It is also worth mentioning that RELIC, a causal-related approach focused on different augmentations, is outperformed by three of the four MSR-based models in **Table 2**. This

Methods	CIFAR10		CIFAR100		STL-10		Tiny ImageNet	
	linear	5-nn	linear	5-nn	linear	5-nn	linear	5-nn
SimCLR [8]	91.80	88.42	66.83	56.56	90.51	85.68	48.84	32.86
BYOL [106]	91.73	89.45	66.60	56.82	91.99	88.64	51.00	36.24
W-MSE [22]	91.99	89.87	67.64	56.45	91.75	88.59	49.22	35.44
ReSSL [107]	90.20	88.26	63.79	53.72	88.25	86.33	46.60	32.39
LMCL [108]	91.91	88.52	67.01	56.86	90.87	85.91	49.24	32.88
SSL-HSIC [37]	91.95	89.99	67.23	57.01	92.09	88.91	51.37	36.03
RELIC [109]	91.96	89.35	67.24	56.88	91.15	86.21	49.17	32.97
SimCLR + MSR	92.34	89.47	67.59	57.64	92.03	86.94	50.12	32.88
BYOL + MSR	92.26	**90.12**	66.97	**57.97**	**93.22**	**89.36**	52.54	**37.54**
LMCL + MSR	**92.45**	89.38	**67.99**	57.71	91.56	87.73	**52.61**	32.35
ReSSL + MSR	91.77	89.06	65.12	55.07	89.91	88.06	47.17	33.03

A linear classifier and a 5-nearest neighbors classifier are selected as the candidate classifiers, and the feature extractor is achieved by using ResNet-18.

Table 2.
Comparisons of benchmark methods and the proposed MSR. The bold entries highlight the best-performing results.

highlights that background information acts as a confounding factor in learning robust feature representations.

We identify two potential reasons for the cases where the performance improvement is less than 1%. First, MSR may be better suited for datasets with higher-resolution images. For instance, the improvement is often below 1% on datasets with low resolutions, such as 32×32 for CIFAR-10 and CIFAR-100, where background information is inherently limited. Second, the performance of MSR could be sensitive to the hyperparameter n. For computational efficiency, we fixed $n = 6$ across all datasets, which may not be optimal for all scenarios.

6. Discussion

This chapter summarizes and analyzes the deep representation learning algorithm guided by unbiased prior knowledge based on three levels, and finds a series of issues worthy of in-depth study. To this end, corresponding theoretical analysis and improvement methods are proposed for deep representation learning methods guided by unbiased prior knowledge at different levels, and the rationality and effectiveness of the proposed algorithm are proven from both theoretical and experimental aspects. The main contributions are summarized as follows:

- According to the problems of self-supervised contrastive learning technology in deep representation learning guided by unbiased prior knowledge at the task-level, that is, low sample efficiency, we focus on the issue of the excessive demand for sample pairs in self-supervised contrastive learning technology, and a meta feature augmentation network based on margin injection is proposed to directly learn feature augmentation, which aims to obtain an informative and collapse-resistant feature representation, and the corresponding experimental verification demonstrates the effectiveness and performance superiority of the proposed method.

- We further research the deep representation learning guided by unbiased prior knowledge within the feature-level, and find that this learning paradigm aims to obtain features from general or specific human knowledge bases to guide the training of deep representation learning models. However, it faces the challenge of the lack of knowledge introduction roadmap. According to the research related to the knowledge introduction roadmap based on knowledge bases, focusing on the problem that large-scale pre-trained visual-language models are difficult to obtain information with rich semantic information, we explore the use of knowledge graphs to efficiently obtain features with rich semantic information, thereby constructing the corresponding prompt method. The algorithm further follows the first principle of Granger causality and performs causal pruning on the label-related knowledge graph subgraphs. A large number of experiments prove the superior performance and robustness of this algorithm.

- In order to solve the problem of incomplete exploration of the theories of deep representation learning, we mainly explore the theoretical improvement of the deep representation learning paradigm guided by unbiased prior knowledge at the interpretable-level based on the causal inference theory and propose an optimized deep representation learning model according to the corresponding theory. Aiming to explore the factual causal relationship between various variable elements in deep representation learning, we revisit the self-supervised contrastive learning method from the perspective of causal inference, and a structural causal model is established to explain the current problems of self-supervised contrastive learning. Under the guidance of this theoretical framework based on the structural causal model, a regularization method based on backdoor adjustment is proposed. The proposed method is further demonstrated and verified theoretically and experimentally, and the results can prove the effectiveness and robustness of the proposed method.

7. Conclusion

The chapter explores cross-level unbiased prior knowledge-guided deep representation learning, addressing task-level, feature-level, and interpretability-level challenges. It highlights the limitations of traditional deep representation learning methods, including low sample efficiency, limited generalization, and reliance on domain-biased data. The proposed solutions include meta feature augmentation for task-level learning, knowledge graph-based prompt construction for feature-level learning, and a structural causal model-guided framework for interpretability-level learning. These approaches demonstrate superior performance and robustness in both theoretical and experimental validations.

However, challenges remain. The integration of unbiased prior knowledge into deep learning models still lacks a unified theoretical framework. Additionally, task-level methods face difficulties in enhancing sample efficiency under highly constrained data settings. Feature-level approaches require more efficient algorithms for extracting and utilizing knowledge from large-scale knowledge graphs. Interpretability-level methods need further exploration of causal relationships to improve model robustness and generalization.

Future directions include developing a comprehensive theoretical framework for unbiased knowledge integration, improving the scalability of knowledge graph-based methods, and advancing causal inference techniques to refine interpretability. Addressing these challenges will contribute to creating more efficient, generalizable, and interpretable deep learning models.

Acknowledgements

This work is supported by National Natural Science Foundation of China No. 62406313, Postdoctoral Fellowship Program, Grant No. GZC20232812, China Postdoctoral Science Foundation, Grant No. 2024M753356, 2023 Special Research Assistant Grant Project of the Chinese Academy of Sciences.

Author details

Jiangmeng Li[1*] and Fei Song[1,2]

1 Institute of Software, Chinese Academy of Sciences, Beijing, China

2 University of Chinese Academy of Sciences, Beijing, China

*Address all correspondence to: jiangmeng2019@iscas.ac.cn

References

[1] Shalf J. The future of computing beyond Moore's law. Philosophical Transactions of the Royal Society A. 2020;**378**(2166):20190061

[2] He K, Zhang X, Ren S, Sun J. Deep residual learning for image recognition. In: 2016 IEEE Conference on Computer Vision and Pattern Recognition, CVPR 2016, Las Vegas, NV, USA, June 27-30, 2016. IEEE Computer Society; 2016. pp. 770-778. DOI: 10.1109/CVPR.2016.90

[3] Jie H, Shen L, Albanie S, Sun G, Enhua W. Squeeze-and-excitation networks. IEEE Transactions on Pattern Analysis and Machine Intelligence. 2020; **42**(8):2011-2023

[4] Zoph B, Le QV. Neural architecture search with reinforcement learning. In: 5th International Conference on Learning Representations, ICLR 2017, Toulon, France, April 24-26, 2017, Conference Track Proceedings. OpenReview.net; 2017. Available from: https://openreview.net/forum?id=r1Ue8Hcxg

[5] Baker B, Gupta O, Naik N, Raskar R. Designing neural network architectures using reinforcement learning. In: 5th International Conference on Learning Representations, ICLR 2017, Toulon, France, April 24-26, 2017, Conference Track Proceedings. OpenReview.net; 2017. Available from: https://openreview.net/forum?id=S1c2cvqee

[6] Deng J, Dong W, Socher R, Li L-J, Li K, Fei-Fei L. Imagenet: A large-scale hierarchical image database. In: 2009 IEEE Computer Society Conference on Computer Vision and Pattern Recognition (CVPR 2009); 20-25 June 2009; Miami, Florida, USA. IEEE Computer Society; 2009. pp. 248-255. DOI: 10.1109/CVPR.2009.5206848

[7] Tian Y, Krishnan D, Isola P. Contrastive multiview coding. In: Vedaldi A, Bischof H, Brox T, Frahm J-M, editors. Computer Vision - ECCV 2020 - 16th European Conference; August 23-28, 2020; Glasgow, UK, Proceedings, Part XI, Lecture Notes in Computer Science. Vol. 12356. Springer; 2020. pp. 776-794. DOI: 10.1007/978-3-030-58621-8_45

[8] Chen T, Kornblith S, Norouzi M, Hinton GE. A simple framework for contrastive learning of visual representations. In: Proceedings of the 37th International Conference on Machine Learning, ICML 2020, 13-18 July 2020, Virtual Event. Proceedings of Machine Learning Research. Vol. 119. PMLR; 2020. pp. 1597-1607. Available from: http://proceedings.mlr.press/v119/chen20j.html

[9] He K, Fan H, Wu Y, Xie S, Girshick RB. Momentum contrast for unsupervised visual representation learning. In: 2020 IEEE/CVF Conference on Computer Vision and Pattern Recognition, CVPR 2020; 13-19 June 2020; Seattle, WA, USA. Computer Vision Foundation/IEEE; 2020. pp. 9726-9735. DOI: 10.1109/CVPR42600.2020.00975

[10] Schick T, Schütze H. Exploiting cloze-questions for few-shot text classification and natural language inference. In: Merlo P, Tiedemann J, Tsarfaty R, editors. Proceedings of the 16th Conference of the European Chapter of the Association for Computational Linguistics: Main Volume, EACL 2021, Online, April 19-23, 2021. Association for Computational Linguistics; 2021. pp. 255-269. DOI: 10.18653/v1/2021.eacl-main.20

[11] Gao P, Geng S, Zhang R, Ma T, Fang R, Zhang Y, et al. Clip-adapter: Better

vision-language models with feature adapters. International Journal of Computer Vision. 2024;**132**(2): 581-595. DOI: 10.1007/s11263-023-01891-x

[12] Jin W, Cheng Y, Shen Y, Chen W, Ren X. A good prompt is worth millions of parameters: Low-resource prompt-based learning for vision-language models. In: Muresan S, Nakov P, Villavicencio A, editors. Proceedings of the 60th Annual Meeting of the Association for Computational Linguistics (Volume 1: Long Papers), ACL 2022, Dublin, Ireland, May 22-27, 2022. Association for Computational Linguistics; 2022. pp. 2763-2775. DOI: 10.18653/v1/2022.acl-long.197

[13] Pearl J, Glymour M, Jewell NP. Causal Inference in Statistics: A Primer. John Wiley & Sons; 2016

[14] Caron M, Misra I, Mairal J, Goyal P, Bojanowski P, Joulin A. Unsupervised learning of visual features by contrasting cluster assignments. In: Larochelle H, Ranzato M'A, Hadsell R, Balcan M-F, Lin H-T, editors. Advances in Neural Information Processing Systems 33: Annual Conference on Neural Information Processing Systems 2020, NeurIPS 2020, December 6-12, 2020, Virtual. 2020. Available from: https://proceedings.neurips.cc/paper/2020/hash/70feb62b69f16e0238f741fab228fec2-Abstract.html

[15] Tian Y, Sun C, Poole B, Krishnan D, Schmid C, Isola P. What makes for good views for contrastive learning? In: Larochelle H, Ranzato M, Hadsell R, Balcan M-F, Lin H-T, editors. Advances in Neural Information Processing Systems 33: Annual Conference on Neural Information Processing Systems 2020, NeurIPS 2020, December 6-12, 2020, Virtual. 2020. Available from: https://proceedings.neurips.cc/paper/2020/hash/4c2e5eaae9152079b9e95845750bb9ab-Abstract.html

[16] Hénaff OJ. Data-efficient image recognition with contrastive predictive coding. In: Proceedings of the 37th International Conference on Machine Learning, ICML 2020, 13-18 July 2020, Virtual Event, Proceedings of Machine Learning Research. Vol. 119. PMLR; 2020. pp. 4182-4192. Available from: http://proceedings.mlr.press/v119/henaff20a.html

[17] Misra I, van der Maaten L. Self-supervised learning of pretext-invariant representations. In: 2020 IEEE/CVF Conference on Computer Vision and Pattern Recognition, CVPR 2020; June 13-19, 2020; Seattle, WA, USA. Computer Vision Foundation/IEEE; 2020. pp. 6706-6716. Available from: https://openaccess.thecvf.com/content_CVPR_2020/html/Misra_Self-Supervised_Learning_of_Pretext-Invariant_Representations_CVPR_2020_paper.html

[18] Li J, Zhou P, Xiong C, Hoi SCH. Prototypical contrastive learning of unsupervised representations. In: 9th International Conference on Learning Representations, ICLR 2021, Virtual Event, Austria, May 3-7, 2021. OpenReview.net; 2021. Available from: https://openreview.net/forum?id=KmykpuSrjcq

[19] Chen T, Kornblith S, Swersky K, Norouzi M, Hinton GE. Big self-supervised models are strong semi-supervised learners. In: Larochelle H, Ranzato M, Hadsell R, Balcan M-F, Lin H-T, editors. Advances in Neural Information Processing Systems 33: Annual Conference on Neural Information Processing Systems 2020, NeurIPS 2020, December 6-12, 2020, Virtual. 2020. Available from: https://proceedings.neurips.cc/paper/2020/

hash/fcbc95ccdd551da181207c0c1400c655-Abstract.html

[20] Verma V, Luong T, Kawaguchi K, Pham H, Le QV. Towards domain-agnostic contrastive learning. In: Proceedings of the 38th International Conference on Machine Learning, ICML 2021, 18-24 July 2021, Virtual Event, Proceedings of Machine Learning Research. Vol. 139. PMLR; 2021. pp. 10530-10541. Available from: http://proceedings.mlr.press/v139/verma21a.html

[21] Xiao T, Wang X, Efros AA, Darrell T. What should not be contrastive in contrastive learning. In: 9th International Conference on Learning Representations, ICLR 2021, Virtual Event, Austria, May 3-7, 2021. OpenReview.net; 2021. Available from: https://openreview.net/forum?id=CZ8Y3NzuVzO

[22] Ermolov A, Siarohin A, Sangineto E, Sebe N. Whitening for self-supervised representation learning. In: Meila M, Zhang T, editors. Proceedings of the 38th International Conference on Machine Learning, ICML 2021, 18-24 July 2021, Virtual Event, Proceedings of Machine Learning Research. Vol. 139. PMLR; 2021. pp. 3015-3024. Available from: http://proceedings.mlr.press/v139/ermolov21a.html

[23] Devon Hjelm R, Fedorov A, Lavoie-Marchildon S, Grewal K, Bachman P, Trischler A, et al. Learning deep representations by mutual information estimation and maximization. In: 7th International Conference on Learning Representations, ICLR 2019, New Orleans, LA, USA, May 6-9, 2019. OpenReview.net; 2019. Available from: https://openreview.net/forum?id=Bklr3j0cKX

[24] van den Oord A, Li Y, Vinyals O. Representation learning with contrastive predictive coding. CoRR. 2018; abs/1807.03748. Available from: http://arxiv.org/abs/1807.03748

[25] Gutmann M, Hyvärinen A. Noise-contrastive estimation: A new estimation principle for unnormalized statistical models. In: Teh YW, Titterington DM, editors. Proceedings of the Thirteenth International Conference on Artificial Intelligence and Statistics, AISTATS 2010, Chia Laguna Resort, Sardinia, Italy, May 13-15, 2010, JMLR Proceedings. Vol. 9. JMLR.org; 2010. pp. 297-304. Available from: http://proceedings.mlr.press/v9/gutmann10a.html

[26] Goldberger J, Gordon S, Greenspan H. An efficient image similarity measure based on approximations of kl-divergence between two gaussian mixtures. In: 9th IEEE International Conference on Computer Vision (ICCV 2003); 14-17 October 2003; Nice, France. IEEE Computer Society; 2003. pp. 487-493. DOI: 10.1109/ICCV.2003.1238387

[27] Bachman P, Hjelm RD, Buchwalter W. Learning representations by maximizing mutual information across views. In: Wallach HM, Larochelle H, Beygelzimer A, d'Alché-Buc F, Fox EB, Garnett R, editors. Advances in Neural Information Processing Systems 32: Annual Conference on Neural Information Processing Systems 2019, NeurIPS 2019, December 8-14, 2019, Vancouver, BC, Canada. 2019. pp. 15509-15519. Available from: https://proceedings.neurips.cc/paper/2019/hash/ddf354219aac374f1d40b7e760ee5bb7-Abstract.html

[28] Chen X, Fan H, Girshick RB, He K. Improved baselines with momentum contrastive learning. CoRR. 2020; abs/2003.04297. Available from: https://arxiv.org/abs/2003.04297

[29] Chuang C-Y, Robinson J, Lin Y-C, Torralba A, Jegelka S. Debiased contrastive learning. In: Larochelle H, Ranzato M'A, Hadsell R, Balcan M-F, Lin H-T, editors. Advances in Neural Information Processing Systems 33: Annual Conference on Neural Information Processing Systems 2020, NeurIPS 2020, December 6-12, 2020, Virtual. 2020. Available from: https://proceedings.neurips.cc/paper/2020/hash/63c3ddcc7b23daa1e42dc41f9a44a873-Abstract.html

[30] Robinson JD, Chuang C-Y, Sra S, Jegelka S. Contrastive learning with hard negative samples. In: 9th International Conference on Learning Representations, ICLR 2021, Virtual Event, Austria, May 3-7, 2021. OpenReview.net; 2021. Available from: https://openreview.net/forum?id=CR1XOQ0UTh-

[31] Elkan C, Noto K. Learning classifiers from only positive and unlabeled data. In: Proceedings of the 14th ACM SIGKDD International Conference on Knowledge Discovery and Data Mining; August 24-27, 2008; Las Vegas, Nevada, USA. ACM; 2008. pp. 213-220. DOI: 10.1145/1401890.1401920

[32] du Plessis MC, Niu G, Sugiyama M. Analysis of learning from positive and unlabeled data. In: Ghahramani Z, Welling M, Cortes C, Lawrence ND, Weinberger KQ, editors. Advances in Neural Information Processing Systems 27: Annual Conference on Neural Information Processing Systems 2014; December 8-13 2014; Montreal, Quebec, Canada. 2014. pp. 703-711. Available from: https://proceedings.neurips.cc/paper/2014/hash/35051070e572e47d2c26c241ab88307f-Abstract.html

[33] Sridharan K, Kakade SM. An information theoretic framework for multi-view learning. In: Servedio RA, Zhang T, editors. 21st Annual Conference on Learning Theory - COLT 2008, Helsinki, Finland, July 9-12, 2008. Omnipress; 2008. pp. 403-414. Available from: http://colt2008.cs.helsinki.fi/papers/94-Sridharan.pdf

[34] Tsai Y-HH, Wu Y, Salakhutdinov R, Morency L-P. Self-supervised learning from a multi-view perspective. In: 9th International Conference on Learning Representations, ICLR 2021, Virtual Event, Austria, May 3-7, 2021. OpenReview.net; 2021. Available from: https://openreview.net/forum?id=-bdp_8Itjwp

[35] Chen X, He K. Exploring simple siamese representation learning. In: IEEE Conference on Computer Vision and Pattern Recognition, CVPR 2021, Virtual, June 19-25, 2021. Computer Vision Foundation/IEEE; 2021. pp. 15750-15758. Available from: https://openaccess.thecvf.com/content/CVPR2021/html/Chen_Exploring_Simple_Siamese_Representation_Learning_CVPR_2021_paper.html

[36] Grill J-B, Strub F, Altché F, Tallec C, Richemond PH, Buchatskaya E, et al. Bootstrap your own latent - A new approach to self-supervised learning. In: Larochelle H, Ranzato M, Hadsell R, Balcan M-F, Lin H-T, editors. Advances in Neural Information Processing Systems 33: Annual Conference on Neural Information Processing Systems 2020, NeurIPS 2020, December 6-12, 2020, Virtual. 2020. Available from: https://proceedings.neurips.cc/paper/2020/hash/f3ada80d5c4ee70142b17b8192b2958e-Abstract.html

[37] Li Y, Pogodin R, Sutherland DJ, Gretton A. Self-supervised learning with kernel dependence maximization. In: Ranzato M, Beygelzimer A, Dauphin YN, Liang P, Vaughan JW, editors. Advances in Neural Information Processing

Systems 34: Annual Conference on Neural Information Processing Systems 2021, NeurIPS 2021, December 6-14, 2021, Virtual. 2021. pp. 15543-15556. Available from: https://proceedings.neurips.cc/paper/2021/hash/83004190b1793d7aa15f8d0d49a13eba-Abstract.html

[38] Gretton A, Bousquet O, Smola AJ, Schölkopf B. Measuring statistical dependence with Hilbert-Schmidt norms. In: Jain S, Simon HU, Tomita E, editors. Algorithmic Learning Theory, 16th International Conference, ALT 2005; October 8-11, 2005; Singapore, Proceedings, Lecture Notes in Computer Science. Vol. 3734. Springer; 2005. pp. 63-77. DOI: 10.1007/11564089_7

[39] Berners-Lee T, Hendler J, Lassila O. The semantic web. Scientific American. 2001;**284**(5):34-43

[40] Miller GA. Wordnet: A lexical database for English. Communications of the ACM. 1995;**38**(11):39-41

[41] Suchanek FM, Kasneci G, Weikum G. Yago: A core of semantic knowledge. In: Williamson CL, Zurko ME, Patel-Schneider PF, Shenoy PJ, editors. Proceedings of the 16th International Conference on World Wide Web, WWW 2007, Banff, Alberta, Canada, May 8-12, 2007. ACM; 2007. pp. 697-706. DOI: 10.1145/1242572.1242667

[42] Auer S, Bizer C, Kobilarov G, Lehmann J, Cyganiak R, Ives ZG. Dbpedia: A nucleus for a web of open data. In: Aberer K, Choi K-S, Noy NF, Allemang D, Lee K-I, Nixon LJB, Golbeck J, Mika P, Maynard D, Mizoguchi R, Schreiber G, Cudré-Mauroux P, editors. The Semantic Web, 6th International Semantic Web Conference, 2nd Asian Semantic Web Conference, ISWC 2007 + ASWC 2007, Busan, Korea, November 11-15, 2007, Lecture Notes in Computer Science. Vol. 4825. Springer; 2007. pp. 722-735. DOI: 10.1007/978-3-540-76298-0_52

[43] Bollacker KD, Evans C, Paritosh PK, Sturge T, Taylor J. Freebase: A collaboratively created graph database for structuring human knowledge. In: Wang JT-L, editor. Proceedings of the ACM SIGMOD International Conference on Management of Data, SIGMOD 2008, Vancouver, BC, Canada, June 10-12, 2008. ACM; 2008. pp. 1247-1250. DOI: 10.1145/1376616.1376746

[44] Vrandecic D, Krötzsch M. Wikidata: A free collaborative knowledgebase. Communications of the ACM. 2014;**57**(10):78-85

[45] Carlson A, Betteridge J, Kisiel B, Settles B, Hruschka ER Jr, Mitchell TM. Toward an architecture for never-ending language learning. In: Fox M, Poole D, editors. Proceedings of the Twenty-Fourth AAAI Conference on Artificial Intelligence, AAAI 2010; July 11-15, 2010; Atlanta, Georgia, USA. AAAI Press; 2010. pp. 1306-1313. DOI: 10.1609/aaai.v24i1.7519

[46] Bo X, Yong X, Liang J, Xie C, Liang B, Cui W, et al. CN-DBpedia: A never-ending Chinese knowledge extraction system. In: Benferhat S, Tabia K, Ali M, editors. Advances in Artificial Intelligence: From Theory to Practice - 30th International Conference on Industrial Engineering and Other Applications of Applied Intelligent Systems, IEA/AIE 2017; June 27-30, 2017; Arras, France, Proceedings, Part II, Lecture Notes in Computer Science. Vol. 10351. Springer; 2017. pp. 428-438. DOI: 10.1007/978-3-319-60045-1_44

[47] Speer R, Chin J, Havasi C. Conceptnet 5.5: An open multilingual graph of general knowledge. In: Singh S, Markovitch S, editors. Proceedings of the

Thirty-First AAAI Conference on Artificial Intelligence; February 4-9, 2017; San Francisco, California, USA. AAAI Press; 2017. pp. 4444-4451. DOI: 10.1609/aaai.v31i1.11164

[48] Harland L. Open PHACTS: A semantic knowledge infrastructure for public and commercial drug discovery research. In: ten Teije A, Völker J, Handschuh S, Stuckenschmidt H, d'Aquin M, Nikolov A, et al. Knowledge Engineering and Knowledge Management - 18th International Conference, EKAW 2012; October 8-12, 2012; Galway City, Ireland. Proceedings, Lecture Notes in Computer Science. Vol. 7603. Springer; 2012. pp. 1–7. DOI: 10.1007/978-3-642-33876-2_1

[49] Ferrucci DA, Brown EW, Chu-Carroll J, Fan J, Gondek D, Kalyanpur A, et al. Building Watson: An overview of the deepqa project. AI Magazine. 2010; **31**(3):59-79

[50] Tang J, Zhang J, Yao L, Li J, Zhang L, Zhong S. Arnetminer: Extraction and mining of academic social networks. In: Li Y, Liu B, Sarawagi S, editors. Proceedings of the 14th ACM SIGKDD International Conference on Knowledge Discovery and Data Mining; August 24-27, 2008; Las Vegas, Nevada, USA. ACM; 2008. pp. 990-998. DOI: 10.1145/1401890.1402008

[51] Ji S, Pan S, Cambria E, Marttinen P, Philip SY. A survey on knowledge graphs: Representation, acquisition, and applications. IEEE Transactions on Neural Networks and Learning Systems. 2022;**33**(2):494-514

[52] Dong X, Gabrilovich E, Heitz G, Horn W, Lao N, Murphy K, et al. Knowledge vault: A web-scale approach to probabilistic knowledge fusion. In: Macskassy SA, Perlich C, Leskovec J, Wang W, Ghani R, editors. The 20th ACM SIGKDD International Conference on Knowledge Discovery and Data Mining, KDD '14, New York, NY, USA - August 24 - 27, 2014. ACM; 2014. pp. 601-610. DOI: 10.1145/2623330.2623623

[53] Dettmers T, Minervini P, Stenetorp P, Riedel S. Convolutional 2D knowledge graph embeddings. In: McIlraith SA, Weinberger KQ, editors. Proceedings of the Thirty-Second AAAI Conference on Artificial Intelligence, (AAAI-18), the 30th Innovative Applications of Artificial Intelligence (IAAI-18), and the 8th AAAI Symposium on Educational Advances in Artificial Intelligence (EAAI-18), New Orleans, Louisiana, USA, February 2-7, 2018. AAAI Press; 2018. pp. 1811-1818. DOI: 10.1609/aaai.v32i1.11573

[54] Nguyen DQ, Nguyen TD, Nguyen DQ, Phung DQ. A novel embedding model for knowledge base completion based on convolutional neural network. In: Walker MA, Ji H, Stent A, editors. Proceedings of the 2018 Conference of the North American Chapter of the Association for Computational Linguistics: Human Language Technologies, NAACL-HLT; June 1-6, 2018; New Orleans, Louisiana, USA, Volume 2 (Short Papers). Association for Computational Linguistics; 2018. pp. 327-333. DOI: 10.18653/v1/n18-2053

[55] Nguyen DQ, Thanh V, Nguyen TD, Nguyen DQ, Phung DQ. A capsule network-based embedding model for knowledge graph completion and search personalization. In: Burstein J, Doran C, Solorio T, editors. Proceedings of the 2019 Conference of the North American Chapter of the Association for Computational Linguistics: Human Language Technologies, NAACL-HLT 2019; June 2-7, 2019; Minneapolis, MN, USA, Volume 1 (Long and Short Papers). Association for Computational Linguistics; 2019. pp. 2180-2189. DOI: 10.18653/v1/n19-1226

[56] Yao L, Mao C, Luo Y. KG-BERT: BERT for knowledge graph completion. CoRR. 2019; abs/1909.03193. Available from: http://arxiv.org/abs/1909.03193

[57] Pearl J. Causal inference in statistics: An overview. Statistics Surveys. 2009;**3**: 96-146

[58] Lopez-Paz D, Nishihara R, Chintala S, Schölkopf B, Bottou L. Discovering causal signals in images. In: 2017 IEEE Conference on Computer Vision and Pattern Recognition, CVPR 2017; July 21-26, 2017; Honolulu, HI, USA. IEEE Computer Society; 2017. pp. 58-66. DOI: 10.1109/CVPR.2017.14

[59] He Y, Shen Z, Cui P. Towards non-iid image classification: A dataset and baselines. Pattern Recognition. 2021;**110**: 107383

[60] Tan W, Zhou C, Sun Q, Zhang H. Causal attention for unbiased visual recognition. In: IEEE/CVF International Conference on Computer Vision, ICCV 2021; October 10-17, 2021; Montreal, QC, Canada. IEEE; 2021. pp. 3071-3080. DOI: 10.1109/ICCV48922.2021.00308

[61] Lv F, Liang J, Li S, Zang B, Liu CH, Wang Z, et al. Causality inspired representation learning for domain generalization. In: IEEE/CVF Conference on Computer Vision and Pattern Recognition, CVPR 2022; June 18-24, 2022; New Orleans, LA, USA. IEEE; 2022. pp. 8036-8046. DOI: 10.1109/CVPR52688.2022.00788

[62] Li J, Zhang Y, Qiang W, Si L, Jiao C, Hu X, et al. Disentangle and remerge: Interventional knowledge distillation for few-shot object detection from a conditional causal perspective. In: Williams B, Chen Y, Neville J, editors. Thirty-Seventh AAAI Conference on Artificial Intelligence, AAAI 2023, Thirty-Fifth Conference on Innovative Applications of Artificial Intelligence, IAAI 2023, Thirteenth Symposium on Educational Advances in Artificial Intelligence, EAAI 2023, Washington, DC, USA, February 7-14, 2023. AAAI Press; 2023. pp. 1323-1333. DOI: 10.1609/aaai.v37i1.25216

[63] Li J, Qiang W, Zheng C, Bing S, Razzak F, Wen J-R, et al. Modeling multiple views via implicitly preserving global consistency and local complementarity. IEEE Transactions on Knowledge and Data Engineering. 2023; **35**(7):7220-7238. DOI: 10.1109/TKDE.2022.3198746

[64] Chopra S, Hadsell R, LeCun Y. Learning a similarity metric discriminatively, with application to face verification. In: 2005 IEEE Computer Society Conference on Computer Vision and Pattern Recognition (CVPR'05); San Diego, CA, USA; 20-26 June 2005. IEEE Computer Society; 2005. pp. 539-546. DOI: 10.1109/CVPR.2005.202

[65] Hadsell R, Chopra S, LeCun Y. Dimensionality reduction by learning an invariant mapping. In: 2006 IEEE Computer Society Conference on Computer Vision and Pattern Recognition (CVPR'06); 17-22 June 2006; New York, NY, USA. IEEE Computer Society; 2006. pp. 1735-1742. DOI: 10.1109/CVPR.2006.100

[66] Zbontar J, Jing L, Misra I, LeCun Y, Deny S. Barlow twins: Self-supervised learning via redundancy reduction. In: Meila M, Zhang T, editors. Proceedings of the 38th International Conference on Machine Learning, ICML 2021, 18-24 July 2021, Virtual Event, Proceedings of Machine Learning Research. PMLR; 2021. Available from: http://proceedings.mlr.press/v139/zbontar21a.html

[67] Finn C, Abbeel P, Levine S. Model-agnostic meta-learning for fast

adaptation of deep networks. In: Precup D, Teh YW, editors. Proceedings of the 34th International Conference on Machine Learning, ICML 2017, Sydney, NSW, Australia, 6-11 August 2017, Proceedings of Machine Learning Research. Vol. 70. PMLR; 2017. pp. 1126-1135. Available from: http://proceedings.mlr.press/v70/finn17a.html

[68] Liu S, Davison AJ, Johns E. Self-supervised generalisation with meta auxiliary learning. In: Wallach HM, Larochelle H, Beygelzimer A, d'Alché-Buc F, Fox EB, Garnett R, editors. Advances in Neural Information Processing Systems 32: Annual Conference on Neural Information Processing Systems 2019, NeurIPS 2019, December 8-14, 2019, Vancouver, BC, Canada. 2019. pp. 1677-1687. Available from: https://proceedings.neurips.cc/paper/2019/hash/92262bf907af914b95a0fc33c3f33bf6-Abstract.html

[69] Zhang Y, Tang H, Jia K. Fine-grained visual categorization using meta-learning optimization with sample selection of auxiliary data. In: Ferrari V, Hebert M, Sminchisescu C, Weiss Y, editors. Computer Vision - ECCV 2018 - 15th European Conference, Munich, Germany, September 8-14, 2018, Proceedings, Part VIII, Lecture Notes in Computer Science. Vol. 11212. Springer; 2018. pp. 241-256. DOI: 10.1007/978-3-030-01237-3_15

[70] Li J, Qiang W, Zheng C, Bing S, Xiong H. Metaug: Contrastive learning via meta feature augmentation. In: Chaudhuri K, Jegelka S, Song L, Szepesvári C, Niu G, Sabato S, editors. International Conference on Machine Learning, ICML 2022, 17-23 July 2022, Baltimore, Maryland, USA, Proceedings of Machine Learning Research. Vol. 162. PMLR; 2022. pp. 12964-12978. Available from: https://proceedings.mlr.press/v162/li22r.html

[71] Krizhevsky A, Hinton G, et al. Learning Multiple Layers of Features from Tiny Images. Toronto, ON, Canada: University of Toronto; 2009

[72] Coates A, Ng A, Lee H. An analysis of single-layer networks in unsupervised feature learning. In: Gordon GJ, Dunson DB, Dudík M, editors. Proceedings of the Fourteenth International Conference on Artificial Intelligence and Statistics, AISTATS 2011; April 11-13, 2011; Fort Lauderdale, USA, JMLR Proceedings. Vol. 15. JMLR.org; 2011. pp. 215-223. Available from: http://proceedings.mlr.press/v15/coates11a/coates11a.pdf

[73] Donahue J, Krähenbühl P, Darrell T. Adversarial feature learning. In: 5th International Conference on Learning Representations, ICLR 2017, Toulon, France, April 24-26, 2017, Conference Track Proceedings. OpenReview.net; 2017. Available from: https://openreview.net/forum?id=BJtNZAFgg

[74] Bojanowski P, Joulin A. Unsupervised learning by predicting noise. In: Precup D, Teh YW, editors. Proceedings of the 34th International Conference on Machine Learning, ICML 2017, Sydney, NSW, Australia, 6-11 August 2017, Proceedings of Machine Learning Research. Vol. 70. PMLR; 2017. pp. 517-526. Available from: http://proceedings.mlr.press/v70/bojanowski17a.html

[75] Krizhevsky A, Sutskever I, Hinton G. Imagenet classification with deep convolutional neural networks. In: Bartlett PL, Pereira FCN, Burges CJC, Bottou L, Weinberger KQ, editors. Advances in Neural Information Processing Systems 25: 26th Annual Conference on Neural Information Processing Systems 2012. Proceedings of a meeting held December 3-6, 2012, Lake Tahoe, Nevada, United States. 2012. pp. 1106-1114. Available from: https://

proceedings.neurips.cc/paper/2012/hash/c399862d3b9d6b76c8436e924a68c45b-Abstract.html

[76] Radford A, Kim JW, Hallacy C, Ramesh A, Goh G, Agarwal S, et al. Learning transferable visual models from natural language supervision. In: Meila M, Zhang T, editors. Proceedings of the 38th International Conference on Machine Learning, ICML 2021, 18-24 July 2021, Virtual Event, Proceedings of Machine Learning Research. Vol. 139. PMLR; 2021. pp. 8748-8763. Available from: http://proceedings.mlr.press/v139/radford21a.html

[77] Jia C, Yang Y, Xia Y, Chen Y-T, Parekh Z, Pham H, et al. Scaling up visual and vision-language representation learning with noisy text supervision. In: Proceedings of the 38th International Conference on Machine Learning, ICML 2021, 18-24 July 2021, Virtual Event, Proceedings of Machine Learning Research. Vol. 139. PMLR; 2021. pp. 4904-4916. Available from: http://proceedings.mlr.press/v139/jia21b.html

[78] Zhou K, Yang J, Loy CC, Liu Z. Learning to prompt for vision-language models. International Journal of Computer Vision. 2022;**130**(9):2337-2348. DOI: 10.1007/s11263-022-01653-1

[79] Derakhshani MM, Sanchez E, Bulat A, da Costa VGT, Snoek CGM, Tzimiropoulos G, et al. Bayesian prompt learning for image-language model generalization. In: IEEE/CVF International Conference on Computer Vision, ICCV 2023; October 1-6, 2023; Paris, France. IEEE; 2023. pp. 15191-15200. DOI: 10.1109/ICCV51070.2023.01398

[80] Khattak MU, Rasheed HA, Maaz M, Khan SH, Khan FS. MaPLe: Multi-modal prompt learning. In: IEEE/CVF Conference on Computer Vision and Pattern Recognition, CVPR 2023; June 17-24, 2023; Vancouver, BC, Canada. IEEE; 2023. pp. 19113-19122. DOI: 10.1109/CVPR52729.2023.01832

[81] Nilsback M-E, Zisserman A. Automated flower classification over a large number of classes. In: Sixth Indian Conference on Computer Vision, Graphics & Image Processing, ICVGIP 2008; 16-19 December 2008; Bhubaneswar, India. IEEE Computer Society; 2008. pp. 722-729. DOI: 10.1109/ICVGIP.2008.47

[82] Fei-Fei L, Fergus R, Perona P. Learning generative visual models from few training examples: An incremental bayesian approach tested on 101 object categories. In: IEEE Conference on Computer Vision and Pattern Recognition Workshops, CVPR Workshops 2004; June 27 - July 2, 2004; Washington, DC, USA. IEEE Computer Society; 2004. p. 178. DOI: 10.1109/CVPR.2004.383

[83] Zhu X, Zhang R, He B, Zhou A, Wang D, Zhao B, et al. Not all features matter: Enhancing few-shot clip with adaptive prior refinement. In: IEEE/CVF International Conference on Computer Vision, ICCV 2023; October 1-6, 2023; Paris, France. IEEE; 2023. pp. 2605-2615. DOI: 10.1109/ICCV51070.2023.00246

[84] Lin Z, Yu S, Kuang Z, Pathak D, Ramanan D. Multimodality helps unimodality: Cross-modal few-shot learning with multimodal models. In: IEEE/CVF Conference on Computer Vision and Pattern Recognition, CVPR 2023; June 17-24, 2023; Vancouver, BC, Canada. IEEE; 2023. pp. 19325-19337. DOI: 10.1109/CVPR52729.2023.01852

[85] Dosovitskiy A, Beyer L, Kolesnikov A, Weissenborn D, Zhai X, Unterthiner T, et al. An image is worth 16×16 words:

Transformers for image recognition at scale. In: 9th International Conference on Learning Representations, ICLR 2021, Virtual Event, Austria, May 3-7, 2021. OpenReview.net. 2021

[86] Vaswani A, Shazeer N, Parmar N, Uszkoreit J, Jones L, Gomez AN, et al. Attention is all you need. In: Guyon I, von Luxburg U, Bengio S, Wallach HM, Fergus R, Vishwanathan SVN, et al. Advances in Neural Information Processing Systems 30: Annual Conference on Neural Information Processing Systems 2017, December 4-9, 2017, Long Beach, CA, USA. 2017. pp. 5998-6008. Available from: https://proceedings.neurips.cc/paper/2017/hash/3f5ee243547dee91fbd053c1c4a845aa-Abstract.html

[87] Sennrich R, Haddow B, Birch A. Neural machine translation of rare words with subword units. In: Proceedings of the 54th Annual Meeting of the Association for Computational Linguistics, ACL 2016; Berlin, Germany; August 7-12, 2016. Volume 1: Long Papers. The Association for Computer Linguistics; 2016. DOI: 10.18653/v1/p16-1162

[88] Wang H, Zhao M, Xie X, Li W, Guo M. Knowledge graph convolutional networks for recommender systems. In: Liu L, White RW, Mantrach A, Silvestri F, McAuley JJ, Baeza-Yates R, Zia L, editors. The World Wide Web Conference, WWW 2019, San Francisco, CA, USA, May 13-17, 2019. ACM; 2019. pp. 3307-3313. DOI: 10.1145/3308558.3313417

[89] Granger C. Investigating causal relations by econometric models and cross-spectral methods. Econometrica. 1969;**37**:424-438

[90] Granger CW. Testing for causality: A personal viewpoint. Journal of Economic Dynamics and Control. 1980; **2**:329-352

[91] Goldstein A, Kapelner A, Bleich J, Pitkin E. Peeking inside the black box: Visualizing statistical learning with plots of individual conditional expectation. Journal of Computational and Graphical Statistics. 2015;**24**(1):44-65

[92] Lin W, Lan H, Li B. Generative causal explanations for graph neural networks. In: Meila M, Zhang T, editors. Proceedings of the 38th International Conference on Machine Learning, ICML 2021, 18-24 July 2021, Virtual Event, Proceedings of Machine Learning Research. PMLR; 2021. Available from: http://proceedings.mlr.press/v139/lin21d.html

[93] Krause J, Stark M, Deng J, Fei-Fei L. 3D object representations for fine-grained categorization. In: 2013 IEEE International Conference on Computer Vision Workshops, ICCV Workshops 2013December 1-8, 2013; Sydney, Australia. IEEE Computer Society; 2013. pp. 554-561. DOI: 10.1109/ICCVW.2013.77

[94] Maji S, Rahtu E, Kannala J, Blaschko MB, Vedaldi A. Fine-grained visual classification of aircraft. CoRR. 2013; abs/1306.5151. Available from: http://arxiv.org/abs/1306.5151

[95] Parkhi OM, Vedaldi A, Zisserman A, Jawahar CV. Cats and dogs. In: 2012 IEEE Conference on Computer Vision and Pattern Recognition; June 16-21, 2012; Providence, RI, USA. IEEE Computer Society; 2012. pp. 3498-3505. DOI: 10.1109/CVPR.2012.6248092

[96] Bossard L, Guillaumin M, Van Gool L. Food-101 - Mining discriminative components with random forests. In: Fleet DJ, Pajdla T, Schiele B, Tuytelaars T, editors. Computer Vision - ECCV

2014 - 13th European Conference; September 6-12, 2014; Zurich, Switzerland, Proceedings, Part VI, Lecture Notes in Computer Science. Vol. 8694. Springer; 2014. pp. 446-461. DOI: 10.1007/978-3-319-10599-4_29

[97] Xiao J, Hays J, Ehinger KA, Oliva A, Torralba A. SUN database: Large-scale scene recognition from abbey to zoo. In: The Twenty-Third IEEE Conference on Computer Vision and Pattern Recognition, CVPR 2010; 13-18 June 2010; San Francisco, CA, USA. IEEE Computer Society; 2010. pp. 3485-3492. DOI: 10.1109/CVPR.2010.5539970

[98] Soomro K, Zamir AR, Shah M. UCF101: A dataset of 101 human actions classes from videos in the wild. CoRR. 2012; abs/1212.0402. Available from: http://arxiv.org/abs/1212.0402

[99] Cimpoi M, Maji S, Kokkinos I, Mohamed S, Vedaldi A. Describing textures in the wild. In: 2014 IEEE Conference on Computer Vision and Pattern Recognition, CVPR 2014; June 23-28, 2014; Columbus, OH, USA. IEEE Computer Society; 2014. pp. 3606-3613. DOI: 10.1109/CVPR.2014.461

[100] Helber P, Bischke B, Dengel A, Borth D. Eurosat: A novel dataset and deep learning benchmark for land use and land cover classification. IEEE Journal of Selected Topics in Applied Earth Observations and Remote Sensing. 2019;**12**(7):2217-2226

[101] Zeiler MD, Fergus R. Visualizing and understanding convolutional networks. In: Fleet DJ, Pajdla T, Schiele B, Tuytelaars T, editors. Computer Vision - ECCV 2014 - 13th European Conference; September 6-12, 2014; Zurich, Switzerland, Proceedings, Part I, Lecture Notes in Computer Science. Vol. 8689. Springer; 2014. pp. 818-833. DOI: 10.1007/978-3-319-10590-1_53

[102] Zhou B, Khosla A, Lapedriza A, Oliva A, Torralba A. Learning deep features for discriminative localization. In: 2016 IEEE Conference on Computer Vision and Pattern Recognition, CVPR 2016; June 27-30, 2016; Las Vegas, NV, USA. IEEE Computer Society; 2016. pp. 2921-2929. DOI: 10.1109/CVPR.2016.319

[103] Borodachov SV, Hardin DP, Saff EB. Discrete Energy on Rectifiable Sets. Vol. 4. Springer; 2019

[104] Cohn H, Kumar A. Universally optimal distribution of points on spheres. Journal of the American Mathematical Society. 2007;**20**(1):99-148

[105] Wang T, Isola P. Understanding contrastive representation learning through alignment and uniformity on the hypersphere. In: Proceedings of the 37th International Conference on Machine Learning, ICML 2020, 13-18 July 2020, Virtual Event, Proceedings of Machine Learning Research. Vol. 119. PMLR; 2020. pp. 9929-9939. Available from: http://proceedings.mlr.press/v119/wang20k.html

[106] Grill J-B, Strub F, Altché F, Tallec C, Richemond P, Buchatskaya E, et al. Bootstrap your own latent-a new approach to self-supervised learning. Advances in Neural Information Processing Systems. 2020;**33**:21271-21284

[107] Zheng M, You S, Wang F, Qian C, Zhang C, Wang X, et al. Ressl: Relational self-supervised learning with weak augmentation. In: Ranzato M, Beygelzimer A, Dauphin YN, Liang P, Vaughan JW. Advances in Neural Information Processing Systems 34: Annual Conference on Neural Information Processing Systems 2021, NeurIPS 2021, December 6-14, 2021, Virtual. 2021. pp. 2543-2555. Available

from: https://proceedings.neurips.cc/paper/2021/hash/14c4f36143b4b09cbc320d7c95a50ee7-Abstract.html

[108] Chen S, Niu G, Gong C, Li J, Yang J, Sugiyama M. Large-margin contrastive learning with distance polarization regularizer. In: Meila M, Zhang T, editors. Proceedings of the 38th International Conference on Machine Learning, ICML 2021, 18-24 July 2021, Virtual Event, Proceedings of Machine Learning Research. Vol. 139. PMLR; 2021. pp. 1673-1683. Available from: http://proceedings.mlr.press/v139/chen21n.html

[109] Mitrovic J, McWilliams B, Walker JC, Buesing LH, Blundell C. Representation learning via invariant causal mechanisms. In: 9th International Conference on Learning Representations, ICLR 2021, Virtual Event; May 3-7, 2021; Austria. OpenReview.net; 2021. Available from: https://openreview.net/forum?id=9p2ekP904Rs

Chapter 3

Leveraging Mobile Applications to Boost Smallholder Farmers' Productivity in the Eastern Cape, South Africa: Effects on Sustainable Food Security

Lelethu Mdoda, Mzuyanda Christian, Ikechi Agbugba and Denver Naidoo

Abstract

This chapter examines the role of mobile applications in enhancing the productivity of smallholder farmers in the Eastern Cape Province of South Africa. It examines their implications for sustainable food security. Utilizing a mixed-methods approach, the study analyzed data from 220 smallholder farmers to assess their socio-economic characteristics, mobile application usage patterns, and the benefits and challenges associated with technology adoption. The findings indicate that many farmers actively use mobile applications, especially WhatsApp and Facebook, to access vital agricultural information, manage farm operations, and communicate with peers. However, the study further highlights critical barriers to adoption, including high costs, limited network coverage, and varying levels of digital literacy. The analysis reveals that education, income, and social networks influence the likelihood of mobile application usage among farmers. This suggests the need for targeted interventions to promote digital literacy and enhance access to technology. The results suggest that, when effectively integrated into agricultural practices, mobile applications have the potential to significantly improve smallholder farmers' productivity and contribute to food security. This chapter advocates for strategic policies that empower smallholder farmers through infrastructure development, educational initiatives, and community support mechanisms. The results highlight the critical role of mobile technology in strengthening agricultural resilience and enhancing the quality of life for smallholder farmers in the area.

Keywords: mobile applications, smallholder farmers, digital literacy, agricultural productivity, food security

1. Introduction

In the contemporary agricultural landscape, smallholder farmers face complex challenges, prompting an urgent need for innovative technological solutions that can bolster productivity and enhance food security. These farmers, defined as those cultivating small plots of land, play a pivotal role in ensuring food security in developing countries, particularly in sub-Saharan Africa. As reported by the Food and Agriculture Organization [1], smallholder farmers contribute to over 80% of food production in several regions, underscoring their significance to local and national economies. Despite their significance, these farmers often grapple with systemic issues such as limited access to resources, insufficient infrastructure, and ineffective communication channels, all of which can hinder their productivity and profitability [2].

The advent of information and communication technologies (ICTs), particularly mobile applications, has emerged as a transformative force in addressing many of the challenges faced by smallholder farmers. Mobile applications enable instant access to vital information regarding market trends, agricultural advice, weather forecasts, and best farming practices. According to Aker and Mbiti [3], the increasing penetration of mobile phones in rural areas has substantially improved the flow of information among farmers, allowing them to make informed decisions regarding their farming practices. This advancement is particularly relevant in the Eastern Cape Province of South Africa, where smallholder farmers often rely on outdated methods and face difficulties in adapting to modern agricultural techniques.

Research has shown that mobile technology can effectively narrow the information gap, reduce transaction costs, and enhance market participation for smallholder farmers. A study by Ezinne et al. [4] highlights that mobile applications not only facilitate communication but also provide a platform for sharing agricultural content that can lead to higher yields and better marketing opportunities. By leveraging mobile technology, farmers can engage more effectively with suppliers, access timely information, and respond more swiftly to market changes. This shift toward digitized agriculture presents an opportunity for smallholder farmers to enhance their productivity and achieve greater food security [5].

Despite the potential benefits associated with mobile applications, many smallholder farmers still encounter barriers to fully utilizing such technologies. Research conducted by Lubua and Kyobe [6] indicates that socio-economic factors, such as education levels, economic conditions, and age, significantly influence the adoption of mobile applications among farmers. This theme is echoed by Musungwini et al. [7], who emphasize the need for targeted interventions to improve access to mobile technology and foster digital literacy. Understanding these factors is crucial for formulating effective strategies aimed at promoting mobile application use and leveraging technology to enhance agricultural productivity.

The Eastern Cape Province provides a unique case study for investigating the impact of mobile applications on smallholder farmers. Historically, this region has been characterized by challenges such as poverty, limited access to market information, and reliance on subsistence farming practices [8]. However, as the demand for food production rises, addressing the barriers faced by smallholder farmers has become a priority for policymakers. Investigating the dynamics that affect mobile application usage in this context will contribute to the growing body of knowledge on agricultural innovation and technology adoption, thereby equipping stakeholders with the insights needed to design better interventions.

This chapter focuses on examining the social and economic elements that impact the adoption of mobile apps by small-scale farmers in South Africa's Eastern Cape Province. Through a comprehensive evaluation that incorporates theoretical frameworks such as Diffusion Theory and the Theory of Planned Behavior, we will explore

DOI: http://dx.doi.org/10.5772/intechopen.1011306

farmers' experiences, perceptions, and challenges while utilizing mobile technology for agricultural purposes. This investigation endeavors not only to highlight the critical role of mobile applications in smallholder agriculture but also to contribute to the ongoing discourse on achieving sustainable food security through innovative technologies. By analyzing these components, the chapter seeks to inform policy recommendations that can enhance the productivity and livelihoods of smallholder farmers in the region.

2. Theoretical framework

The study, titled "*Leveraging Mobile Applications to Boost Smallholder Farmers' Productivity in the Eastern Cape, South Africa: Effects on Sustainable Food Security*," is grounded in two prominent theories: Diffusion Theory (DT) and the Theory of Planned Behavior (TPB). Diffusion Theory (DT) plays a crucial role in understanding how mobile applications, as innovations, are adopted by smallholder farmers in the Eastern Cape. It examines the spread of new technologies across different social systems, highlighting the importance of communication channels, the role of social networks, and the pace at which farmers adopt these mobile solutions to enhance their productivity. The Theory of Planned Behavior (TPB) further contributes by explaining the psychological factors that drive farmers' intentions to adopt these mobile applications. TPB focuses on how attitudes toward mobile technology, subjective norms (i.e., the influence of peers or community), and perceived behavioral control (farmers' belief in their ability to use the technology effectively) impact their actual behavior. By integrating both theories, this study provides a comprehensive framework to understand how mobile applications can improve agricultural practices and productivity, while also influencing sustainable food security through the adoption process.

3. Diffusion theory

Diffusion Theory, first proposed by Rogers [9], offers valuable insights into how new innovations, such as mobile technologies, are adopted within particular social systems. The theory outlines a multi-phase progression in the adoption process: awareness, evaluation, choice, application, and affirmation. In the initial phase, individuals gain familiarity with the innovation, whereas in the subsequent phase, they develop a perspective on it by assessing its benefits and alignment with their needs. The decision stage involves weighing the benefits against possible risks, leading to the adoption or rejection of the innovation [10].

In the context of agricultural technology, several studies have explored how diffusion patterns impact smallholder farmers' adoption of mobile applications. For instance, Khou and Suresh [11] found that perceived ease of use and perceived usefulness significantly influenced farmers' intentions to adopt mobile farming applications. This highlights the importance of ensuring that mobile applications are user-friendly and demonstrate clear benefits to users, thereby facilitating the diffusion process. Moreover, Asif et al. [12] emphasize that individual and community factors, such as social networks and cultural norms, play an essential role in the technological adoption process, emphasizing the need for tailored approaches to foster acceptance.

4. Theory of planned behavior

The Theory of Planned Behavior (TPB) complements Diffusion Theory by focusing on the psychological aspects influencing an individual's intention to adopt a behavior [13]. According to the TPB, behavioral intentions are influenced by three key components: attitudes toward the behavior, subjective norms, and perceived behavioral control. Attitudes encompass a person's positive or negative evaluations of performing a particular action; subjective norms pertain to social pressures that may encourage or discourage the adoption of the behavior; and perceived behavioral control refers to the perception of one's ability to carry out the action successfully [13].

In agricultural contexts, the TPB has been effectively employed to analyze farmers' intentions concerning technology adoption. A study by Chen and Sima [14] applied the TPB framework to examine farmers' intentions to use precision agriculture technologies and found that both attitudes and perceived social norms significantly influenced their adoption intentions. Additionally, the study highlights that perceived behavioral control, often impacted by access to resources and knowledge, can either facilitate or hinder the adoption of new technologies among smallholder farmers. This aspect is critical, as it suggests that increasing farmers' confidence in using mobile applications through training and awareness programs can bolster adoption rates.

5. Integrating theoretical frameworks

The integration of Diffusion Theory and the Theory of Planned Behavior provides a holistic understanding of the factors that influence smallholder farmers' adoption of mobile applications. Diffusion Theory emphasizes the importance of social systems and communication networks in disseminating information about innovations, while the TPB captures the psychological and social dynamics at play in farmers' decision-making processes regarding technology adoption [15]. Together, these frameworks illustrate that successful adoption of mobile technologies for agriculture requires not merely the presence of technology but also supportive social networks that foster positive attitudes and perceived control over using the technology effectively [16].

Consequently, the implications for policymakers and practitioners are far-reaching. The findings indicate a pressing need to enhance farmers' access to educational resources, create supportive peer networks, and align technical support with local agricultural practices. As highlighted by Masuka et al. [17], agricultural extension services must evolve to incorporate mobile technology as a primary tool for knowledge dissemination, marking a paradigm shift in how farmers interact with agricultural innovations.

The theoretical frameworks of Diffusion Theory and the Theory of Planned Behavior provide invaluable insights into understanding the factors influencing the adoption of mobile applications by smallholder farmers in the Eastern Cape Province. By situating farmers' experiences within these frameworks, stakeholders can better craft interventions that address specific barriers and facilitate the effective use of mobile technology. Continuous research informed by these theories will contribute to the broader dialog surrounding agricultural innovation, development policy, and food security in South Africa.

6. Materials and methods

The research was conducted in South Africa's Eastern Cape Province, a region characterized by its vast land area of 168,966 km^2. Established in 1994, the province emerged from the Xhosa-dominated territories of Transkei and Ciskei. It ranks as the third most populous region in the country, with 6,562,053 residents, accounting for 12.7% of the national population. In comparison, Gauteng and KwaZulu-Natal Provinces have populations of 12,272,263 (23.7%) and 10,267,300 (19.2%), respectively [8, 18]. The province is predominantly rural, with communities relying on agriculture, tourism, and formal employment for their livelihoods.

Situated between the subtropical climate of KwaZulu-Natal and the Mediterranean climate of the Western Cape, the region experiences a bimodal rainfall pattern, with winter rains in the west and summer rains in the east. Unpredictable weather conditions result in varying growing seasons across the area. Despite this, the climate supports agricultural activities, including the cultivation of perennial, arable, and horticultural crops, as well as livestock farming (ruminant and monogastric). The area is primarily inhabited by emerging crop farmers who depend on agriculture for their livelihood.

6.1 Sample size and sampling procedure

The study focused on smallholder farmers in South Africa who utilize mobile phones to enhance productivity and address knowledge gaps in agriculture. A mixed-methods approach, combining qualitative and quantitative techniques, was employed for data collection and analysis. A descriptive survey design was adopted, with data gathered through semi-structured questionnaires.

A multi-stage sampling method was used to select participants. The first stage involved identifying District Municipalities actively engaged in agricultural production. Four districts—Chris Hani, OR Tambo, Amatole, and Alfred Nzo—were chosen. In the second stage, two Local Municipalities within each district, known for their farming activities, were purposively selected. The final stage involved selecting 16 villages based on the presence of active smallholder vegetable farmers. Respondents were randomly chosen from lists of vegetable farmers in these villages. A total sample size of 220 farmers was selected, with 80% (176) being mobile phone users and 20% (44) non-users. This stratification ensured a robust comparison of the impact of mobile phone usage on agricultural productivity.

6.2 Data collection

Primary data were collected through face-to-face interviews using a semi-structured questionnaire developed after a thorough literature review. The questionnaire was pretested and administered by skilled enumerators fluent in IsiXhosa. The final version was overseen by farm supervisors or heads to ensure accuracy. The survey captured data on farmers' socio-demographic characteristics, resource availability, media access, mobile phone usage for agricultural purposes, the impact of mobile phones on productivity and welfare, factors influencing mobile phone adoption, and challenges faced in accessing and using mobile technology. The survey was conducted from August 20 to November 15, 2019, in the Eastern Cape Province.

Variable	Description	Measurement
X_1	Farmers' gender	1 = male, 0 = otherwise
X_2	Farmers' age	Actual years
X_3	Farmers' marital status	1 = married, 0 = otherwise
X_4	Farmers' family size	1 = > 4, 0 = otherwise
X_5	Number of years spent in formal education	1 = actual years spent in school, 0 = otherwise
X_6	Farmers' source of income	1 = social grants, 0 = otherwise
X_7	Number of years spent in farming	Actual years of farming
X_8	Distance/closeness to the market place	1 = 10 km, 0 = otherwise
X_9	Access to extension agents by the farmer	1 = access to extension agents, 0 = otherwise
X10	Access to a financial institution by the farmer	1 = access to a financial institution, 0 = otherwise
X11	Member of farm organization	1 = member of farm organization, 0 = otherwise
X12	Household monthly income	1= > 1500, 0 = otherwise
X13	Occupation by the household head	1 = full time farmer, 0 = otherwise
X14	Farming as the only source of income	1 = farming as an only income source, 0 = otherwise
X15	Knowledge of using mobile phones for agricultural purposes	1 = can use mobile phone for agricultural purposes, 0 = otherwise

Source: Researchers' Initiative, 2021.

Table 1.
Description of variables used in the study.

6.3 Data

The variables for this study were identified in consultation with experts and professionals familiar with the region and its agricultural context. These variables were carefully selected to ensure the study's relevance and comprehensiveness. Data collected are shown in **Table 1**.

7. Analytical framework

This section examines two analytical approaches. The first involves descriptive statistics, such as frequencies, percentages, and mean values, to summarize the profiles and characteristics of farmers in the study area. The second approach employs a logistic regression model to identify factors influencing the adoption of mobile phones by smallholder farmers for productivity enhancement.

8. Logistic regression

The study utilized the logit regression model to assess the factors driving the use of mobile phones among smallholder farmers. The term "logit" refers to log-likelihoods, which estimate the probability of an event occurring within one of two categories based on specific explanatory variables [19]. According to Mdoda et al. [20] and Chauke et al. [21], logistic regression is suitable for analyzing the probabilistic relationship between independent variables in a model. The logit model was chosen for this study due to the binary nature of the dependent variable, which categorizes respondents into mobile phone users and non-users. Mobile phone usage in this context refers to farmers who have adopted mobile technology to improve productivity.

The regression analysis involves two distinct outcomes. Since the dependent variable is binary, the study employs a binomial logistic model, where 0 represents farmers who do not use mobile phones on their farms and 1 represents those who do.

For this study, the two categories are "mobile phone users" and "non-users." The binary regression model is designed to explain Y = 1, indicating farmers who use mobile phones, and Y = 0, representing those who do not. As outlined by Wooldridge [19], X denotes the set of explanatory variables, while p represents the probability of Y = 1. The relationship between these variables is expressed as follows:

$$p(Y=1) = 1 + e\beta\chi \tag{1}$$

$$p(Y=0) = 1 - \frac{e\beta\chi}{1+e\beta\chi} = \frac{1}{1+e\beta\chi} \tag{2}$$

where Eq. (2) is the subsidiary response level, that is, the possibility that small holder farmers employ the usage of handsets on their farms, as this will likely be revealed using the logistic regression approach. The computations simultaneously show the logit adjustment results with probability proportions explained thus:

$$[\theta(x) \operatorname{logit}[\theta(x)] = \log] = \alpha + \beta_1 X_1 + \beta_2 X_2 + \beta_3 X_3 + \ldots\ldots\ldots L + \beta_n X_n \; 1 - \theta(x) \tag{3}$$

Asides from authorizing its estimate as a direct regression, the following representations relate:

Θ = logistic amendment of the contingency fraction; = the intercept span

β = explanatory or critical variables; and.

X_i = predictor or forecaster variables.

The preceding procedures were feasible inside the STATA. More so, Eq. (3) indicates the perusal generated the chances of relations depleting the highest expectation technique. The logistic deterioration in this study can be stated as follows:

$$Y1 = \alpha + \beta 1X1 + \beta 2X2 + n\beta 3X3 + \beta 4X4 + \beta 5X5L + Un \tag{4}$$

where

Yi (mobile phones usage) = the reliance on variable distinct as mobile phones usage = 1 and 0 otherwise α = constant.

β = slope of the distinct forecaster variables.

X_i = forecaster variables.

U_n = alteration or variation error term.

9. Results and discussion

9.1 Socio-economic characteristics of smallholder farmers

The study examined the socio-economic characteristics of smallholder farmers in the Eastern Cape, who use mobile applications for enhancing agricultural productivity. The data revealed a diverse demographic profile among the 220 surveyed farmers, with a significant majority (70%) actively using mobile applications for agricultural purposes. More importantly, the majority of respondents were female (88%), highlighting women's critical role in agriculture and food production in the region. This finding aligns with Sikundla et al. [22], who noted that female farmers often manage household and agricultural activities, thus contributing significantly to food security.

The data also indicated that most farmers were aged between 28 and 50 years, suggesting a relatively youthful demographic among smallholder farmers in the Eastern Cape. Age is a critical factor in technology adoption, as younger farmers tend to be more receptive to innovative farming practices and technologies [21]. In conjunction with education levels, where the average farmer had approximately 7 years of formal education, these findings suggest that education plays a vital role in an individual's ability to utilize mobile applications effectively. According to Mwalupaso et al. [2], education enhances farmers' capabilities to access information and adopt new technologies, positively impacting productivity.

9.2 Mobile applications usage patterns

The survey results concerning specific mobile applications revealed that WhatsApp (54%) and Facebook (27%) were the most frequently utilized platforms among farmers. These findings are consistent with the observations of Huq et al. [23], who underscored the increasing reliance on social media tools for agricultural information dissemination. Farmers reported using WhatsApp primarily for sharing agricultural information, managing farm operations, and communicating with peers. This reflects a shift toward leveraging social media not only as a communication tool but also as a medium for fostering agricultural collaboration. **Tables 2** and **3** show the mobile application use.

The frequency of mobile phone usage for agricultural purposes indicated that 62% of respondents used mobile applications daily, while 15% reported weekly usage. This high level of engagement suggests that smallholder farmers recognize the importance of real-time information for day-to-day decisions in their farming activities. The implications of such usage patterns are significant; farmers who utilize mobile technologies

Categories	Frequency	Percentage (%)
WhatsApp	120	54
Facebook	60	27
Newspapers	30	14
Twitter	10	5

Table 2.
Frequency distribution showing the extent of usage of mobile phone apps for agricultural information dissemination.

Categories	Frequency	Percentage (%)
Daily	136	62
Weekly	34	15
1–4 times a week	20	9
2–3 times a month	30	14

Source: [24].

Table 3.
Frequency of mobile phone usage for agricultural information.

can enhance their awareness of critical issues like market prices, weather conditions, and agricultural best practices, resulting in improved agricultural outputs [4].

9.3 Main purpose of using mobile phones by smallholder farmers

The adoption of mobile phone applications by smallholder farmers plays a vital role in adapting to evolving agricultural practices and leveraging modern technology to enhance productivity and profitability. **Table 4** outlines the key purposes for which smallholder farmers utilize mobile phones.

The findings of the study reveal that a significant portion of mainstream farmers, approximately 18%, rely on mobile phones to set reminders for essential farm management tasks, as they often forget these activities. This aligns with Chisama's [25] research, which highlights that most farmers prefer using mobile phones to stay updated on their farm-related responsibilities. Beyond reminders, mobile phones serve various other purposes in agriculture, including soil fertility management and

Categories	Frequency	Percentage (%)	Rank
Farmers' usage of mobile phones and the Internet for extension advice	10	5	8
Farmers' usage of mobile phone for agriculture business	30	13.64	3
Farmers using mobile phones for traceability	20	9.00	6
Farmer groups and money transfer	10	5	10
Pasture management and livestock distribution	5	2.27	12
Weather updates	10	5	9
Fertilizer application rates	22	10	5
Improved crop varieties and market information	15	6.82	7
Access training and improved product marketing	28	12.73	4
Reminders on farm management activities	40	18.00	1
Soil fertility management and agricultural prices	32	14.55	2
Irrigation practices	8	3.64	11

**Results appearing in multiple responses with frequencies and percentages (N = 220).*
Source: [24].

Table 4.
Frequency of farmers' usage of mobile phones.

monitoring agricultural prices (15%), facilitating agricultural business operations (13.6%), accessing farming training and enhancing product marketing (12.7%), determining fertilizer application rates (10%), ensuring traceability (9%), obtaining information on improved crop varieties and market trends (6.8%), seeking extension advice and Internet access (5%), coordinating farmer groups and enabling money transfers (5%), receiving weather updates (5%), and managing irrigation practices (3.6%). The least common use of mobile phones among smallholder farmers was for pasture management and livestock distribution, accounting for only 2.3%. Overall, mobile phones are a crucial tool in boosting smallholder productivity by delivering timely and accessible information to farmers.

9.4 Benefits of mobile applications

The analysis of benefits derived from mobile application usage by farmers further illuminated the substantial impact of technology on agricultural productivity. The benefits of using mobile by smallholder farmers are shown in **Table 5**. A significant majority of respondents reported increased access to high-yielding seeds (77%), market pricing information (73%), and knowledge of optimal crop production techniques (59%). These results echo findings from studies such as those conducted by Aker and Mbiti [3], which demonstrate that mobile information services can contribute to enhanced agricultural productivity by providing timely and relevant information.

Moreover, the ability to quickly access market data through mobile applications can empower farmers to negotiate better prices for their produce, thus improving their income and livelihoods. Research by Adam and Hassan [26] suggests that when smallholder farmers are equipped with market information, they are more likely to engage in profitable trading practices, ultimately leading to improved food security at the household level.

9.5 Challenges faced by smallholder farmers

Despite the numerous advantages linked to mobile application usage, the study also identified significant challenges hindering farmers' ability to maximize the potential of mobile technology. Challenges are shown in **Table 6**. The findings revealed that 66% of respondents cited high costs associated with mobile phones as

Variable	Frequency	Percentage (%)
High-yielding seeds	170	77
Fertilizer use	110	50
Market information and pricing	160	73
Crop and livestock production techniques	130	59
Pesticides and herbicides use	80	37
Training from agricultural extension services	90	45
General agricultural news	90	45
Source: [24].		

Table 5.
Benefits of using mobile by smallholder farmers.

Problem	Frequency	Percentage (%)	Rank
Expensive	145	66	1
Mobile phone operating problem	115	52	2
Network coverage problems	110	50	3
The high cost of repairing	95	43	4
Technical problems	90	41	5
Difficulty in using mobile phones	88	40	6

Source: [24].

Table 6.
Problem faced by smallholder farmers in using mobile phones.

a major barrier to utilization. This aligns with the work of Lubua and Kyope [6], who note that economic constraints diminish farmers' capabilities to invest in necessary technologies.

Moreover, issues such as network coverage (50%) and mobile phone operating difficulties (52%) emerged as significant challenges, which negatively impacted the consistency of information access and utilization. As highlighted by Mwalupaso et al. [2], the lack of reliable telecommunications infrastructure in rural areas can contribute to disparities in access to mobile-based agricultural resources, perpetuating existing inequalities.

9.6 Econometric analysis of mobile application usage

The logistic regression analysis indicated a formidable relationship between socioeconomic variables and mobile application usage among smallholder farmers. The model's findings highlighted that education levels and income, along with family size, were significantly correlated with mobile application use. Specifically, each additional year of education was associated with a 0.163% increase in the likelihood of adopting mobile applications for agricultural purposes. This supports findings from Masuka et al. [17], which emphasize the importance of educational interventions to improve farmers' technology adoption. **Table 7** illustrates the factors influencing the media usage by smallholder farmers.

Conversely, the analysis indicated that older farmers exhibited lower mobile application usage due to barriers such as limited exposure to novel technologies. For instance, each additional year in a farmer's age reduced the likelihood of mobile app usage by 0.287%. Findings from Asif et al. [12] corroborate this assertion, emphasizing that older adults may be less inclined to engage with new technologies, unless provided with adequate training and support.

9.7 Implications for food security

The findings of this study illuminate the potential for mobile applications to significantly contribute to agricultural productivity and by extension, food security among smallholder farmers in the Eastern Cape Province. By facilitating timely access to critical agricultural information, mobile technology serves as a conduit for improving crop yields and market competitiveness. As highlighted by the FAO [1],

Variable	Coefficient	Std. error	Significance	dy/dx
Intercept	−1.948	0.613	0.002***	0.2123
Age	−0.287	0.651	0.043 **	0.2242
Years spent in school	0.163	0.058	0.004***	0.1903
Family size	0.163	0.058	0.004***	0.2003
Farming experience	−0.681	0.425	0.023**	0.1530
Total income level	0.423	0.145	0.038***	0.2156
Number of observers = 220 Pseudo $R^2 = 0.72$	−2 log-likelihood 148.569 Adjusted R square = 0.70		Prob (chi-square) = 0.000 DF = 8.00	

*Standard errors: **p < 0.05, ***p < 0.001.*
Source: [24].

Table 7.
Factors influencing the use of media by smallholder farmers.

smallholder farmers are pivotal to achieving food security, and the adoption of mobile applications can enhance their productivity, thereby contributing to sustainable agricultural development in South Africa.

While challenges persist in the adoption of mobile technologies, the findings underscore the importance of addressing these barriers in order to empower smallholder farmers effectively. Policymakers, agricultural extension services, and nongovernmental organizations (NGOs) can play instrumental roles in facilitating the integration of mobile technology into agricultural practices. Incentives for mobile technology adoption, coupled with tailored educational programs focused on digital literacy, can foster a conducive environment for smallholder farmers to thrive.

10. Conclusion

This chapter has explored the critical role of mobile applications in enhancing the productivity of smallholder farmers in the Eastern Cape Province of South Africa and their implications for sustainable food security. The findings indicate that mobile technology acts as a significant enabler, providing farmers with timely access to vital agricultural information, which in turn enhances their decision-making processes and farming practices. The data demonstrated that a substantial proportion of farmers were utilizing mobile applications, particularly WhatsApp and Facebook, as effective tools for sharing knowledge, managing farm operations, and accessing market information. This underscores the transformative potential of mobile technology in bridging communication gaps and facilitating collaboration among farmers.

Despite the evident benefits associated with mobile application usage, the study highlighted several barriers that must be addressed to maximize the potential of mobile technologies for agricultural development. Key challenges included the high costs of mobile devices, limited network coverage, and varying levels of digital literacy among farmers. These findings resonate with similar studies on agricultural technology adoption, which emphasize that access to resources and infrastructure play a pivotal role in shaping the ability of smallholder farmers to leverage innovations effectively. To counter these challenges, targeted interventions by government and NGOs are essential to enhance farmers' access to technology, improve infrastructure, and provide training on how to utilize mobile applications effectively.

From a socio-economic perspective, the analysis of factors influencing mobile application usage revealed that education, income, and family dynamics significantly affected the likelihood of farmers adopting these technologies. Specifically, higher education levels were associated with greater use of mobile applications, suggesting that robust educational initiatives can empower farmers to embrace modern farming techniques. Additionally, the role of social networks and community support was emphasized, as interconnected farmers were more likely to engage with mobile technology for agricultural purposes. Thus, fostering collective action and peer-to-peer learning within agricultural communities can serve as a catalyst for broader technology adoption.

It is critical for stakeholders to recognize that the successful integration of mobile technology into the agricultural landscape is not solely reliant on technology availability. The socio-cultural and economic contexts in which these farmers operate must be understood and addressed to enable meaningful and sustainable adoption. Policymakers should focus on creating an enabling environment that promotes agricultural innovation through infrastructure development, financial support, and digital literacy initiatives specifically tailored for smallholder farmers.

Future research should continue to investigate the evolving nature of mobile applications in agriculture, particularly their integration with other technologies such as drones and Internet of Things (IoT) systems. Longitudinal studies can provide deeper insights into how sustained engagement with mobile applications influences agricultural productivity and food security over time. Finally, as the landscape of global agriculture continues to evolve, it is crucial that the voices and experiences of smallholder farmers remain at the forefront of this discourse, guiding the development of policies and initiatives that aim to harness technology for agricultural resilience.

In conclusion, mobile applications represent a significant opportunity for enhancing the livelihoods of smallholder farmers in the Eastern Cape Province of South Africa. By addressing the barriers to technology adoption and fostering an enabling environment for innovation, stakeholders can empower these farmers, ultimately contributing to greater food security and sustainable agricultural development in the region. Implementing strategic interventions and continuing to support farmers in navigating the complexities of agricultural technology will be vital for achieving a resilient agricultural future.

Author details

Lelethu Mdoda[1]*, Mzuyanda Christian[2], Ikechi Agbugba[3,4,5] and Denver Naidoo[6]

1 Discipline of Agricultural Economics, University of KwaZulu-Natal, Pietermaritzburg, South Africa

2 School of Agricultural Sciences, University of Mpumalanga, Mbombela, South Africa

3 Department of Agricultural and Applied Economics, Faculty of Agriculture, Rivers State University, Port Harcourt, Nigeria

4 Business Management Programme, York St. John University, London, United Kingdom

5 Agribusiness Management Programme, Rome Business School (Nigerian Campus), Ikeja, Lagos State, Nigeria

6 African Centre for Food Security (ACFS), University of KwaZulu-Natal, Pietermaritzburg, South Africa

*Address all correspondence to: mdodal@ukzn.ac.za

References

[24] Food and Agriculture Organization (FAO). The State of Food and Agriculture 2016: Climate Change, Agriculture, and Food Security. Rome: FAO; 2016. Available from: chrome-extension://efaidnbmnnnibpcajpcglclefindmkaj/https://openknowledge.fao.org/server/api/core/bitstreams/07bc7c6e-72e5-488d-b2f7-3c1499d098fb/content

[25] Mwalupaso GE, Wang S, Xu Z, Tian X. Towards auspicious agricultural informatization-implication of farmers' behavioral intention apropos of Mobile phone use in agriculture. Sustainability. 2019;**11**:6282. DOI: 10.3390/su11226282

[26] Aker JC, Mbiti IM. Mobile phones and economic development in Africa. The Journal of Economic Perspectives. 2010;**24**(3):207-232. DOI: 10.1257/jep.24.3.207

[27] Ezinne ME, Liz T, Katharina D. The revolution of mobile phone-enabled services for agricultural development (m-Agri services) in Africa; the challenges for sustainability. Sustainability. 2020;**12**:485. DOI: 10.3390/su12020485

[28] Agbugba IK, Agbagwa SK, Anumudu C, Ekwebelem OC, Al-Sharify ZT, Isaac-Bamgboye FJ, et al. The evolving state of food security in Nigeria amidst the COVID-19 pandemic – A review. Open Agriculture. 2022;7:899-909

[29] Lubua EW, Kyobe ME. The influence of socioeconomic factors on the use of Mobile phones in the agricultural sector of Tanzania. The African Journal of Information Systems. 2019;**11**(4):352-366

[30] Musungwini S. Mobile phone use by Zimbabwean smallholder farmers: A baseline study. The African Journal of Information and Communication (AJIC). 2018;**22**:29-52. DOI: 10.23962/10539/26171

[31] Mdoda L, Obi A. Analysis of profitability of smallholder irrigated food plots in the eastern Cape Province of South Africa. Journal of Agribusiness and Rural Development. 2019;**3**(53):225-232

[32] Rogers EM. Diffusion of Innovations. 5th ed. New York: Free Press; 2003

[33] Mdoda L, Obi A, Tamako N, Naidoo D, Baloyi R. Resource use efficiency of potato production among smallholder irrigated farmers in the Eastern Cape Province of South Africa. Sustainability. 2023;**15**(19):14457

[34] Khou A, Suresh KR. A study on the role of social media mobile applications and its impact on agricultural marketing in the Puducherry region. Journal of Management. 2018;**5**(6):28-35. Available from: http://www.iaeme.com/JOM/issues.asp?JType=JOM&VType=5&IType=6

[35] Asif AS, Uddin MN, Dev DS, Miah MAM. Factors affecting Mobile phone usage by the farmers in receiving information on vegetable cultivation in Bangladesh. Journal of Agricultural Informatics. 2017;**8**(1):33-43

[36] Ajzen I. The theory of planned behavior. Organizational Behavior and Human Decision Processes. 1991;**50**(2):179-211. DOI: 10.1016/0749-5978(91)90020-T

[37] Chen Y, Sima H. Study on farmers' adoption of precision agriculture technologies: An empirical analysis based on the theory of planned behavior.

Sustainability. 2017;**9**(8):1435. DOI: 10.3390/su9081435

[38] Agbugba IK. Brain Re-engineering concept and reimagination: Strategy form rebranding agriculture and youth engagement in promoting food production. European Modern Studies Journal. 2023;7(5):213-223

[39] Park HJ, Camara MB, Agbugba IK. Solar-powered parboiling rice machine and its relevance to sustainability. European Modern Studies Journal. 2023;7(6):1-15

[40] Masuka B, Matenda T, Chipomho J, Mapope N, Mupeti S, Tatsvarei S, et al. Mobile phone use by small-scale farmers: The potential to transform production and Marketing in Zimbabwe. South African Journal of Agricultural Extension. 2016;**44**(2):121-135. DOI: 10.17159/2413-3221/2016/v44n2a406

[41] Hlomendlini PH. Key factors influencing smallholder market participation in the former homelands of South Africa: Case study of the Eastern Cape [MSc dissertation]. South Africa: Stellenbosch University, RSA; 2015

[42] Wooldridge JM. Introductory Econometrics, A Modern Approach. 4th ed. USA: Michigan State University; 2009

[43] Mdoda L, Meleni S, Mujuru N, Alaka KO. Agricultural credit effects on smallholder crop farmers input utilisation in the Eastern Cape Province, South Africa. Journal of Human Ecology. 2019;**66**(1-3):45-55

[44] Chauke PK, Motlhatlhana ML, Pfumayaramba TK, Anim FDK. Factors influencing access to credit: A case study of smallholder farmers in the Capricorn District of South Africa. African Journal of Agricultural Research. 2013;**8**(7):582-585

[45] Sikundla T, Mushunje A, Akinyemi BE. Socioeconomic drivers of Mobile phone adoption for marketing among smallholder irrigation farmers in South Africa. Cogent Social Sciences. 2018;**4**(1):1505415

[46] Huq M, Farhana K, Rahman A. Application of mobile phone in agricultural marketing in Bangladesh. IOSR Journal of Business and Management. 2017;**19**(1):77-82

[47] Mdoda L, Christian M, Agbugba I. Use of information systems (Mobile phone app) for enhancing smallholder farmers' productivity in eastern Cape Province, South Africa: Implications on food security. Journal of the Knowledge Economy. 2024;**15**:1-17. DOI: 10.1007/s13132-023-01212-0

[48] Chisama BF. Farmers' use of mobile phone technology for agricultural information services in Lilongwe District, Malawi. Open Access Theses. 934. Published MSc Thesis, Purdue University, and West Lafayette, Indiana. 2016. Available from: https://docs.lib.purdue.edu/open_access_theses/934

[49] Adam SAS, Hassan TA. Socio-economic factors influencing small scale farmer's livelihoods and food security in Central Darfur state – Sudan. International Journal of Current Research in Life Sciences. 2015;**4**(11):464-468

Chapter 4

Unlocking Collective Wisdom: The Power of Knowledge Sharing in Modern Organizations

Sarika Singh, Gour C. Saha and Mukesh Singh

Abstract

In today's fast-paced work environment, knowledge sharing is increasingly vital for organizational success. Despite a decrease in employee turnover in India post-pandemic, high-employee mobility in a dynamic job market continues to challenge knowledge retention. Frequent workforce transitions result in the loss of expertise can upset organizational continuity. Additionally, inefficiencies in accessing knowledge by employees lead to wasted resources, redundancy, and disengagement, impacting morale and productivity. Traditional knowledge management systems focused on saving information often fall short in enabling seamless access. While digital tools have improved knowledge storage, the key challenge lies in effectively sharing knowledge with those who need it. Modern knowledge-sharing practices are supported by AI-driven tools and collaborative platforms and a strong knowledge-sharing culture enable an ecosystem for dynamic, interaction-based sharing, and innovation. This chapter discusses the impact of knowledge sharing on firm's performance and identifies important factors for building knowledge-sharing capabilities. These include individual, and organizational and cultural factors. Finally, the chapter examines the evolution of knowledge-sharing practices in few Indian firms. It explores how digital systems for explicit and tacit knowledge sharing can improve collaboration. With these insights, senior managers can enhance innovation, efficiency, and competitiveness, ensuring long-term growth and success in a rapidly evolving business landscape.

Keywords: explicit knowledge sharing, tacit knowledge sharing, knowledge management, innovation, business performance

1. Introduction

In today's fast-paced work environment, knowledge sharing has become essential for organizational success. While employee turnover and job hopping have slightly decreased in Indian organizations following the pandemic, the 18% job attrition rate recorded in 2023 still remains a significant challenge for knowledge sharing. Frequent workforce transitions often result in the loss of valuable expertise, insights, and organizational memory, disrupting daily operations and hindering long-term growth and innovation.

In large organizations in India, inefficiencies in accessing knowledge are becoming a serious challenge. According to an informal interview with senior managers from five consulting firms, employees often spend about 20% of their work time, searching for answers that their colleagues already know. The issue stems from a lack of awareness about whom to approach or where to find the needed information. This disconnect leads to redundancy, as employees spend time on work that has already been done, and it wastes valuable time and resources. Beyond inefficiencies, this also contributes to employee disengagement. When employees feel unsupported in accessing the information they need or experience repeated frustrations, their morale and motivation may decline. This disengagement can ripple across teams, negatively impacting productivity and collaboration.

In the digital age, where systems are highly interconnected, the IT industry, in particular, faces additional challenges. Cybersecurity threats are on the rise, and managing these risks requires effective cross-functional knowledge sharing. Organizations must focus on building a strong knowledge-sharing culture to improve efficiency, keep employees engaged, and address emerging risks effectively. A powerful example of addressing the knowledge sharing issue is Google's G2G, or "Googlers-to-Googlers," network. This initiative highlights how a well-designed knowledge-sharing culture can transform organizational dynamics. At Google, regardless of role or hierarchy, employees are encouraged to reach out to their colleagues, seek guidance, share expertise, or learn new skills. This open access to collective knowledge not only makes work processes smoother but also fosters a sense of community and support, contributing to Google's reputation for having an exceptional work culture.

The Indian workforce is undergoing a significant transformation, characterized by a unique generational mix. Senior management largely consists of seasoned professionals, the mid-management tier is predominantly composed of Gen Y, and the new recruits entering the workforce are primarily Gen Z. Each of these generations brings distinct working styles, values, and approaches to the table, often leading to friction in the workplace. However, this generational diversity also presents a valuable opportunity to foster a culture of knowledge sharing where organizations can enable employees to learn from one another.

Traditionally, organizations have approached knowledge sharing through knowledge management systems that focused primarily on storing and organizing information. These systems allowed employees to upload documents, insights, and data into centralized repositories. However, while these repositories were useful for storing knowledge, they often fell short in enabling seamless access to the right information at the right time. Employees frequently struggled to find what they needed, as there was no clear mechanism for guiding access to specific knowledge or expertise within the organizations. Certain mechanisms, such as cross-functional teams, customer-focused units, work groups, and communities of practice, were established to promote collaboration and knowledge exchange. However, these efforts often lacked a cohesive approach to recognize and facilitate genuine knowledge sharing. As a result, even though systems and processes were in place, they did not fully address the need for dynamic and targeted knowledge exchange.

In modern organizations, digital tools have revolutionized how knowledge is stored, making it easier to access and manage large amounts of information. However, a key challenge persists: channelling this stored knowledge to the employees who need it most. Many organizations rely on static knowledge management practices, which focus on depositing knowledge without ensuring it reaches the intended audience. This creates disconnect, as employees may be unaware of the resources available or unsure how to access them effectively.

By contrast, knowledge sharing goes beyond static storage. It is dynamic and interaction-focused, aiming to actively connect people with the information, skills, and expertise they require. It emphasizes building networks, encouraging collaboration, and fostering open communication among employees. Modern knowledge-sharing practices use tools like AI-driven recommendations, collaborative platforms, and social learning to ensure that knowledge flows seamlessly across teams and functions. This approach not only enhances accessibility but also boosts innovation, efficiency, and employee engagement, making knowledge sharing an indispensable element of successful organizations today.

This chapter aims to explore the adoption of knowledge-sharing practices in Indian and global firms, analysing the factors that influence knowledge-sharing processes worldwide. It provides a comprehensive overview through a summary of literature reviews and case studies, addressing two key objectives:

i. To gain a deeper understanding of how knowledge sharing in different organizational contexts impacts firm performance.

ii. To identify and evaluate the critical knowledge-sharing factors necessary for developing a framework that offers actionable guidelines to enhance organizational performance.

By examining these objectives, the chapter seeks to bridge theoretical insights with practical strategies, enabling firms to harness the full potential of knowledge sharing for improved outcomes.

2. Knowledge sharing and organizational performance

Knowledge, encompassing elements such as management systems, brand identity, customer information, and corporate reputation, is a vital strategic asset for organizations. Its effective sharing among employees plays a critical role in enhancing organizational performance and leveraging intellectual capital. Research highlights the importance of knowledge-based tasks, reporting that 99% of organizational activities rely on knowledge [1].

The knowledge-based theory of the firm emphasizes the role of knowledge sharing in fostering innovation and building a strong foundation for organizational success [2]. This process enables individuals to learn not only from their own experiences but also from others through feedback, advice, and shared insights. The reciprocal nature of knowledge sharing generates new ideas while enriching both the giver and the receiver [3].

Organizational performance is influenced by the types of knowledge shared and the methods used to manage it. Tacit knowledge, resembling wisdom in an information value chain, embodies deeply ingrained expertise and insights [4]. McKinsey & Company and Bain & Company utilize "people-to-people" methods, connecting global networks of experts to share tacit knowledge through meetings, calls, emails, and video conferences, ensuring alignment with company culture and customer needs [5]. Conversely, Accenture's "people-to-documents" model emphasizes the sharing of anonymized explicit knowledge, treating knowledge objects as reusable templates for core insights across industries, thereby enhancing operational efficiency. While explicit knowledge sharing improves efficiency by distributing valuable information, tacit knowledge sharing fosters dialog, shared experiences, and collective problem-solving, driving innovation and collaboration [6].

Empirical studies highlight that innovation culture mediates the relationship between knowledge sharing and firm performance [7, 8]. Knowledge sharing fosters collaboration and the exchange of ideas, creating a foundation for innovative thinking. An innovation culture ensures shared knowledge is actively applied to improve processes, products, and services, driving business performance. Firms with strong knowledge-sharing practices and an innovation-focused environment achieve greater adaptability, efficiency, and market success.

In summary, the relationship between knowledge sharing and organizational performance is multifaceted, encompassing improved collaboration, innovation, and the development of structures that optimize knowledge utilization. This reinforces the importance of embedding knowledge-sharing practices within organizational strategies to achieve sustained growth and competitiveness.

3. Factors affecting knowledge sharing: Conceptual framework

Research on knowledge sharing explores how firms utilize knowledge to gain a competitive advantage. Studies identify culture, attitude, and infrastructure as key enablers of knowledge-sharing capabilities. Effective knowledge sharing hinges on balancing "intrinsic" factors, such as motivation and trust, with "extrinsic" factors, like infrastructure and reward systems. For instance, job security fosters intrinsic motivation, encouraging employees to share knowledge through strong relationships and reciprocity [9]. In contrast, extrinsic motivators, such as robust knowledge infrastructure, promote self-interest and operational efficiency. Organizations that harmonize intrinsic and extrinsic factors create a mutually reinforcing system, boosting competitive advantage and performance. Knowledge sharing is crucial for a company's success, but there is little research on how companies develop this ability. Companies vary in how they adopt practices to improve knowledge sharing. A knowledge-sharing culture is shaped by how a company is organized and operates. Key factors include leadership, trust, technology, rewards, and company culture. Good leadership sets clear goals, defines success, and helps manage power to encourage sharing. Trust builds teamwork and support, though it can be hard to maintain as the company grows. A strong culture shifts from "What do we think?" to "What do we know?" Companies with effective knowledge-sharing treat knowledge as an important asset, making it part of their values and decision-making.

Business analytics and data mining technologies have further revolutionized knowledge sharing by converting raw data into actionable insights that drive decision-making and innovation. These tools enable organizations to extract, analyse, and disseminate valuable information, fostering collaboration and informed strategies. Data mining uncovers hidden patterns and trends, facilitating explicit knowledge sharing in a structured and accessible format. Analytics platforms promote real-time knowledge exchange by integrating insights into workflows and providing personalized recommendations. This seamless sharing of data-driven insights enhances operational efficiency, empowers organizations to adapt to market changes, and cultivates a culture of continuous learning and improvement.

The study highlights that the adoption of knowledge sharing is influenced by a variety of external and internal factors (**Figure 1**). It draws upon the Theory of Reasoned Action (TRA), which emphasizes the significance of the knowledge-sharing

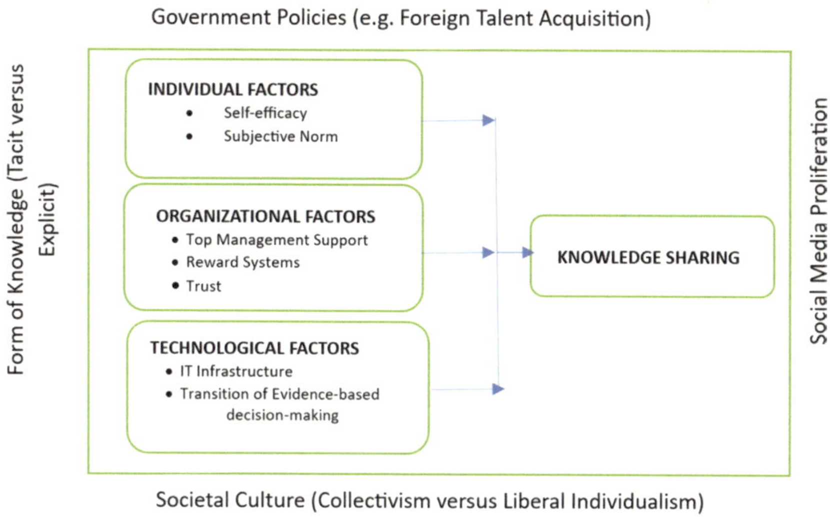

Figure 1.
Knowledge-sharing framework.

process. Theory of reasoned action examines individuals' intentions, willingness, and engagement in specific knowledge-sharing behaviors [10]. The theory identifies three key drivers of behavior: the attitude toward the sharing behavior, subjective norms, and the intention to perform or refrain from the behavior [11]. Further research explored factors affecting knowledge-sharing behavior within organizations [12].

Self-efficacy, defined as an individual's belief in their ability to successfully perform and achieve a specific task or goal, plays a crucial role in shaping knowledge-sharing behaviors. Introduced by Albert Bandura as part of Social Cognitive Theory, self-efficacy influences an individual's attitude toward engaging in the knowledge-sharing process [13]. A high level of self-efficacy enhances an individual's willingness and confidence to share knowledge, fostering active participation.

Organizational support significantly impacts the success of knowledge-sharing initiatives. Effective managers play a vital role in recognizing and leveraging the unique expertise of employees. By explicitly identifying and acknowledging individuals' skills—for example, expertise in customer acquisition—managers facilitate "knowledge handshakes," or collaborative exchanges of information. Integrating these practices into routine workflows and incentivizing participation through rewards further cultivate a culture of knowledge sharing within the organization.

Technology serves as an enabler of knowledge sharing by streamlining the diffusion and assimilation of knowledge into business processes. According to Technology Assimilation Theory, the effective infusion of technology enhances organizational performance by embedding it into routine activities [14]. While knowledge sharing is not solely dependent on hardware, two critical technological factors identified in this study are ICT infrastructure and the shift toward evidence-based decision-making. These elements support the seamless exchange and utilization of knowledge within organizations.

The three internal factors—individual, organizational, and technological—are influenced by four external factors: government policy, societal culture, the type of knowledge shared, and social media. For example, in difficult job markets, policies supporting foreign talent can weaken networks, leading individuals to withhold knowledge to protect their jobs. In individualistic societies, people share knowledge mainly for personal gain or career growth, often sharing only when it benefits them. In collectivist societies, sharing knowledge is focused on helping the group, with more collaboration. In these cultures, how much people share can be uncertain because both the risks and rewards influence their choices. The type of knowledge also matters. Knowledge deeply rooted in an organization's practices is easier to share, while knowledge from external sources is harder to transfer. A recent study discusses the impact of social media on knowledge sharing [15]. The researchers suggest that factors like altruism, online attachment motivation, and online relationship commitment influence knowledge sharing. The use of social media has evolved from traditional tools such as email and face-to-face meetings to modern platforms such as enterprise social networks, Google Docs, wikis, discussion forums, and blogs.

4. Knowledge sharing in Indian organizations: Few evidences

The Government of India launched the Digital India program on 2 July 2015, with the aim of transitioning India into a digitally empowered society. This initiative sought to enhance online infrastructure, making public and private services accessible to citizens electronically. By enabling smoother and more transparent transactions, digitization curbed the existence of a parallel economy and encouraged widespread adoption of digital systems. The government leveraged the advancements in digital enterprise to drive socio-economic stability and achieve development goals. Initiatives such as 'Make in India' fostered public-private partnerships, promoting collaboration across industries and facilitating technology transfer and knowledge sharing.

Digitization integrates business processes, enhances operational efficiency, and improves customer service. It has augmented both manufacturing and services sector, key growth avenues for the Indian economy. Growth in the manufacturing sector spurred expansion in several service sub-sectors due to ancillary requirements. Additionally, digitization transformed numerous non-tradable services into tradable ones. These developments expanded exports, employment opportunities, and foreign direct investment [16].

While the regulatory environment encourages collaboration and innovation, the key to remaining competitive in a dynamic marketplace is dissemination of knowledge. In addition, hierarchical organizational structures, typical of most Indian organizations, together with high-employee mobility calls for robust knowledge management. A typical workforce includes individuals from multiple generations who bring varied perspectives. However, differences in language, cultural backgrounds, and attitudes require innovative communication strategies. Knowledge sharing is the exchange of information, expertise, and insights between employees, teams and organizations enhancing collaboration and business outcomes. As Indian firms embrace digital systems for knowledge sharing, they have to be prepared for wide-ranging transformation. Building organizational trust is crucial for nurturing a culture of knowledge sharing. Furthermore, a combination of cultural, technological, and leadership factors determines the success of these practices. The Indian culture, which values interpersonal relationships, mutual respect, and adaptability, provides a unique opportunity to strengthen organizational culture. By embracing these cultural strengths, organizations can foster a collaborative environment that promotes knowledge sharing and innovation. Prioritizing employee well-being and engagement enhances organizational trust. The commitment of the leadership team and rewards for knowledge sharing enhance employee's confidence and participation.

In the following section, the authors explore knowledge sharing initiatives in Indian organizations with an emphasis on the industry context, challenges, platforms, tools, and business value.

4.1 Knowledge sharing in IT security industry

4.1.1 Introduction

Industry leaders in IT security sector have leveraged advanced technology and organized knowledge-sharing frameworks, to enhance their operational efficiency and mitigate security risks to their client's IT infrastructure and networks. In this domain, knowledge sharing is vital for organizational growth, innovation, and operational resilience.

4.1.2 Industry context

Information technology-related security crimes are on the rise and are impacting firm productivity. Considering the potential financial impact of IT breaches on firms, effective IT security becomes the cornerstone of firm performance.

The efficient production of goods and services requires the integration of intelligent machines, storage systems, and smart production systems. With the aim of furthering business goals, firms across multiple sectors are integrating digital technologies such as big data, cloud computing, artificial intelligence, machine learning, robotics, data analytics, and blockchain. Organizational systems undergoing digital transformation are also becoming highly complex, involving multiple actors and interactions. The systems are interconnected with IOT by using wireless sensor networks, communication protocols, distributed control systems, and cloud computing. The interconnection of systems implies being exposed to cybersecurity risks, which can cause damage to the data in computer systems, or disrupt operations. As the interconnections make the system more vulnerable and exposed, cybersecurity has to go hand in hand with digital industrial transformation.

Rising frequency and sophistication of cyber threats necessitates real-time knowledge sharing and documentation. Knowledge sharing helps ensure that employees, partners, and clients are equipped to respond to emerging risks. When employees participate in collaborative networks, they gain access to implicit knowledge, experience, and skills.

4.1.3 Challenges in knowledge sharing

Despite their technological expertise, organizations in the IT security domain face significant challenges. The fast-paced evolution of cybersecurity makes it difficult for employees to keep up-to-date with the latest developments. The teams are overwhelmed with abundant data from threat intelligence, research reports, and customer feedback making it difficult for them to filter and disseminate relevant information. Besides, high-employee turnover rates, in technical roles, risks the loss of critical institutional knowledge. Teams operating in different regions or domains often work in isolation, leading to duplication of efforts and missed opportunities for collaboration. Employees from different cultural and professional backgrounds are hesitant to share knowledge due to lack of trust or fear of criticism.

4.1.4 Strategies for knowledge sharing

Clients demand stable products that tackle cyber security threats in real time while improving their quality of work and life. Different teams work together to devise security solutions for client organizations. This requires innovation and necessitates effective knowledge-sharing mechanisms. The key lies in documenting knowledge at each stage and direct communication within and across teams. The workforce includes cybersecurity researchers, product management, development and engineering, quality assurance, documentation, UX, marketing, sales, and support teams distributed globally. While the work of some, such as product managers, begins long before the solution is released, the work of others, such as the support and documentation teams start in the middle of the product life cycle and continues until the end-of-life date is declared. Given this context, firms in this domain have adopted a knowledge-sharing ecosystem with a multi-faceted approach.

- *Centralized knowledge repository*: A centralized repository, using *Microsoft SharePoint*, enable seamless storage and retrieval of documents, reports, and training materials.

    o Salesforce knowledge base enables teams to document internal articles and resolutions to customer issues. These platforms enable knowledge sharing between traditionally distinct departments, customer issue resolution, and product development. They can either use the same platform or use different platforms that feed into one another. These platforms support multiple data types, such as text, scripts, images, videos, and training modules. For example, a customer issue that is resolved is used to create an internal article for future reference.

    o *Threat intelligence sharing platform*: A dedicated platform integrated with a system that provides detailed and explainable threat intelligence allows real-time sharing of knowledge across teams and external partners. Atlassian's Confluence is a platform for documenting research and competitor knowledge, timelines and progress updates, cross-team discussions, and demos.

    o *Collaboration tools*: Dedicated channels for focused discussions, specific projects, and research topics. Asana and Atlassian's Jira are some alternatives that offer a platform for moving forward events, such as product development, resolving customer issues, documentation, as well as the full range of events that must take place during the course of the product lifecycle.

- Tools like *Slack* and *Microsoft Teams* facilitate instant communication and file sharing.

- *Learning management system (LMS)*: Learning management system that provides structured training and certifications on cybersecurity topics. Gamification elements incentivized participation and knowledge retention.

- *Peer-to-peer learning programs*: Regular webinars, hackathons, and "lunch and learn" sessions encourage knowledge sharing among employees. Subject matter experts (SMEs) conduct sessions to bridge skill gaps.

- *Customer and partner portals*: Secure portals for customers and partners, allowing them to access threat reports, product updates, and troubleshooting guides.
- The organization's community portal, which is typically a platform for sharing and responding to customer issues by customers, partners, support, and other teams, is a great resource for knowledge sharing among all the stakeholders of key product developments, customer issues, and pain-points and workarounds.

4.1.5 Business value

Comprehensive knowledge-sharing initiatives deliver tangible benefits to the organization and its stakeholders. Centralizing information allowed faster access to data, improved decision-making and response times for customer service, and product development teams. Real-time threat intelligence sharing enabled rapid identification and mitigation of cyber threats, enhancing client trust and reducing incidents. Cross-functional collaboration also stimulates innovation. Leveraging shared knowledge led to advanced threat detection algorithms and cloud security solutions. A customer portal with timely updates strengthened client relationships. This helps position the firm as a trusted advisor in cybersecurity.

Reduced duplication of efforts and improved operational efficiency translated to considerable cost savings. Initiatives in knowledge sharing and innovation enhance the firm's reputation as a forward-thinking organization, attracting top talent and new business opportunities. Knowledge-sharing initiatives fostered a sense of community and professional growth. New opportunities for learning and collaboration, resulting in higher job satisfaction and low turnover.

4.2 Knowledge sharing in Edayar pharmaceuticals

4.2.1 Introduction

Edayar Pharma, a leading pharmaceutical company specializing in different formulations, exemplifies the essence of knowledge sharing in a competitive and innovation-driven industry. The firm recognized early on that knowledge sharing is vital for staying ahead in a competitive market. With a workforce comprising of researchers, production experts, and regulatory professionals, the organization developed robust capabilities to harness and disseminate knowledge effectively.

4.2.2 Industry context

The pharmaceutical sector is characterized by stringent regulatory requirements, rapid scientific advancements, and the need for seamless collaboration between cross-functional teams. Challenges such as preserving institutional memory and ensuring compliance with evolving global standards underscored the importance of a structured approach to knowledge management.

4.2.3 Challenges in knowledge sharing

The pharmaceutical industry operates under stringent regulations, enforced by the authorities such as Food and Drug Administration (FDA) and European Medicines Agency (EMA). These rules dictate how information is shared internally and externally. For instance, sharing clinical trial data must comply with data protection laws like General Data Protection Regulation (GDPR) or Health Insurance Portability and Accountability Act, of 1996 (HIPAA), while intellectual property (IP) laws limit the dissemination of proprietary research. A fear of non-compliance with these regulations may create a culture of caution, slowing knowledge sharing within the organization.

As the organization invests heavily in Research and Development (R&D), in certain instances, the management may prioritize safeguarding proprietary information over an environment of collaboration. Organizations are structured into functional silos that hinder seamless communication and collaboration. Knowledge may remain confined to specific teams, leading to duplication of efforts. Besides, the firm generates vast amounts of data, from clinical trial results to real-world evidence and genomic research. Integrating and managing this data is a significant challenge. Employees may also hesitate to share knowledge due to concerns about losing their perceived value within the company or the risk of sharing incorrect information in a highly regulated environment. Collaborations between pharmaceutical companies, academia, and external partners are fraught with challenges. Differences in organizational goals, misaligned incentives, and legal complexities surrounding data ownership and usage hinder external knowledge sharing.

4.2.4 Knowledge-sharing framework

Edayar Pharma institutionalized knowledge sharing, on two pillars: technological tools and cultural practices. The firm uses a Pharma Knowledge Management System (PKMS), a digital platform for retrieval and distribution of medical knowledge, used for decision-making in production and research settings. Knowledge sharing on the PKMS supports the iteration and advancement of product and process understanding across the product development lifecycle. It facilitates the management team in attainment of product quality management and process performance, alongside continual improvement. The PKMS is best used in combination with other software programs such as CRM systems and Electronic Health Records. Knowledge sharing on this system facilitates understanding the big picture, improve the quality of risk assessment, and make connections to support technology transfer, and scale-up and change management initiatives. The knowledge management framework is built on the following pillars:

4.2.4.1 Centralized knowledge repository

The PKMS hosts a centralized repository called "Knowledge Hub" that serves as the backbone of knowledge-sharing practices. A repository of updated SOPs is made accessible to all employees, ensuring compliance and consistency across operations.

Research and development insights: Documentation of past and ongoing research projects includes experiment results, methodologies, and lessons learnt. The system captures and stores information on a variety of clinical trials and outcomes, and provides advanced analytics and reports assisting R&D professionals in evaluating the safety and efficacy of drugs. With predictive analytics and real-time data insights, research and development teams can identify possible challenges and improve trial outcomes.

Regulatory guidelines: The knowledge management system provides robust compliance and regulatory intelligence updated in real time for different markets. By making updated regulatory information, easily accessible, the organization ensures adherence to statutory requirements in products and processes, mitigates risk, and facilitates the approval for new drugs.

4.2.4.2 AI-powered search and recommendations

Smart search: AI integrated with the PKMS allows employees to get targeted insights from clinical trial data, scientific literature, and patents. Users can search for specific topics, keywords, or questions and retrieve relevant documents, expert contacts, and related case studies and present information in an organized manner. The system also suggests resources, training modules, or experts based on an employee's role, past activities, and current projects.

4.2.4.3 Communities of practice

Edayar pharma encourages communities of practice to facilitate peer-to-peer knowledge exchange. These communities support extensive information exchange and collaboration among cross-functional teams such as research teams, regulatory affairs, and clinical development units. Typically, these CoPs are structured around areas such as formulation development, quality assurance, and regulatory compliance. Monthly virtual and in-person meetings enable members to share insights, troubleshoot challenges, and discuss emerging trends. Senior employees act as facilitators, ensuring discussions remain productive and inclusive. Dedicated channels on the Knowledge Hub for each CoP allow asynchronous discussions and document sharing.

- *AI-powered onboarding modules* tailored to individual roles ensure that new employees quickly assimilate into the company's knowledge ecosystem.

- *Mentorship* is encouraged as a means for transferring tacit knowledge. New hires shadow experienced mentors who guide them through organizational processes, technical skills, and cultural nuances.

- *Collaborative tools and platforms*: The firm leverages digital collaboration tools to facilitate real-time knowledge sharing across geographies. Project management systems are integrating digital twin technology that presents a simulated environment for drug manufacturing. This helps monitor equipment performance, optimize manufacturing, and ensure product quality resulting in efficient and cost-effective production. Platforms such as Asana and Trello enable teams to document progress, share updates, and store project-specific knowledge in a centralized location.

- Video conferencing and chat tools integrated with the knowledge hub ensure seamless communication and document sharing. Interactive dashboards present complex data in an intuitive format, aiding decision-making and fostering cross-functional understanding. These platforms facilitate seamless information exchange, cross-functional collaboration on drug development and regulatory compliance.

A user-friendly design with simplified interfaces and intuitive navigation was used to minimize resistance. In addition, the HR team ensured widespread adoption of the knowledge hub by organizing hands-on workshops and tutorials. The leadership endorsed a culture of open knowledge sharing and recognized contributions by rewarding employees. The objective was to make sure that employees feel comfortable sharing mistakes and lessons learnt.

4.2.5 Continuous learning and development

Knowledge sharing is closely tied to the firm's L&D initiatives. The company offers AI-curated courses that align with individual career paths and organizational goals. Regular sessions feature internal and external experts to address industry trends, regulatory changes, and innovative practices. Employees participate in events such as Hackathons and Innovation Days to solve complex problems, generating new knowledge in the process.

4.2.6 Business value

The organization's approach to knowledge sharing demonstrates the transformative impact of combining technology with a strong organizational culture. By encouraging continuous learning and preserving institutional memory, Edayar pharmaceuticals is positioned as an industry leader. The firm witnessed a 20% increase in new product launches over 3 years. Streamlined access to past R&D insights and cross-functional collaboration accelerated product development and the centralized repository for regulatory guidelines reduced compliance errors by 25%. AI-powered tools reduced time spent searching for information by 30%, allowing employees to focus on high-value tasks. These capabilities ensured faster market approvals and fewer disruptions. The mentorship programs and personalized L&D initiatives boosted employee engagement and retention, with a 15% decrease in turnover rates.

5. Implications for Indian organizations

As digital systems and services grow in India, knowledge sharing is key for firms seeking growth and efficiency.

As client companies adopt new technologies like AI and blockchain, their systems become more vulnerable to cyber security risks. Firms providing IT security services are tasked with responding to these threats in real time. The key lies in integrating diverse operations across the business value chain and knowledge sharing. However, challenges, such as vast amount of data, evolving customer needs, and high-employee turnover, can hinder knowledge sharing. Tools such as centralized repositories (e.g. SharePoint), threat intelligence platforms (e.g. confluence), collaboration tools (e.g. Slack, Teams), learning management systems, peer learning through webinars, and customer portals can help improve competitiveness. The integration of business analytics and data mining tools into these platforms can maximize the impact of knowledge sharing.

Firms in the pharmaceutical industry have to meet stringent regulatory requirements and attain global standards. Edayar pharma highlights the need for balancing intrinsic factors like trust and motivation with extrinsic factors like robust knowledge management systems. A pharma knowledge management system together with a knowledge hub and collaborative platforms such as Asana and Trello enhanced problem-solving and decision-making capabilities. With practices prioritizing

DOI: http://dx.doi.org/10.5772/intechopen.1010249

employee well-being, leadership support, and rewards, the management team created an environment for knowledge sharing. Such an ecosystem cultivated an agile workforce that is well-equipped to adapt to challenges and seize new opportunities.

6. Conclusion

The objective of the chapter is to explore how knowledge sharing impacts firm performance and identify key factors essential for developing an effective knowledge-sharing framework. Important factors that influence knowledge sharing are individual capability, organizational support, and technological infrastructure. Other factors such as type of knowledge, societal culture, government policies, and social media also impact the extent of knowledge shared. While easy access to document knowledge improves efficiency, sharing of expertise and insights fosters dialog, and problem-solving. Seamless information flow along the business value chain reduces cost and enhances client satisfaction. Even as the organization benefits from collective intelligence, a culture of openness, trust, and inclusive leadership improves employee morale.

The IT security sector with an evolving technological environment and the pharmaceutical sector with stringent government regulations provide a good testing ground for our analysis. The first case study refers to a firm in the IT security sector that has deployed an integrated knowledge management system to respond to evolving cyber threats. Unified knowledge sharing allows for the development of advanced security solutions and prompt client response. The business gains through an improved market reputation, increased business opportunities, and reduced employee turnover. In contrast, our second case analyses a firm that operates within stringent government requirements that prioritize data security. Edayar Pharmaceuticals invests in R&D to attain global standards, while at the same time adheres to strict rules for information sharing. The firm deployed an integrated PKMS alongside practices that prioritized employee well-being, leadership support, and rewards. This alignment shaped a sustainable knowledge-sharing culture and strengthened the firm's competitive position in the market.

Evidence from the industry validates that an effective knowledge sharing framework is shaped by strengthening individual, and organizational and technological capabilities. A well-structured knowledge-sharing culture helps leverage intellectual capital and achieve long-term success. The findings from both literature and industry cases underscore the importance of knowledge-sharing as a key driver of business growth in an increasingly competitive landscape.

Acknowledgements

The authors acknowledge the use of Open AI for language polishing of the manuscript.

Conflict of interest

The authors declare no conflict of interest.

Author details

Sarika Singh[1*], Gour C. Saha[2] and Mukesh Singh[3]

1 School of Inspired Leadership, Gurugram, Haryana, India

2 Faculty of Data Science and Analytics, Sir Padampat Singhania University, Udaipur, India

3 Encube Ethicals Pvt. Ltd., Goa, India

*Address all correspondence to: prof.sarika.singh@gmail.com

References

[50] Wah L. Making Knowledge Stick. In: The Knowledge Management Yearbook 2000-2001. 1st ed. Routledge; 2000. 12 p. Available from: https://archive.org/details/knowledgemanagem0000wood

[51] Kengatharan NK. A knowledge-based theory of the firm. International Journal of Manpower. 2019;**40**(6):1056-1074. DOI: 10.1108/IJM-03-2018-0096

[52] Davenport TH, Prusak L. Working knowledge: How organizations manage what they know. Ubiquity. 1998:1-15. Available from: http://www.acm.org/ubiquity/book/t_davenport_1.html

[53] Tobin DR. The Knowledge-Enabled Organization: Moving from "Training" to "Learning" to Meet Business Goals. New York, NY: AMACON; 1998. Available from: https://archive.org/details/knowledgeenabled00tobi/page/n5/mode/2up

[54] Hansen MT, Nohria N, Tiemey T. What's your strategy for managing knowledge. Harvard Business Review. 1999;**77**(2):106-116. Available from: https://hbr.org/1999/03/whats-your-strategy-for-managing-knowledge

[55] Matthew CT, Sternberg RJ. Developing experience-based (tacit) knowledge through reflection. Learning and Individual Differences. 2009;**19**(4):530-540. DOI: 10.1016/j.lindif.2009.07.001

[56] Arsawan IWE, Wirga IW, Rajiani I, Suryantini NPS. Harnessing knowledge sharing practice to enhance innovative work behavior: The paradox of social exchange theory. Polish Journal of Management Studies. 2020;**21**(2):60-73. DOI: 10.17512/pjms.2020.21.2.05

[57] Wang Z, Wang N. Knowledge sharing, innovation and firm performance. Expert Systems with Applications. 2012;**39**(10):8899-8908. DOI: 10.1016/j.eswa.2012.02.017

[58] Casimir G, Lee K, Loon M. Knowledge sharing: Influences of trust, commitment and cost. Journal of Knowledge Management. 2012;**16**(5):740-753. DOI: 10.1108/13673271211262781

[59] Fishbein M, Ajzen I. Belief, Attitude, Intention, and Behavior. 1st ed. Addison Wesley Publishing Company; 1975. Available from: https://archive.org/details/beliefattitudein0000fish

[60] Godin G, Kok G. The theory of planned behavior: A review of its applications to health-related behaviors. American Journal of Health Promotion. 1996;**11**(2):87-98. DOI: 10.4278/0890-1171-11.2.87

[61] Bock GW, Kim YG. Breaking the myths of rewards. Information Resources Management Journal. 2002;**15**(2):14-21. DOI: 10.4018/irmj.2002040102

[62] Bandura A. Self-efficacy: Toward a unifying theory of behavioral change. Psychological Review. 1977;**84**(2):191-215. DOI: 10.1037/0033-295X.84.2.191

[63] Fichman RG, Kemerer CF. The assimilation of software process innovations: An organizational learning perspective. Management Science. 1997;**43**(10):1345-1363. DOI: 10.1287/mnsc.43.10.1345

[64] Ma WWK, Chan A. Knowledge sharing and social media: Altruism, perceived online attachment motivation and perceived online relationship commitment. Computers in Human

Behavior. 2014;**39**:51-58. DOI: 10.1016/j.chb.2014.06.015

[65] Lal K. Information and Communication Technologies in the Context of Globalization: Evidence from Developing Countries. London: Palgrave Macmillan; 2007. DOI: 10.1057/9780230597877

Chapter 5

Cross-Domain Knowledge Transfer in Large Models: Transforming Knowledge Management Dynamics

Weiqiang Jin and Biao Zhao

Abstract

In today's rapidly evolving technological landscape, large models—particularly large language models—are reshaping the dynamics of knowledge management. In this chapter, we explore how these advanced models facilitate cross-domain knowledge transfer—a critical capability in an era marked by increasingly interconnected global challenges and data overload—enabling the integration of information from diverse research fields. By leveraging the capabilities of large language models (LLMs), organizations can break down silos, foster innovation, and enhance decision-making processes. We systematically examine the mechanisms through which cross-domain knowledge transfer occurs in large language models, discuss the challenges such as data privacy and model bias, and highlight the implications for businesses operating in transformative environments. Case studies and current research provide insights into optimizing knowledge management strategies to harness the full potential of artificial intelligence in a multidisciplinary context. Overall, we hope that this chapter provides a foundational framework for scholars studying human-artificial intelligence (AI) collaboration and offers practitioners criteria to evaluate LLM adoption risks. We believe the findings in this chapter are critical for organizations seeking to balance agility with ethical accountability in the upcoming artificial general intelligence (AGI) era.

Keywords: knowledge management, cross-domain knowledge transfer, large language models, transformative environment, artificial intelligence, machine learning

1. Introduction

The fragmentation of knowledge across organizational silos and disciplines has become a key bottleneck for innovation in the twenty-first century [1]. As industries face pressures to adapt to rapid technological shifts and sustainability demands, traditional knowledge management (KM) systems struggle to bridge the gap between specialized expertise and cross-functional collaboration [2–4]. Knowledge management (KM) has traditionally relied on structured repositories, workflows, and human expertise to organize and disseminate information. However, the rise of artificial intelligence has disrupted these practices, bringing about a paradigm shift in how organizations approach the creation, storage, and utilization of knowledge [5].

The rapid integration of generative artificial intelligence (GenAI), that is, large language models (LLMs), into organizational workflows has created unprecedented opportunities and challenges for KM [6–8]. While existing studies have documented GenAI's technical capabilities, few have systematically explored how GenAI fundamentally redefines KM paradigms across industries or evaluated its long-term implications for interdisciplinary collaboration and decision-making. This research addresses this gap by analyzing the transformative role of GenAI in KM, with a focus on LLMs, to provide actionable frameworks for scholars and practitioners navigating this evolving landscape [9, 10]. This study addresses the following research questions:

- How do LLMs overcome the limitations of traditional KM systems in integrating tacit and cross-domain knowledge?
- What ethical and operational risks emerge from LLM-driven KM, and how can they be mitigated?
- What frameworks can guide organizations in balancing the democratization of expertise with governance requirements?

By addressing these gaps, this research contributes to both academic discourse and practical KM strategies. For scholars, it offers a taxonomy of LLM capabilities in cross-domain contexts and identifies underexplored risks such as epistemic dependency on AI-generated content. For practitioners, the proposed frameworks empower organizations to navigate the tension between innovation and governance, ensuring LLMs drive sustainable value rather than operational fragility.

1.1 The historical evolution of knowledge management systems

Knowledge management (KM) as a formal discipline emerged in the late twentieth century, emphasizing the collection, storage, and dissemination of knowledge [4, 5]. Early systems primarily relied on databases and hierarchical structures, which were excellent at preserving explicit knowledge—facts, procedures, and policies that could be codified. However, these rigid systems often resulted in the development of organizational silos, where departments and teams operated in isolation, limiting cross-functional collaboration and knowledge exchange [8, 9].

Intranets, wikis, and collaborative tools that emerged in the early 2000s sought to mitigate these challenges by enabling more fluid sharing of information [10]. For instance, platforms like SharePoint allowed employees to access centralized repositories, while tools such as Confluence encouraged team-driven content creation. Despite these advancements, traditional KM systems still struggled to integrate tacit knowledge—the intuitive, experience-based insights often held by individuals—and bridge knowledge gaps across departments, industries, or disciplines. These limitations, compounded by the exponential growth of unstructured data in the 2010s, exposed critical vulnerabilities in conventional KM approaches and underscored the need for adaptive, AI-powered solutions [10–13].

1.2 The role of AI in augmenting traditional knowledge processes

Artificial intelligence (AI) has transformed KM by introducing advanced capabilities such as automation, pattern recognition, and real-time insights [2, 3, 6]. Unlike earlier systems, which required manual input and organization, AI tools powered by machine learning and natural language processing (NLP) can autonomously analyze unstructured data, extract key insights, and provide contextual recommendations.

For example, modern AI-driven KM systems can process vast amounts of data—from emails and reports to social media—and identify trends or risks in real-time [7–9]. In industries like healthcare, this capability has enabled organizations to predict patient outcomes by synthesizing clinical records with research data. Similarly, in the financial sector, AI tools are used to conduct comprehensive risk assessments by combining historical economic data with current geopolitical developments. Furthermore, AI's ability to adapt and learn ensures that KM systems remain relevant in dynamic environments. For instance, chatbots and virtual assistants can continuously improve their responses by learning from user interactions, offering a personalized knowledge experience for employees and customers alike. By pushing KM beyond static information storage, AI facilitates a transition toward dynamic, real-time learning environments [11, 12].

However, current research predominantly focuses on narrow applications of AI in KM (e.g., document classification or chatbot deployment), overlooking systemic questions about scalability, ethical governance, and the integration of human-AI hybrid intelligence. While prior work has focused on automating discrete KM tasks, it often assumes AI's role as a passive tool rather than an active driver of organizational transformation. This overlooks the systemic shifts required to integrate human and machine intelligence in dynamic environments [10, 12, 13]. This study seeks to expand this discourse by examining how AI reshapes KM holistically—not just as a tool but as a catalyst for reimagining organizational learning and innovation.

1.3 Introducing large language models (LLMs)

Large language models (LLMs) represent a groundbreaking advancement in AI-driven knowledge management [2, 3]. Unlike traditional systems that rely on predefined rules and structured datasets, LLMs leverage vast and diverse datasets encompassing text, images, and other modalities to understand context, generate insights, and synthesize knowledge across domains.

For example, LLMs like GPT-4, DeepSeek, and Llama can process technical documents, business reports, and scientific studies simultaneously, extracting commonalities and actionable insights that drive decision-making. This cross-domain synthesis is particularly valuable in multidisciplinary environments, where knowledge from multiple fields must be integrated to address complex challenges.

One real-world application of LLMs is in pharmaceutical research. Here, models can analyze clinical trial data, patient feedback, and molecular biology research to identify promising drug candidates. Similarly, in the field of education, LLMs are being used to create adaptive learning systems that tailor content to individual learning styles and progress levels.

What truly sets LLMs apart is their ability to generate new knowledge by identifying patterns and connections that may not be immediately apparent to human analysts. For instance, an LLM can combine insights from environmental science and economics to propose sustainable business strategies that balance profitability with ecological impact. This capacity for fluid integration and adaptation makes LLMs indispensable tools for organizations looking to thrive in complex, rapidly evolving landscapes [12, 14].

Our analysis shows that LLMs make three key contributions to KM: (1) cross-domain knowledge accessibility, enabling seamless knowledge sharing across isolated fields; (2) context-aware knowledge integration, synthesizing real-time data and contextual signals for optimized decision-making; (3) governance and risk mitigation, addressing challenges like bias and privacy issues. We stress the need to balance AI efficiency with human oversight, and emphasize ethical governance and sustainable practices to fully realize the potential of LLMs in KM.

These contributions redefine KM paradigms: LLMs are not merely tools but active agents of organizational transformation. For researchers, this work establishes a framework to study human-AI symbiosis in cross-domain contexts; for practitioners, it provides actionable guidelines to balance innovation with ethical governance.

1.3.1 Structure of the chapter

This chapter explores the transformative role of large language models (LLMs) in knowledge management (KM) through three key contributions: cross-domain knowledge accessibility, context-aware knowledge integration, and governance and risk mitigation. Each section provides technical evaluations, real-world applications, and governance strategies.

- *Section 2*: Examines the architectural foundations of LLMs (e.g., transformer models and few-shot learning) that enable cross-domain knowledge retrieval and processing.

- *Section 3*: Explores how LLMs break down organizational silos through case studies in healthcare (e.g., integrating clinical data with patient feedback) and manufacturing (e.g., unifying engineering and marketing insights).

- *Section 4*: Confronts ethical and operational risks of LLMs, proposing solutions such as federated learning for data privacy, adversarial debiasing for fairness, and transparency frameworks for accountability.

- *Section 5*: Highlights the implications for business decision-making, such as financial institutions using LLMs to predict market risks by correlating geopolitical events with historical trends.

- *Section 6*: Outlines future directions, including personalized knowledge systems, green AI practices, and decentralized architectures, to ensure responsible scaling of LLM applications.

- *Section 7*: Critically synthesizes the findings in relation to prior literature, highlights new insights, and demonstrates how this study contributes to the broader discourse on AI-driven KM.

- *Section 8*: Concludes the study by summarizing the theoretical and managerial implications, outlining future research directions, and providing a call to action for ethical governance and sustainability in LLM-driven KM.

By addressing these themes, the chapter provides a comprehensive framework for scholars and practitioners to harness the transformative potential of LLMs while navigating their challenges.

2. Understanding large models and cross-domain knowledge transfer

2.1 Architecture and capabilities of large models

Large language models (LLMs), such as OpenAI's GPT series or Google's BERT, are sophisticated neural networks designed to process and generate human-like text [2, 3]. At their core lies the transformer architecture, which allows them to handle sequences of text with unparalleled efficiency. The transformer model uses attention mechanisms to identify relationships between words, phrases, or concepts within vast datasets, enabling it to understand and predict text contextually.

LLMs' strength lies in their scale. Trained on billions of data points across multiple domains, they develop a generalized understanding of language and knowledge that extends beyond isolated fields. These models can generate coherent essays, translate languages, summarize texts, and even create programming code, showcasing their versatility and cross-functional capabilities. An additional innovation is their ability to handle fine-tuning [7–9]. Organizations can train LLMs on specific datasets, tailoring their knowledge to meet specialized needs—from financial forecasting to molecular biology research—while retaining their broad foundational knowledge.

2.2 Mechanisms of cross-domain knowledge transfer

Cross-domain knowledge transfer occurs when insights or patterns identified in one field are adapted and applied to another [4–6]. For example, techniques from computational biology can inspire innovations in AI-driven diagnostics, or supply chain optimization methods can inform pandemic response strategies. LLMs are uniquely equipped for this task because they:

1. *Recognize shared patterns:* LLMs analyze diverse datasets, identifying recurring principles or analogies across fields. For instance, a model trained on economic theory and climate data might find parallels in resource scarcity models.

2. *Abstract core concepts:* By generalizing knowledge, LLMs distill complex ideas into universal principles that are applicable across disciplines. For example, concepts of risk assessment in finance can inform project management strategies in engineering.

3. *Facilitate communication:* LLMs bridge the gap between disciplines by translating technical jargon into universally understandable language. This makes them ideal for interdisciplinary teams working on complex problems.

One mechanism driving this capability is "few-shot learning," where LLMs adapt to new tasks with minimal additional data [13, 14]. For example, when exposed to a handful of examples from a niche domain, the model quickly grasps the context and applies its pre-existing knowledge to generate relevant outputs.

2.3 Real-world examples

1. *Pharmaceutical innovation:* Pharmaceutical companies leverage LLMs to analyze medical literature, clinical trial data, and patient feedback to identify potential treatments. For example, Pfizer's AI-driven drug discovery programs use models to cross-reference molecular biology findings with real-world patient outcomes, accelerating research timelines significantly.

2. *Business sustainability:* Corporations are using LLMs to combine insights from environmental science and business data to craft sustainable strategies. For instance, a major retailer integrated climate models and economic predictions to optimize their supply chain, reducing carbon emissions by 30.

3. *Multidisciplinary academic research*: Universities increasingly rely on LLMs to facilitate collaboration among departments. In one case, an AI research team worked with environmental scientists to create predictive models for wildfire spread by integrating climate data with historical wildfire patterns. This interdisciplinary approach enabled quicker response strategies and more accurate risk assessments.

4. *Financial risk management:* Financial institutions are deploying LLMs to merge economic indicators, geopolitical news, and historical market trends to provide real-time risk analysis. For example, JPMorgan's AI systems identify emerging risks by synthesizing seemingly unrelated data—such as international trade agreements and weather forecasts—to predict potential market disruptions.

5. *Expanding boundaries with LLMs:* As LLMs become more sophisticated, their ability to enable cross-domain knowledge transfer continues to grow. By integrating datasets from multiple disciplines, these models facilitate innovations that were previously unimaginable. In the sections ahead, we will explore how these capabilities address organizational challenges and drive advancements in sectors ranging from healthcare to education.

6. *Architecture and capabilities of large models:* Large models, such as GPT and BERT, are built using neural networks that mimic human reasoning. The transformer architecture, specifically, empowers these models to handle sequences of text, making connections between disparate pieces of information.

7. *Mechanisms of cross-domain knowledge transfer:* Cross-domain transfer happens through the model's ability to generalize patterns. For example, knowledge from biology can inform medical device design, while insights from environmental science can guide business sustainability efforts. LLMs learn to abstract core principles and apply them across varying contexts.

Overall, organizations use LLMs for tasks such as drafting multidisciplinary reports, predicting market behavior, and synthesizing cross-industry trends. A pharmaceutical company, for instance, could leverage LLMs to combine chemical research with healthcare data for innovative solutions.

3. Breaking down silos: Integrating knowledge across domains

3.1 Overcoming challenges of knowledge silos

Organizational silos, long seen as a barrier to efficiency and innovation, arise when departments or teams operate in isolation [7, 10]. This fragmentation often leads to duplication of efforts, gaps in communication, and a failure to leverage shared expertise. Historically, silos have been perpetuated by cultural, structural, and technological factors. For example, different divisions within a company may use incompatible software systems, making cross-departmental collaboration cumbersome [1]. LLMs are poised to dismantle these barriers by creating centralized hubs where all data and knowledge converge [2, 3].

Through natural language processing (NLP) capabilities, LLMs can ingest and synthesize information from disparate systems, generating cohesive insights that are accessible to everyone within an organization. For instance, a global manufacturing firm struggling with disjointed processes across its R&D, production, and marketing departments could use LLMs to unify knowledge. The model would harmonize data from technical manuals, supply chain records, and market research reports, enabling teams to work with a shared understanding.

In addition, LLMs foster transparency by making organizational knowledge universally searchable and retrievable. They act as a bridge between teams, ensuring that critical insights are not lost in isolated systems but instead contribute to the collective intelligence of the organization.

3.1.1 Facilitating interdisciplinary collaboration

True innovation often occurs at the intersection of disciplines. However, facilitating collaboration between teams with distinct expertise—such as engineers and marketers, or scientists and policymakers—can be challenging due to differences in terminology, methodologies, and priorities. LLMs excel in translating complex, technical jargon into accessible language, enabling diverse groups to collaborate effectively.

For example, in the healthcare industry, a team of medical researchers, software engineers, and data analysts might work together to develop an AI-driven diagnostic tool. Each group brings unique expertise, but their differing vocabularies can create misunderstandings. An LLM can mediate this collaboration by generating plain-language summaries of technical specifications, aligning goals, and even proposing actionable steps based on the collective input.

Another way LLMs facilitate interdisciplinary work is by providing contextual insights. A marketing team launching a new product might need input from the engineering department about manufacturing feasibility. Instead of wading through dense technical documents, the marketers can use an LLM to generate concise summaries that highlight relevant details, streamlining communication and decision-making.

Case study 1: Streamlining Product Development Cycles A multinational consumer electronics company faced significant delays in product development due to a lack of coordination between R&D, supply chain, and marketing teams. By implementing an LLM-driven knowledge management platform, the company created a centralized repository of insights that all departments could access [1]. For example, R&D teams could instantly retrieve market feedback analyzed by the marketing department, while supply chain managers could align inventory forecasts with new product launches. This integration reduced product development cycles by 25%, saving both time and resources.

Case study 2: Advancing Climate Action through Collaboration A consortium of environmental organizations and government agencies sought to develop actionable strategies for mitigating climate change. The project required expertise from climatologists, economists, urban planners, and policymakers. Using an LLM, the consortium synthesized data from diverse sources, such as scientific research papers, economic models, and policy briefs. The model also generated multilingual summaries for stakeholders worldwide, enabling seamless collaboration across regions and disciplines. As a result, the consortium produced a comprehensive climate action plan in half the expected time.

Case study 3: Enhancing Supply Chain Resilience During the COVID-19 pandemic, a global logistics company experienced disruptions due to fluctuating demand and border closures. By deploying an LLM, the company integrated data from international trade agreements, weather forecasts, and real-time shipment tracking systems [1]. The model provided predictive insights into potential delays and recommended alternative routes, ensuring timely deliveries. This application not only improved operational efficiency but also strengthened relationships with clients by maintaining service reliability.

3.2 The transformative power of integration

LLMs are more than just tools for efficiency—they are enablers of cultural change within organizations. By breaking down silos, they promote a mindset of shared ownership and collaboration, where teams are empowered to work together toward common goals. For example, in a large consulting firm, the integration of an LLM-based platform transformed team dynamics, allowing consultants across global offices to share best practices and client insights in real-time, fostering a culture of innovation and shared expertise.

As businesses increasingly operate in complex, fast-changing environments, the ability to integrate knowledge across domains will become a defining factor for success. Companies that embrace LLMs for integration are more agile, adaptive, and competitive in responding to market demands.

3.3 Overcoming challenges of knowledge silos

Organizational silos restrict knowledge flow. Departments often work independently, limiting innovation [4, 10]. LLMs address this by creating centralized hubs where data from all departments converge. For instance, a financial institution adopted an LLM to unify fragmented customer data across departments, improving client engagement and significantly reducing service redundancies. Additionally, these models facilitate democratized access to knowledge. Employees at all levels can leverage LLMs to retrieve relevant insights, ensuring that decision-making is not limited to a few individuals with specialized knowledge.

3.4 Facilitating interdisciplinary collaboration

By translating complex technical jargon into accessible language, LLMs allow diverse teams—from engineers to marketers—to collaborate effectively. For instance,

DOI: http://dx.doi.org/10.5772/intechopen.1011821

in the energy sector, LLMs helped project managers align renewable energy engineers with policy analysts to design actionable plans for meeting sustainability goals. The LLM acted as a mediator, summarizing regulatory frameworks for engineers and technical blueprints for analysts, ensuring alignment across all stakeholders. They streamline workflows by acting as intermediaries, ensuring all parties work with synchronized information. Beyond this, LLMs can proactively highlight potential bottlenecks in collaborative projects by analyzing workflow data and suggesting solutions, enabling teams to address issues before they escalate.

Case study 1: Accelerating automotive innovation an automotive company faced delays in rolling out electric vehicle models due to disjointed communication between design and manufacturing teams. By deploying an LLM, the company created a shared knowledge platform that integrated feedback from both teams [1]. This reduced miscommunication, streamlined manufacturing processes, and accelerated time-to-market by 20%.

Case study 2: Advancing precision medicine a biotech firm used an LLM to integrate genetic research with clinical trial data, allowing researchers and healthcare professionals to collaborate more effectively. The platform's ability to synthesize these data sources helped identify promising therapies for rare diseases, significantly reducing the time needed for analysis.

Case study 3: Transforming retail logistics a global retailer implemented an LLM to coordinate logistics, merchandising, and customer support teams. By integrating real-time inventory data with customer feedback, the retailer improved stock management and reduced delivery delays by 30%. This holistic approach enhanced customer satisfaction and streamlined operations.

4. Challenges in cross-domain knowledge transfer

Data privacy and security: As organizations increasingly adopt large language models (LLMs) to enable cross-domain knowledge transfer, concerns around data privacy and security have grown significantly [11–13]. These models are often trained on extensive datasets that may include sensitive or proprietary information. For example, a healthcare organization utilizing an LLM to analyze patient records must ensure that the data is encrypted and anonymized to prevent potential breaches or unauthorized access. Beyond technical safeguards, organizations need robust policies to regulate how data is collected, stored, and shared.

One of the emerging strategies is the adoption of federated learning—a technique that allows models to be trained across decentralized datasets without transferring sensitive data to a central server. For instance, a consortium of hospitals could use federated learning to collaboratively improve diagnostic algorithms while preserving patient privacy. Furthermore, implementing zero-trust architectures and end-to-end encryption ensures that data remains secure throughout its lifecycle.

Addressing bias in models: Bias within LLMs poses a significant challenge, especially in cross-domain knowledge transfer, where diverse datasets with varying degrees of quality and representation are used. Models trained on biased or incomplete data risk perpetuating stereotypes or excluding critical perspectives, leading to flawed outputs. For example, an LLM used in recruitment might inadvertently favor candidates from overrepresented demographics due to historical biases in hiring data.

Addressing this issue requires a multipronged approach. First, datasets must be audited and curated to ensure diversity and fairness. Techniques like adversarial debiasing and bias mitigation algorithms can be applied during the training process to reduce systemic distortions. Additionally, transparency in model decision-making is critical. Explainability tools, such as SHapley Additive exPlanations (SHAP) or Local Interpretable Model-agnostic Explanations (LIME), enable stakeholders to understand and scrutinize the reasoning behind an LLM's predictions, allowing biases to be identified and corrected.

Ethical and governance concerns: The rapid deployment of LLMs raises profound ethical questions. For instance, should an LLM-generated recommendation in a healthcare context carry the same weight as a decision made by a human professional? Similarly, how do we address the risks of misuse, such as generating misleading content or automating discriminatory practices?

To navigate these challenges, organizations must establish comprehensive AI governance frameworks. These should include ethical guidelines, accountability structures, and clear protocols for model deployment and usage. For example, a financial institution employing an LLM for credit risk assessment might require periodic audits to ensure compliance with anti-discrimination laws. Furthermore, organizations should engage diverse stakeholders—including ethicists, legal experts, and end-users—in the development and oversight of AI initiatives.

Emerging challenges and future directions: While current challenges like data privacy, bias, and ethics are well-documented, new issues are emerging as LLMs become more integrated into organizational workflows [6, 14]. One such challenge is the environmental impact of training and maintaining these models. The computational power required for LLMs contributes to significant carbon emissions, prompting organizations to explore greener AI practices. Techniques like model pruning, knowledge distillation, and the use of energy-efficient hardware are gaining traction as potential solutions.

Another frontier is the challenge of ensuring contextual accuracy in cross-domain applications. While LLMs are proficient at synthesizing information, they can sometimes generate outputs that are factually incorrect or contextually irrelevant. Reinforcing human oversight and incorporating domain-specific fine-tuning can mitigate these risks, ensuring that outputs align with organizational goals and standards.

By proactively addressing these challenges, organizations can unlock the full potential of LLMs while ensuring that their deployment aligns with ethical, legal, and societal expectations. The use of LLMs introduces concerns about data leaks and breaches. Sensitive organizational knowledge must be protected through robust encryption and ethical AI practices.

Addressing bias in large language models: Bias in training datasets can lead to flawed outcomes. For example, skewed historical data might reinforce existing inequalities. Organizations must actively audit and retrain models to mitigate biases. AI's growing role necessitates comprehensive governance frameworks. Misuse of LLMs, such as generating misleading content, must be countered through transparency and accountability.

5. Implications for business and decision-making

5.1 Enabling informed decision-making

Large language models (LLMs) are revolutionizing business decision-making by providing real-time, actionable insights derived from analyzing complex and multidimensional datasets [2, 3]. Unlike traditional decision-support systems that rely on predefined algorithms and structured data, LLMs are capable of interpreting vast amounts of unstructured information, including text, audio, and even images. This capability allows organizations to uncover hidden patterns, predict trends, and make decisions with a level of confidence previously unattainable.

5.2 Enhanced predictive capabilities

One of the primary ways LLMs support informed decision-making is through enhanced predictive capabilities. By analyzing historical and real-time data, these models can forecast outcomes across multiple domains. For instance, in supply chain management, LLMs can predict potential disruptions by synthesizing data from weather forecasts, geopolitical developments, and market trends. Businesses can then proactively adjust their strategies, mitigating risks and minimizing losses.

In marketing, LLMs help organizations identify shifting consumer preferences by analyzing social media, customer feedback, and industry reports. These insights enable companies to design campaigns that resonate with their target audience, increasing engagement and return on investment.

5.3 Real-time contextual understanding

Unlike traditional systems, which often require human intervention to contextualize insights, LLMs can process and interpret data within their context. For example, an LLM integrated into a financial institution's operations can monitor global news, identify events that may impact the market (such as policy changes or natural disasters), and provide actionable recommendations tailored to specific investment portfolios. This capability ensures that decision-makers are always informed by the most relevant and timely information.

5.4 Democratizing decision-making

Another significant impact of LLMs is the democratization of decision-making. By making advanced analytical tools accessible to non-technical stakeholders, these models empower employees across all levels of an organization to contribute to strategic discussions. For instance, a project manager without a background in data science can use an LLM-powered dashboard to explore potential project risks and develop contingency plans based on data-driven insights.

5.5 Automating routine decisions

In addition to supporting high-level strategic decisions, LLMs are also transforming routine decision-making processes. For example, in e-commerce, LLMs can automate inventory restocking decisions by analyzing sales data, seasonal trends, and supplier availability. Similarly, in HR management, LLMs can assist with workforce planning by predicting staffing needs based on historical patterns and projected business growth.

As LLMs continue to evolve, their role in decision-making will expand, enabling businesses to navigate increasingly complex environments with greater agility and precision.

LLMs provide actionable insights by analyzing complex datasets in real-time. Businesses can make agile decisions, such as adapting supply chains to global events or tailoring marketing strategies to emerging trends.

5.6 Industry-specific applications

- Healthcare: LLMs are advancing precision medicine by integrating genomic data, clinical research, and patient feedback to identify personalized treatment options. For example, they are being used to predict patient outcomes and recommend therapies tailored to specific genetic profiles, significantly enhancing the efficacy of treatment plans.

- Finance: Financial institutions are leveraging LLMs for comprehensive risk assessment by synthesizing global economic indicators, policy changes, and historical market trends. They also aid in fraud detection by analyzing transaction patterns and identifying anomalies in real-time.

- Education: In education, LLMs are revolutionizing learning by creating adaptive learning paths that cater to individual student needs. By combining cognitive science with pedagogical data, they offer customized content delivery and real-time feedback to improve student engagement and outcomes.

- Manufacturing: LLMs are optimizing production processes by analyzing supply chain data, predicting equipment failures, and enhancing quality control through cross-referencing historical data with current performance metrics.

- Energy sector: Renewable energy companies use LLMs to integrate weather patterns, market trends, and policy updates to optimize energy production and distribution, ensuring efficiency and sustainability.

5.7 Driving innovation

LLMs are not only solving existing problems but also uncovering opportunities for innovation. By synthesizing vast amounts of interdisciplinary data, companies can identify emerging market trends and anticipate consumer needs. For example:

- Exploring new markets: Companies are using LLMs to analyze demographic, cultural, and economic data to identify opportunities in previously untapped regions.

- Developing cutting-edge products: Research and development teams use LLMs to generate design ideas, simulate product performance, and optimize prototypes based on customer feedback and market research.

- Adapting to disruptions: LLMs provide real-time analytics on external disruptions such as pandemics, natural disasters, or geopolitical shifts, allowing businesses to quickly pivot strategies and maintain operational continuity.

6. Future directions in AI and knowledge

Artificial intelligence and knowledge management are on the cusp of a transformative era, marked by several emerging trends that promise to redefine how organizations operate and innovate. These trends leverage the latest advancements in AI and LLMs to address complex challenges and unlock new opportunities [7, 12].

6.1 Personalized knowledge systems

As AI models become more sophisticated, the focus has shifted toward creating highly personalized knowledge systems. These systems use advanced machine learning algorithms to deliver tailored insights to individual users based on their specific roles, preferences, and real-time needs. For example, a sales manager could receive personalized market trend analyses, while a researcher might gain access to curated scientific papers relevant to ongoing projects. The integration of LLMs with user behavior analytics allows for dynamic adaptation, ensuring that recommendations remain contextually relevant and actionable.

6.2 Real-time learning and continuous updates

One of the most exciting advancements is the emergence of real-time learning systems. Traditional AI models are often static, requiring periodic updates to incorporate new data. In contrast, modern LLMs are increasingly capable of integrating continuous data streams, enabling them to learn and adapt in real-time. This capability is particularly valuable in industries such as finance and healthcare, where timely insights can significantly impact decision-making. For example, an LLM monitoring global financial markets can instantly adjust risk assessments in response to breaking news or policy changes.

6.3 Multimodal AI integration

The next generation of LLMs is designed to process and synthesize information across multiple modalities, including text, images, audio, and even video. This multimodal integration expands the potential applications of AI in knowledge management. For instance, in the medical field, an LLM could combine textual patient records with diagnostic imaging to provide a comprehensive analysis, enhancing diagnostic accuracy. Similarly, in manufacturing, models could analyze video footage of production lines alongside maintenance logs to predict equipment failures more effectively.

6.4 Decentralized AI architectures

As concerns around data privacy and computational efficiency grow, decentralized AI architectures are gaining traction. Federated learning, a technique where models are trained across distributed datasets without centralizing the data, is becoming a cornerstone of secure and efficient AI systems. Organizations are increasingly adopting this approach to ensure compliance with data protection regulations while still leveraging the power of collective intelligence. For example, a global network of hospitals could use federated learning to train a diagnostic AI model without compromising patient privacy.

6.5 AI-augmented collaboration platforms

AI-powered collaboration tools are revolutionizing how teams work together across geographies and disciplines. These platforms leverage LLMs to facilitate seamless communication, translate technical jargon, and provide real-time insights during collaborative projects. For instance, a cross-functional team developing a new product could use an AI tool to consolidate feedback from engineers, marketers, and designers, ensuring alignment and accelerating time-to-market.

6.6 Sustainability and green AI

The environmental impact of training and deploying LLMs has become a growing concern. The AI community is actively exploring strategies to reduce energy consumption, such as developing energy-efficient algorithms, utilizing renewable energy for data centers, and optimizing model architectures through techniques like pruning and distillation. Organizations are increasingly prioritizing these green AI practices to balance technological advancement with environmental responsibility.

6.7 Democratization of AI tools

The accessibility of AI tools is expanding, enabling even small and medium-sized enterprises (SMEs) to benefit from advanced technologies. Cloud-based LLM platforms and open-source models are reducing the barriers to entry, allowing businesses of all sizes to integrate AI into their knowledge management processes [7]. This democratization fosters innovation across diverse sectors, from local startups to non-profit organizations addressing global challenges.

By embracing these trends, organizations can position themselves at the forefront of the AI revolution, leveraging cutting-edge technologies to drive innovation, improve decision-making, and achieve sustainable growth [6, 14].

- Personalized knowledge systems: Tailored insights for individual users, improving relevance and efficiency.
- Real-time learning: Continuous updates to models ensure adaptability to changing data landscapes.
- Multimodal AI: Combining text, images, and audio to enhance cross-domain applications.

Speculating on the future: In 10 years, knowledge management may become entirely AI-driven, with systems autonomously curating and delivering insights to decision-makers, drastically reducing human effort in repetitive tasks.

7. Discussion on LLMs with KM

This study has explored the transformative role of large language models (LLMs) in enabling cross-domain knowledge transfer and reshaping knowledge management (KM) dynamics. By addressing the research questions outlined in the introduction, this work advances the understanding of how LLMs overcome the limitations of traditional KM systems, mitigate ethical and operational risks, and provide frameworks for balancing innovation with governance. Below, we critically synthesize our findings in relation to prior literature, highlight new insights, and demonstrate how this study contributes to the broader discourse on AI-driven KM.

7.1 Critical synthesis of findings and literature

Cross-domain knowledge transfer and LLMs: Prior research has extensively documented the technical capabilities of LLMs, such as natural language processing (NLP) and pattern recognition [2, 3]. However, existing studies have largely focused on narrow applications, such as document classification or chatbot deployment, without systematically examining how LLMs enable cross-domain knowledge transfer. This study bridges this gap by demonstrating how LLMs integrate tacit and explicit knowledge across traditionally isolated domains, such as healthcare, finance, and logistics. For instance, our case studies reveal that LLMs can unify clinical trial data with patient feedback in pharmaceutical research, or correlate geopolitical events with market trends in financial risk management. These findings align with the literature on knowledge integration but extend it by highlighting LLMs' unique ability to dynamically synthesize multidisciplinary data in real-time.

Overcoming knowledge silos: The fragmentation of knowledge across organizational silos has long been identified as a barrier to innovation [4]. Traditional KM systems, such as intranets and wikis, have attempted to address this challenge but often fail to integrate tacit knowledge or bridge domain-specific gaps. Our findings show that LLMs act as centralized hubs, harmonizing data from disparate sources (e.g., technical manuals and market research reports) and making organizational knowledge universally accessible. This capability aligns with the literature on collaborative KM [5] but introduces a novel dimension: LLMs not only facilitate knowledge sharing but also generate new insights by identifying patterns and connections that are not immediately apparent to human analysts.

Ethical and operational risks: While the literature has highlighted risks such as algorithmic bias [6] and data privacy breaches, this study provides actionable frameworks for mitigating these challenges. For example, we propose federated learning for data anonymization in healthcare and adversarial debiasing techniques to ensure fairness in recruitment algorithms. These solutions build on prior work but emphasize the need for proactive governance and stakeholder engagement, which have been underexplored in the context of LLM-driven KM.

7.2 New insights and contributions

This study advances the reader's understanding of the research problem in several key ways:

- Context-aware knowledge integration: Unlike traditional KM systems, which rely on static repositories, LLMs enable dynamic, real-time synthesis of knowledge. This capability is particularly valuable in multidisciplinary environments, where insights from multiple fields must be integrated to address complex challenges.

- Epistemic dependency: We introduce the concept of epistemic dependency—organizations' reliance on AI-generated content—as a critical theoretical construct. This concept challenges the traditional view of KM as a human-centric process and calls for new frameworks to balance AI-driven efficiency with human oversight.

- Scalability and generalization: Our findings demonstrate that LLMs can be fine-tuned for domain-specific applications while retaining their cross-domain capabilities. This insight addresses a key limitation in the literature, which often assumes a trade-off between specialization and generalization.

7.3 Limitations and future research

While this study provides a comprehensive framework for understanding LLM-driven KM [6, 10–13], several limitations warrant further exploration:

- Epistemic trust: Future research should investigate how organizations can balance reliance on AI-generated insights with human critical thinking, particularly in high-stakes domains like healthcare and finance.

- Scalability vs. ethics: The trade-offs between model size, computational efficiency, and ethical considerations remain underexplored. Future studies should examine how these trade-offs impact equitable access to AI capabilities.

- Human-AI creativity: The role of LLMs in augmenting—rather than replacing—human creativity and innovation requires further investigation.

This study has demonstrated that LLMs are not merely tools for automating KM tasks but active agents of organizational transformation [5, 7–9]. By enabling cross-domain knowledge transfer, breaking down silos, and fostering interdisciplinary collaboration, LLMs redefine how organizations create, store, and utilize knowledge. However, realizing this potential requires addressing ethical, operational, and environmental challenges through proactive governance and stakeholder engagement. As organizations navigate the complexities of the AI era, this study provides a roadmap for harnessing the transformative power of LLMs while ensuring alignment with societal values and sustainability goals.

8. Conclusion and call to action

The transformative potential of large language models (LLMs) in enabling cross-domain knowledge transfer, breaking down silos, and fostering innovation across industries has been a central theme of this book [2, 3]. LLMs have emerged as powerful tools that redefine how organizations manage, integrate, and apply knowledge, offering unprecedented efficiency, adaptability, and scalability. Through real-world applications, we have demonstrated how LLMs streamline operations, facilitate interdisciplinary collaboration, and deliver actionable insights across diverse sectors such as healthcare, finance, education, and logistics. However, the journey toward leveraging LLMs effectively is not without challenges. Issues of data privacy, model bias, ethical concerns, and environmental impact remain critical areas that require proactive strategies. To fully harness the potential of LLMs, organizations must adopt a balanced approach that combines technological innovation with ethical governance and sustainability [6–8].

For simplicity, we structure it into three subsections to address the theoretical and managerial implications of the study, as well as to outline future research directions.

8.1 Theoretical implications

This research contributes to the theoretical understanding of knowledge management (KM) in the era of artificial intelligence by highlighting the role of LLMs as active agents of organizational transformation rather than passive tools. The study bridges a critical gap in the literature by systematically exploring how LLMs enable cross-domain knowledge transfer, a capability that has been underexplored in traditional KM frameworks. By introducing the concept of context-aware knowledge integration, this work provides a new lens through which to examine how LLMs dynamically synthesize information from diverse domains, enabling organizations to address complex, multidisciplinary challenges [12–14].

Furthermore, the study advances the discourse on human-AI collaboration by proposing a taxonomy of LLM capabilities in cross-domain contexts [7, 11]. It underscores the importance of epistemic dependency—the reliance on AI-generated content—as a theoretical construct that warrants further investigation. This research also highlights the need for interdisciplinary approaches to studying AI-driven KM, emphasizing the integration of insights from computer science, organizational behavior, and ethics to develop holistic frameworks for understanding and optimizing human-AI symbiosis.

For practitioners, this research offers actionable insights into how organizations can leverage LLMs to enhance decision-making, foster innovation, and maintain competitive advantage in transformative environments. Key managerial implications include:

1. *Breaking down silos:* Deploy LLMs as centralized hubs to integrate siloed data (e.g., R&D blueprints, customer feedback, and regulatory documents), enabling cross-functional teams to collaborate on shared insights.

2. *Ethical AI governance:* Implement auditable AI frameworks with bias mitigation tools (e.g., adversarial debiasing) and transparency protocols (e.g., SHAP-based explainability) to ensure compliance with regulations like GDPR and build stakeholder trust.

3. *Sustainability in AI deployment:* Prioritize energy-efficient practices (e.g., model pruning and federated learning) and renewable energy adoption to reduce LLMs' carbon footprint while maintaining performance.

8.2 Future research and call to action

8.2.1 Ideas for future research

To advance LLM-driven knowledge management, future studies should focus on:

- *Epistemic trust:* How can organizations balance reliance on AI-generated insights with human critical thinking? What frameworks ensure accountability in high-stakes decisions (e.g., medical diagnostics)?

- *Scalability vs. ethics:* How do trade-offs between model size (e.g., GPT-4's 1.7T parameters) and computational costs impact equitable access to AI capabilities?
- *Human-AI creativity:* Can LLMs augment—rather than replace—human innovation in fields like drug discovery or climate modeling?
- *Green AI:* Develop decentralized architectures (e.g., blockchain-integrated LLMs) to reduce energy consumption while preserving data privacy.
- *Societal equity:* Investigate policies to prevent AI-driven disparities in education, healthcare, and employment, ensuring marginalized communities benefit from LLM advancements.

The potential of LLMs to bridge disciplinary divides and address global challenges—from pandemic response to climate resilience—is unparalleled. Yet, this promise hinges on responsible innovation. Organizations must adopt proactive governance (e.g., ethics boards and impact assessments), invest in human-AI hybrid workflows, and prioritize inclusive design to ensure LLMs empower rather than marginalize. By uniting scholars, practitioners, and policymakers, we can steer AI toward a future where technology amplifies human potential and fosters collective progress.

Acknowledgements

This chapter was conducted by Weiqiang Jin during his research at Xi'an Jiaotong University. The authors would like to thank the editors and anonymous reviewers, who significantly enhanced the quality of this work.

The authors acknowledge the use of DeepSeek-V3 for the language polishing of the manuscript.

Abbreviations

LLM	large language model
KM	knowledge management
AI	artificial intelligence
AGI	artificial general intelligence
GenAI	generative artificial intelligence
NLP	natural language processing
SHAP	SHapley Additive exPlanations
LIME	Local Interpretable Model-agnostic Explanations
GDPR	General Data Protection Regulation
SME	small and medium-sized enterprises
GPT	generative pre-trained transformer
BERT	Bidirectional Encoder Representations from Transformers

Author details

Weiqiang Jin[1,2,3]* and Biao Zhao[1]*

1 School of Information and Communications Engineering, Xi'an Jiaotong University, Xi'an, Shaanxi, China

2 Department of Electrical and Electronic Engineering, The University of Hong Kong (HKU), Hong Kong, China

3 Bioengineering Department and Imperial-X, Imperial College London, London, UK

*Address all correspondence to: weiqiangjin@stu.xjtu.edu.cn
and biaozhao@xjtu.edu.cn

References

[66] Crossan MM. The knowledge-creating company: How Japanese companies create the dynamics of innovation. Journal of International Business Studies. 1996;**27**(1):196-201. DOI: 10.1057/jibs.1996.13 [Accessed: September 1, 2024]

[67] Vaswani A, Shazeer N, Parmar N, Uszkoreit J, Jones L, Gomez AN, et al. Attention is all you need. Advances in Neural Information Processing Systems. 2017;**30**:6000-6010

[68] Brown TB, Mann B, Ryder N, Subbiah M, Kaplan J, Dhariwal P, et al. Language models are few-shot learners. Advances in Neural Information Processing Systems. 2020;**33**:1877-1901

[69] Hislop D. Knowledge Management in Organizations: A Critical Introduction. Oxford, United Kingdom: Oxford University Press; 2013

[70] Davenport TH, Prusak L. Working knowledge: How organizations manage what they know. Ubiquity. 2000;**2000**(August):6. DOI: 10.1145/347634.348775 [Accessed: August 2024]

[71] Mehrabi N, Morstatter F, Saxena N, Lerman K, Galstyan A. A survey on bias and fairness in machine learning. ACM Computing Surveys (CSUR). 2021;**54**(6):1-35

[72] Yao Y, Li Z, Zhao H. GKT: A novel guidance-based knowledge transfer framework for efficient cloud-edge collaboration LLM deployment. In: Ku L-W, Martins A, Srikumar V, editors. Findings of the Association for Computational Linguistics: ACL 2024. Bangkok, Thailand: Association for Computational Linguistics; 2024. pp. 3433-3446. Available from: https://aclanthology.org/2024.findings-acl.204 [Accessed: 2024]

[73] Cassano F, Gouwar J, Lucchetti F, Schlesinger C, Freeman A, Anderson CJ, et al. Knowledge transfer from high-resource to low-resource programming languages for code LLMs. Proceedings of the ACM on Programming Languages. 2024;**8**(OOPSLA2):295. DOI: 10.1145/3689735 [Accessed: October 2024]

[74] Tolegen G, Toleu A, Mussabayev R. Enhancing low-resource NER via knowledge transfer from LLM. In: Nguyen NT et al., editors. Computational Collective Intelligence. ICCCI 2024, Lecture Notes in Computer Science. Vol. 14810. Cham: Springer; 2024. DOI: 10.1007/978-3-031-70816-9_19 [Accessed: 2024]

[75] Yang H, Wang Y, Xu X, Zhang H, Bian Y. Can we trust LLMs? Mitigate overconfidence bias in LLMs through knowledge transfer. arXiv preprint arXiv:2405.16856. 2024. Available from: https://arxiv.org/abs/2405.16856 [Accessed: 2024]

[76] Zhao Z, Cao Y, Gong S, Patras I. Enhancing zero-shot facial expression recognition by LLM knowledge transfer. arXiv preprint arXiv:2405.19100. 2024. Available from: https://arxiv.org/abs/2405.19100 [Accessed: 2024]

[77] Deng A, Gao Z, Choudhuri A, Planche B, Zheng M, Wang B, et al. Seq2Time: Sequential knowledge transfer for video LLM temporal grounding. arXiv preprint arXiv:2411.16932. 2024. Available from: https://arxiv.org/abs/2411.16932 [Accessed: 2024]

[78] Cassano F, Gouwar J, Lucchetti F, Schlesinger C, Freeman A, Anderson CJ,

et al. Knowledge transfer from high-resource to low-resource programming languages for code LLMs. arXiv preprint arXiv:2308.09895. 2024. Available from: https://arxiv.org/abs/2308.09895 [Accessed: 2024]

[79] Patidar M, Sawhney R, Singh A, Chatterjee B, Mausam, Bhattacharya I Few-Shot Transfer Learning for Knowledge Base Question Answering: Fusing Supervised Models with In-Context Learning. 2024. Available from: https://arxiv.org/abs/2311.08894 [Accessed: 2024]

Chapter 6

Knowledge Sharing: Theoretical Lenses and Practical Implications

Samane Sadeghian and Mohammad Ghaffari Feyzabadi

Abstract

Knowledge is recognized as a vital resource for organizations in today's knowledge-based economy. It serves as a key driver for innovation, performance improvement, sustainable competitive advantage, and successful adaptation to environmental changes. However, for knowledge to realize its full potential, it must be effectively shared within the organization. This chapter explores the concept of knowledge sharing, its significance, different types of knowledge (explicit and tacit), various theoretical perspectives on knowledge sharing (including Social Capital Theory, Social Exchange Theory, Theory of Reasoned Action, Theory of Planned Behavior, and Resource-Based View), and factors influencing knowledge-sharing behavior (such as artificial intelligence, gender, social capital, rewards, organizational justice, and leadership). Additionally, potential challenges associated with knowledge sharing, such as knowledge hoarding, free-riding, and different knowledge-sharing states (ideal, free-riding, dormant, and non-utilization), are discussed. Finally, the chapter examines the role of leadership in knowledge sharing and provides recommendations for enhancing knowledge-sharing practices in organizations. The objective of this chapter is to offer a comprehensive overview of knowledge sharing and provide insights for managers to foster a knowledge-sharing culture within their organizations.

Keywords: knowledge, knowledge sharing, social exchange theory, social capital theory, impact of gender on knowledge sharing, impact of leadership on knowledge sharing, types of knowledge sharing

1. Introduction

Human resources play a critical role in organizations. Unlike other resources such as machinery, buildings, and capital, which can be depleted, human capital continuously provides invaluable contributions to organizations that cannot be exhausted. The significance of this notion becomes evident within the framework of the knowledge economy. In today's knowledge-driven economy, most organizations seek to achieve a competitive advantage through their human capital. This is because the current economy has shifted from tangible assets to intangible resources such as knowledge, skills, and individual capabilities, with organizations striving to gain a competitive edge through these intangible assets. In this context, knowledge emerges as the most crucial resource, often considered a key enabler of organizational success [1].

But what is knowledge? "Knowledge is a fluid mix of framed experiences, values, contextual information, and expert insights that provides a framework for evaluating and integrating new experiences and information, playing a vital role in fostering innovation" [2]. Given the significance of knowledge, it is often asserted that "knowledge is power." This statement highlights that knowledge serves as a fundamental resource for both organizations and individuals [3].

Knowledge and information, as powerful tools enabling organizations to adapt to changes in the world, form the foundation of the most critical characteristic of any intelligent twenty-first-century organization. In the modern era, knowledge's role in securing sustainable competitive advantage has significantly increased [4]. A review of the existing literature reveals that knowledge is considered the most crucial prerequisite for innovation, performance improvement, sustainable competitive advantage, environmental change anticipation, and continuous organizational success. It is also recognized as a fundamental resource for maintaining stability in the face of industrial and technological shifts [4–9]. In such an era, the necessity of knowledge management within organizations is more crucial than ever [1].

Given the advantages of knowledge, one might assume that organizations should strictly protect their knowledge assets. However, while safeguarding organizational knowledge is important, an open and unrestricted approach to knowledge within internal processes is equally essential. Without such an approach, knowledge gaps emerge [3]. Thus, knowledge sharing should be a central focus within organizations.

As mentioned earlier, knowledge is power, and knowledge sharing amplifies and strengthens this power [10]. The utilization of knowledge in solving organizational challenges and, consequently, creating competitive advantage [11] is only feasible when individuals share their knowledge and generate new knowledge from others' insights. A study of successful organizations reveals that they actively manage and share their knowledge assets, thereby achieving strategic goals and superior performance [4]. One critical challenge organizations face is that poorly managed and unshared knowledge deteriorates over time. Tacit knowledge, which accumulates in individuals' minds, must be shared. Among all knowledge management processes, knowledge sharing is considered the most essential [9]. If a culture of knowledge sharing is not cultivated, there is a risk of losing valuable knowledge or misusing existing knowledge [12]. For instance, in an employee's absence, if knowledge has not been shared, organizational operations may encounter significant disruptions. Similarly, when an employee leaves the organization, substantial time and financial resources must be invested in training new personnel to regain the knowledge previously acquired by former colleagues [3].

The significance of knowledge sharing can also be analyzed through the Resource-Based View (RBV) theory. According to this theory, resources that are valuable, rare, and inimitable provide organizations with competitive advantages. Given that knowledge possesses these characteristics, it is deemed a crucial resource for sustainable competitive advantage [13].

Regarding knowledge sharing, various theories and influential factors have been proposed. Generally, knowledge sharing is defined as the willingness of individuals to share information and knowledge with others in an organization, primarily occurring through the conversion of tacit knowledge into explicit knowledge and its externalization [3, 9]. Through knowledge sharing, individuals and organizations can attain the previously mentioned benefits of knowledge, including enhanced innovation, improved performance, agility, and sustainable competitive advantage.

Researchers have examined knowledge sharing through multiple theoretical lenses, such as Social Capital Theory, which explores the impact of structural, relational, and cognitive capital on knowledge sharing [6, 14–17]; Social Exchange Theory (SET), which considers individuals as rational actors who assess the benefits of sharing knowledge before engaging in such behavior [15, 18–20]; and the Theory of Reasoned Action (TRA), which examines how attitudes and subjective norms influence individuals' intentions, including knowledge-sharing intentions [21, 22]. Furthermore, the Theory of Planned Behavior (TPB) explores how individuals' intentions translate into actual behaviors, including knowledge-sharing behavior [23, 24]. Some scholars integrate these theories within organizational contexts [25], suggesting that based on SET, organizations can encourage knowledge sharing by offering incentives (both financial and non-financial, such as fostering an environment of respect and appreciation), thereby influencing individuals' attitudes and intentions toward knowledge sharing.

Additionally, the Resource-Based View (RBV) posits that knowledge is a valuable, rare, and inimitable resource that grants organizations a competitive advantage [13].

A review of existing research indicates that most studies on knowledge sharing have been conducted within specific domains, often lacking comprehensiveness and general applicability. They tend to focus on particular theoretical perspectives rather than adopting a holistic approach [26]. Given the increasing importance of knowledge sharing, particularly as a strategic response to dynamic environmental changes, this chapter aims to explore various theoretical perspectives and influential factors affecting knowledge sharing. The ultimate goal is to enhance the comprehensiveness of knowledge-sharing research. Furthermore, in the final section, the practical implications of the discussed concepts for organizational settings are examined.

2. Literature review

2.1 Types of knowledge

By examining the existing literature, we recognize the vast and multifaceted nature of knowledge. However, knowledge is primarily classified into two main types:

1. Explicit knowledge and

2. Tacit knowledge.

Explicit knowledge is defined as codified knowledge that can be easily transmitted through verbal or written communication [27]. As a result, it can be easily documented, transferred, shared, and reused within an organization [28]. In other words, explicit knowledge is formally encoded using a symbolic system or manifested as a tangible physical artifact, making it readily shareable [29]. Examples include procedures, instructions, policies, production plans, forecasts, maps, technical product details, tools, and resources [29]. Information and communication technologies such as electronic databases, data transmission systems, workflows, mailing lists, and video conferences facilitate the capture and dissemination of explicit knowledge [28].

In contrast, tacit knowledge is an intangible asset that includes mental models, schemas, cognitive insights, intuition, and heuristics [29]. It involves timely extraction of relevant insights from vast data sets to derive solutions and is defined as a combination of personal experiences, specific contexts, ideas, values, and emotions, sometimes rooted in aspirations, values, or deeply held beliefs [28]. According to [30], tacit knowledge is valuable, uncodified knowledge that serves as a source of information and creativity. As noted by [28], tacit knowledge refers to intuitive and inexpressible knowledge formed through individuals' past experiences in specific fields. It is difficult to identify, formalize, and transfer to others and evolves dynamically through social interactions and personalization [28].

Tacit knowledge is often regarded as a competitive advantage due to its difficulty in being transferred. Enhancing the sharing and formalization of tacit knowledge presents a managerial challenge in organizations [27, 29] as it is more personal, effort-intensive, and costlier to share compared to explicit knowledge [29]. Employees often resist sharing their valuable knowledge with others [28], Nevertheless, certain aspects of tacit knowledge can be inadvertently shared [31], such as perceptions, beliefs, and experiences [1].

Another classification of knowledge divides it into individual and organizational knowledge. Individual knowledge refers to an individual's ability to judge and make decisions based on their knowledge, whereas organizational knowledge is considered an organizational resource that enables the workforce to make collective decisions based on accumulated knowledge. This collective knowledge is acquired through organizational knowledge management processes [32].

2.2 Knowledge sharing

To understand the evolution of knowledge studies, we must trace their historical development. Since the 1950s, the importance of integrating tacit and explicit knowledge has been emphasized. Consequently, the development of knowledge management began in the early 1960s, when researchers, influenced by the emphasis on learning through best practices and lessons, focused on knowledge codification and explicit knowledge storage.

From the 1990s to the early 2000s, knowledge was recognized as a vital economic resource in the knowledge-based society. Organizations aiming to navigate dynamic changes needed to generate and share knowledge rather than merely processing it efficiently. At this stage of development, researchers increasingly studied and described knowledge-sharing processes and the conversion of tacit knowledge into explicit knowledge to enhance intellectual capital [32].

Today, knowledge sharing is a strategic approach for adapting to environmental changes. Given its significance, numerous definitions have emerged in the literature:

"Knowledge sharing is a behavior based on the reciprocal exchange of expertise, skills, and information among employees" [26].

"The willingness of employees to share information (in the form of ideas, experiences, facts, processes, formulas) with others in the organization" [30].

"The transfer of knowledge between individuals, groups, teams, departments, and organizations" [9].

"Making relevant knowledge accessible to colleagues within the organization" [8].

"A reciprocal exchange of knowledge, encompassing both the collection and donation of explicit and tacit knowledge" [27].

"Knowledge sharing includes the externalization process of converting tacit knowledge into explicit knowledge" [3].

According to Islam et al. [2], knowledge sharing occurs when "individuals possessing knowledge willingly transfer their work experience, techniques, and opinions to others in a tangible manner, expecting others to apply such knowledge in practice at the workplace."

Organizational knowledge has been examined in various studies and contexts. For instance, Wang et al. [17] explored knowledge sharing in online Q&A communities, emphasizing social capital theory and highlighting the significance of social aspects, trust, and feedback systems. Additionally, Liao [33] investigated knowledge sharing in R&D departments, analyzing the role of power from a social exchange perspective. This study concluded that managerial social power and institutional trust significantly influence engineers' knowledge-sharing behavior, underscoring the necessity of fostering a knowledge-sharing culture to maintain competitive advantage.

According to Ref. [6], Fatemi et al. examined the impact of abusive supervision on knowledge sharing, moderated by organizational and peer support [13]. Similarly, Lee et al. [34] studied the enhancement of knowledge sharing through diversity-oriented leadership during crises (e.g., COVID-19), finding that such leadership styles significantly improve knowledge sharing, particularly during turbulent times.

The benefits of knowledge sharing have been extensively documented. It is considered a vital social asset [16], a key driver of organizational learning, an enhancer of individual and organizational performance, and a contributor to sustainable competitive advantage [7]. Furthermore, it fosters innovation at both individual and organizational levels [2], enhances job performance [16], and plays a crucial role in achieving organizational efficiency [16]. It also strengthens memory [27] at both individual and organizational levels and contributes to organizational competitiveness and success [16]. The absence of knowledge sharing threatens organizational survival [6].

Within organizations, tasks are interdependent, and no single individual possesses sufficient knowledge to resolve all organizational challenges [1]. Knowledge sharing enables organizations to respond more swiftly to problems, develop new ideas and insights, and avoid reinventing the wheel or repeating past mistakes [29].

Some sources define knowledge sharing as encompassing both knowledge seeking and knowledge contribution [35–38]. These two elements form a feedback loop, and the absence of either results in an incomplete and unsustainable knowledge-sharing process. For instance, individuals who exclusively seek knowledge without contributing to it are considered "free riders," benefiting from others' knowledge without sharing their own [17].

Knowledge sharing is a behavior that cannot be simply influenced through policies and regulations. While offering flexibility and opportunities to knowledgeable employees can positively impact knowledge sharing [1], a more in-depth examination of the factors that influence knowledge sharing within organizations is necessary. This aspect is explored further in subsequent sections.

2.2.1 States and challenges of knowledge sharing

Knowledge sharing involves two key actors: the sender and the receiver. The act of sharing knowledge requires the active participation of both the sender and the receiver [16]. Thus, two fundamental aspects of knowledge sharing emerge: knowledge collection and knowledge donation. Knowledge collection refers to the process by which individuals acquire knowledge or, in other words, learn, whereas knowledge donation entails transferring one's knowledge to others through communication [2]. Essentially, a receiver engages in knowledge collection, while a sender performs knowledge donation.

According to Lei et al. [27], knowledge sharing can be defined as the reciprocal exchange of knowledge, encompassing both the collection and donation of explicit and tacit knowledge. Based on this perspective, different states and challenges in knowledge sharing can be identified. In Zhang et al. [39], various challenges of knowledge sharing are comprehensively discussed, focusing on two dimensions: knowledge usage and knowledge donation. Consequently, four states are identified:

1. *The ideal state*: In this state, individuals both share their knowledge with others and utilize the knowledge shared by others. This is considered the optimal situation.

2. *The free-rider state*: In this state, individuals only use knowledge without contributing their own. This can be linked to the phenomenon of *knowledge hiding*, which refers to the deliberate concealment or withholding of knowledge from others. Knowledge hiding not only affects financial and operational performance but also negatively impacts organizational culture by damaging relationships and fostering distrust among employees. Conversely, in a scenario where employees recognize that their knowledge could benefit a colleague and share it voluntarily without being explicitly asked, knowledge hiding does not occur [40]. According to Kim et al. [13], knowledge hiding can be analyzed through the lens of *power dynamics*, as knowledge hoarding can serve as a source of personal power and competitive advantage. However, efforts should be made to mitigate this issue. To prevent knowledge hiding, organizations can leverage *knowledge management tools*, promote teamwork, emphasize collective knowledge ownership, and strengthen employees' organizational commitment. If no action is taken to address this state, knowledge sharing within the organization will inevitably decline. This phenomenon can be explained through *Social Exchange Theory (SET)*, which suggests that individuals will reduce knowledge-sharing behaviors if they perceive no future benefits from doing so. If some employees share knowledge while others do not reciprocate, those who initially shared will eventually reduce their efforts due to a lack of perceived return on investment.

3. *The dormant state*: In this state, neither knowledge is shared nor utilized. The lack of knowledge utilization in this case may stem from employees not seeing personal benefits in the shared knowledge, insufficient support from senior management, or the excessive time and effort required by existing knowledge-sharing systems. Similar measures used to counteract knowledge hiding can be applied here to encourage participation.

4. *The non-utilization state*: In this state, knowledge is shared but not put to use. This phenomenon is often referred to as *"reinventing the wheel."* Employees fail to leverage existing knowledge, leading to inefficiencies. To address this, organizations must encourage knowledge utilization through strategies such as clarifying the benefits of using shared knowledge and creating environments where employees can practice and refine acquired knowledge as skills (**Figure 1**).

2.2.2 Sharing best practices?

Two types of knowledge sharing can be considered: sharing best practices and sharing mistakes. While best practices are often the first thought

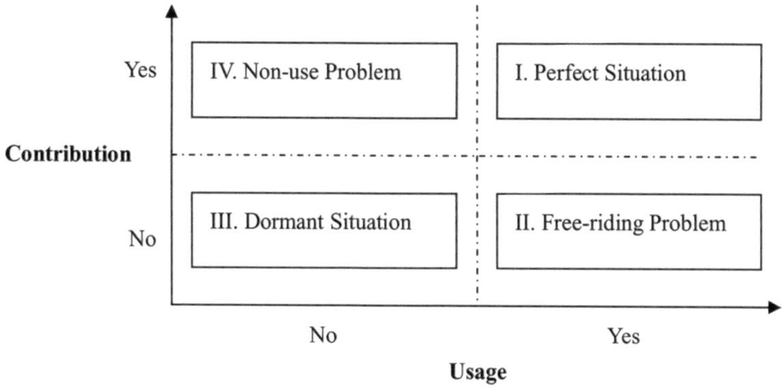

Figure 1.
States of knowledge sharing.

in knowledge-sharing discussions, sharing mistakes is equally important, as errors—despite their undesirable nature—offer valuable learning opportunities for organizations.

The process of sharing mistakes fosters critical reflection on individual experiences, allowing employees to generate new ideas as solutions to workplace challenges. This interactive process in knowledge-sharing enables the transformation of experiences and insights into new understandings through the recombination of knowledge. To promote a culture of mistake-sharing, organizations should reward employees who proactively identify and correct potential system errors [28]. Additionally, according to Social Exchange Theory, if organizations value and incentivize knowledge sharing, employees will be more motivated to share their mistakes and contribute to organizational learning.

2.2.3 Factors influencing knowledge sharing

2.2.3.1 The impact of artificial intelligence on knowledge sharing

Artificial intelligence (AI) can facilitate knowledge sharing in organizations through several mechanisms:

1. Connecting individuals working on similar issues, even when they are geographically dispersed.

2. Creating interconnected and synchronized systems that provide managers with a comprehensive understanding of available knowledge and, in turn, highlight knowledge gaps and limitations.

3. Enhancing collective intelligence by complementing human expertise with AI-driven insights [11].

According to Chowdhury et al. [41], AI can reduce skepticism among employees, positively influencing and ultimately increasing knowledge sharing. To leverage AI for knowledge sharing, managers should establish mechanisms that facilitate knowledge exchange among employees, particularly regarding processes, systems, and applications of AI in human resource activities. Additionally, AI-driven knowledge-sharing mechanisms should include well-structured knowledge storage solutions, ensuring easy accessibility for employees.

In summary, AI enhances knowledge management by stimulating creative thinking, fostering shared memory across teams, and enabling peer feedback and review. However, it is crucial to acknowledge that knowledge creation and management are inherently human-centered processes. Therefore, AI should not replace humans but rather enhance and support knowledge sharing [11].

2.2.3.2 The impact of gender on knowledge sharing

Differences in knowledge sharing between genders are anticipated. On one hand, it is argued that women tend to share knowledge as they strive to overcome traditional stereotypes regarding their professional advancement. On the other hand, it is suggested that women are more cautious and less inclined to share their knowledge with others [6]. It is evident that gender differences manifest across a wide range of behaviors. For example, individuals' willingness to assist others varies depending on their gender. Men and women respond differently to various workplace factors. For instance, differences in reactions may be observed in competitive work environments, abusive supervision, or a lack of trust [42].

According to Social Role Theory, differences in knowledge sharing or knowledge hiding between men and women can be identified. This theory suggests that gender role beliefs stem from the historical division of labor between men and women and the roles they have traditionally played. Consequently, expectations regarding how men and women are (descriptive stereotypes) and how they should behave (prescriptive stereotypes) are formed [43]. From this perspective, women are expected to be communal, compassionate, helpful, attuned to collective needs or the emotions of others, and to seek emotional satisfaction. Conversely, men are expected to be agentic, meaning assertive, independent, competitive, and goal-oriented [44]. Furthermore, according to Regulatory Fit Theory, individuals are aware that others generally expect them to behave in accordance with gender roles. Conforming to these expectations is rewarded, while violating them can result in penalties. Consequently, individuals choose gender roles that align with societal expectations [44]. These two theories collectively influence the relationship between gender and knowledge sharing or knowledge hiding.

Men are more likely than women to conceal knowledge in the workplace and tend to rely more on rationalized knowledge hiding. In contrast, women are more likely to engage in behaviors such as playing dumb (e.g., pretending not to know the answer to a colleague's request for help) and evasive hiding (e.g., promising to provide information at a later time). This behavior reinforces the gender stereotype of female incompetence. Additionally, by failing to fulfill promised knowledge sharing due to the "playing dumb" approach, the social expectation that women are helpful is also explicitly undermined.

Men are more likely to benefit from gendered social expectations beyond the advantages of fulfilling these expectations, as they have the opportunity to conceal and protect their knowledge while choosing the safest way to do so. Meanwhile, under the pressure of gendered social expectations, women select approaches that may be detrimental to them in both the short and long term.

Naturally, the gender composition of the environment plays a crucial role. In male-dominated workplaces, men are less likely to conceal knowledge. Both men and women engage less in playing dumb and evasive hiding. In such environments, knowledge seekers are more likely to be men, whereas in female-dominated environments, they are more likely to be women [45].

2.2.3.3 The impact of social capital on knowledge sharing

According to Ref. [46], Bourdieu defines social capital as an individual's ability to gain value and benefit from a social network. Social capital refers to the connections and interactions among members of a network, facilitating actions and achieving organizational goals through the creation of norms and mutual trust [28]. Trust and social norms are critical aspects of social capital [15]. Social capital can be categorized into three dimensions: (1) structural capital, (2) cognitive capital, and (3) relational capital. Structural capital pertains to the overall structure of social ties among individuals, emphasizing social interactions and communication channels. Relational capital addresses the emotional nature of interpersonal connections, often manifesting as trust and respect, which can develop through social interactions. Cognitive capital refers to shared understandings of tasks and collective goals, as well as the ability to comprehend and apply knowledge during social interactions [17].

Social capital provides a suitable context for social exchange, which is discussed in the following section. Social capital, particularly in its structural dimension (social ties and interactions), enhances access to external resources, facilitates exchanges and knowledge absorption, and improves knowledge transfer efficiency by reducing time and effort through the creation of knowledge-sharing channels. Consequently, social capital plays a crucial role in knowledge sharing. Furthermore, through established social ties, relationships—and subsequently, stable knowledge sharing—are observed. Additionally, the relational dimension of social capital fosters knowledge sharing by promoting trust and reducing perceived risks in interactions. Finally, cognitive social capital is highly significant, as a shared understanding of collective goals and norms enhances knowledge self-efficacy within communities. This, in turn, increases the likelihood of understanding, sharing, and utilizing knowledge to solve problems [6, 17].

According to Social Capital Theory, organizations with strong internal networks benefit from free-flowing communication, close interactions, resource exchange, and enhanced team performance. Thus, an organizational environment that promotes diversity and social interactions makes effective knowledge sharing more feasible [16]. The study by Wang et al. [17] examines the role of social capital in knowledge sharing, suggesting that social capital can act as a mediator between knowledge-seeking behaviors and increased participation in knowledge-sharing processes, ultimately enhancing sustainable knowledge sharing. In essence, individuals' pursuit of knowledge fosters social capital development, which in turn strengthens engagement in knowledge-sharing activities.

2.2.3.4 Social exchange theory and knowledge sharing

Social Exchange Theory begins with a fundamental question: Why do individuals with significant knowledge often hesitate to share it? According to this theory, if knowledge sharing does not offer mutual benefits, it is perceived as a costly action. For example, it is not rational for individuals to share knowledge with those who provide no reciprocal advantage [13].

Social Exchange Theory posits that individuals expect returns for voluntary actions, gaining motivation through exchanges with others. In social exchanges, knowledge, recognition, or approval can be considered valuable resources. Here, individuals are motivated by rewards such as reputation, the satisfaction of helping others, and positive feedback [15].

More precisely, within the framework of Social Exchange Theory, knowledge sharing is seen as the exchange of a valuable resource between two parties. During this exchange, individuals evaluate the costs associated with acquiring and sharing knowledge (which includes work effort and loss of power) against the expected benefits. A person's willingness to share knowledge depends on their assessment of these costs and rewards. Therefore, organizations should offer external incentives to encourage employee knowledge sharing [29]. While individuals may also share knowledge for expected social rewards such as approval and respect, they primarily aim to maximize benefits while minimizing costs. Reflecting on Social Exchange Theory employees who receive rewards are expected to reciprocate with high motivation and engagement in knowledge sharing, thereby supporting the organization [3]. Rewarding and recognizing knowledge-sharing behaviors fosters a positive perception among employees regarding the value of their knowledge-sharing contributions [1].

Thus, according to this theory, rewarding individuals is expected to increase their participation in knowledge sharing. However, a critical issue arises: the strategic management of knowledge. External incentives compel individuals to evaluate the effort required for knowledge sharing in relation to the expected reward [3].

According to Zhang et al. [39], reward systems are beneficial and influential in most knowledge-sharing mechanisms. However, it is essential to note that the relationship between rewards and knowledge sharing is more complex than it appears. External motivational factors must be considered in the context in which individuals engage in knowledge-sharing activities. Therefore, a fair organizational environment—particularly in performance evaluations (which should be just, impartial, and equitable)—can encourage individuals to share knowledge. Specifically, incorporating knowledge-sharing metrics into Key Performance Indicators (KPIs) is crucial for promoting knowledge sharing [1]. Employees who perceive performance evaluations as fair and unbiased develop a positive outlook toward their organization, which strengthens their willingness to engage in knowledge sharing [3]. Furthermore, as previously mentioned, appropriate KPIs should be established to institutionalize the sharing of mistakes within organizations to harness its benefits.

2.2.3.5 The impact of leadership on knowledge sharing

Supervisors' behaviors and leadership styles in an organization can significantly influence knowledge sharing. It is important to note that leadership here does not refer to a specific individual within the organization but rather to the act of leading individuals. It is well established that supervisors' behaviors significantly impact subordinates' behaviors, particularly their discretionary actions. For employees, engaging in some discretionary behaviors, such as organizational citizenship behavior, is considerably less risky and less costly than knowledge sharing. This is because individuals may perceive knowledge sharing as a potential loss of their competitive advantage and expertise. Thus, the way individuals are led in an organization greatly affects their perception of knowledge sharing.

For instance, excessive supervision—referred to as intrusive monitoring—has a negative impact on individuals' willingness to share knowledge. Conversely, empowering leadership positively influences knowledge-sharing behavior [13]. The positive effect of transformational leadership on knowledge sharing has also been examined by Yin et al. [47], confirming that transformational leadership fosters knowledge-sharing behavior. One less frequently explored leadership style is diversity-oriented leadership, in which leaders emphasize the inclusion of employees from diverse backgrounds and characteristics. According to Lee et al. [34], this leadership style positively influences knowledge-sharing behavior. Additionally, Asbari et al. [10] argues that there is a reciprocal relationship between dynamic leadership and knowledge-sharing behavior.

According to Ref. [19], Ahmad et al. explored the relationship between leadership and knowledge-sharing behavior in their study [16]. To understand this relationship, it is first necessary to distinguish between two types of knowledge: task-oriented knowledge and context-framing knowledge. Context-framing knowledge pertains to an individual's understanding of how their knowledge relates to the knowledge of other team members. This type of knowledge helps individuals recognize how their work and expertise contribute to achieving organizational goals. On the other hand, task-oriented knowledge is technical in nature and essential for performing specific job-related tasks, as it pertains to how work is executed.

A leader who demonstrates a high level of job-related competencies has a positive impact on the development of context-framing knowledge. Through this mechanism, employees become aligned with organizational objectives and are more likely to engage in knowledge sharing.

Additionally, enhancing employees' capabilities and competencies strengthens knowledge sharing. In this regard, a leader who actively demonstrates and fosters people-related competencies positively influences the creation and reinforcement of an environment conducive to knowledge sharing. Furthermore, the organizational leader must cultivate a workplace environment characterized by trust, empathy, openness to knowledge sharing, and accessibility to support. These factors encourage individuals to share knowledge.

This aligns closely with social exchange theory, as the aforementioned factors—such as an environment rich in trust, openness, and empathy—create intangible benefits for individuals. Consequently, when employees perceive these non-material advantages, they are more likely to participate in knowledge-sharing activities.

3. Discussion

This research illuminates the multifaceted interaction of individual, organizational, and technological factors that shape knowledge-sharing behavior. The results highlight the importance of leadership, social capital, and organizational rewards, but also identify knowledge hiding, gender, and AI adoption challenges as obstacles to successful knowledge-sharing processes.

Leadership styles directly impact employees' willingness to share knowledge. Empowering and transformational leaders promote cultures that welcome the sharing of knowledge, while close supervision discourages open communication [16, 47]. Transformational leadership, in particular, promotes a culture of cooperation and trust, which is a prerequisite for the open exchange of knowledge [10]. Social capital, especially its structural and relational ones, facilitates knowledge sharing effectiveness *via* strong relationships as well as increasing employees' trust [15, 17].

AI-driven knowledge-sharing technologies improve knowledge management, but their success is dependent on how well they are integrated into human interaction and not as replacements [11].

For example, artificial intelligence may enhance collaboration among teams of various geographical areas; however, the role of the human factor is still vital in delivering contextual insight and the appropriate application of shared knowledge [41]. Gender variation must be considered in formulating knowledge-sharing approaches, as men and women behave differently based on the expectations of societal roles [42, 45]. Social exchange processes suggest that knowledge sharing flourishes in environments where employees perceive fairness and reciprocity in reward and appreciation [13, 39]. Future studies need to investigate the impact of cultural diversity, industry characteristics, and virtual work settings on knowledge-sharing practices, aiming to enhance theoretical models in this field [34]. Furthermore, examining the interaction between leadership styles and social capital in various organizational settings can provide further knowledge regarding the synergistic impacts of these factors on knowledge sharing [6].

4. Theoretical implications

This study contributes to the theoretical discourse on knowledge sharing by integrating multiple theoretical perspectives, including Social Exchange Theory (SET), Social Capital Theory, Resource-Based View (RBV), and Transformational Leadership Theory. The findings reinforce and extend these theoretical constructs in the following ways:

Regarding Social Exchange Theory (SET), this study supports the premise that individuals engage in knowledge sharing when they anticipate reciprocal benefits. The reluctance to share knowledge due to concerns about losing competitive advantage aligns with prior research [13]. Furthermore, the study confirms that fair reward systems, including both monetary and non-monetary incentives, play a pivotal role in fostering knowledge-sharing behaviors [15].

In the context of Social Capital Theory, this study highlights the three key dimensions of social capital—structural, relational, and cognitive capital—and their role in shaping knowledge-sharing behaviors. Strong internal networks and interpersonal trust encourage employees to engage in reciprocal exchanges of knowledge [6, 17]. From the perspective of Resource-Based View (RBV), the study underscores that knowledge is an inimitable and valuable resource that contributes to sustained competitive advantage [13]. Organizations that effectively manage and share their knowledge assets are more likely to maintain long-term competitiveness.

Finally, concerning Transformational Leadership Theory, this research confirms the positive influence of transformational and empowering leadership styles on knowledge-sharing behaviors [47]. Leaders who cultivate trust, inclusivity, and an open communication culture create environments conducive to knowledge exchange.

This study extends existing theoretical discussions by examining the impact of gender differences, AI-enabled knowledge sharing, and leadership diversity, providing a multifaceted perspective on knowledge-sharing dynamics in modern organizations.

5. Managerial implication

For managers, this study offers actionable insights to enhance knowledge sharing within organizations. First, fostering social capital through trust-building and collaborative initiatives can create a supportive environment for knowledge exchange [17]. Second, investing in transformational leadership development can empower employees to share knowledge more openly [47]. Third, leveraging AI tools to connect employees and identify knowledge gaps can streamline knowledge-sharing processes, provided that human interactions remain central [11]. Fourth, addressing gender differences by creating inclusive policies can ensure equitable participation in knowledge sharing [45]. Finally, implementing fair reward systems and promoting a culture of learning from mistakes can further motivate employees to engage in knowledge-sharing behaviors [28, 39].

6. Conclusion

The research results confirm the complex interface of individual, organizational, and technological drivers of knowledge-sharing behavior. Though social capital and several styles of leadership came out as significant predictors of knowledge sharing, the study also revealed obstacles like the hiding of knowledge, gender disparities, and inadequate organizational support.

A major finding is the vital role played by leadership in promoting a climate where knowledge transfer occurs. Transformational and diversity-oriented leadership styles shape the environments that are marked by trust and collaboration, while very formal or authoritarian leadership frameworks hinder employees from facilitating knowledge sharing comfortably. In addition, digital technologies and artificial intelligence also possess the potential to fundamentally change knowledge-sharing tasks; however, their success will depend on their smooth alignment with knowledge-sharing strategies entailing humans.

The results indicate that artificial intelligence must augment and not replace human contact, stressing the need to ensure a balance between technological advancement and interpersonal learning. This study also questions the formulation of organizational policies to support knowledge-sharing activities. Future studies should consider the degree to which cultural variation and industry-specific factors, as well as virtual working environments, influence knowledge-sharing attitudes and behaviors and thereby add to the body of this scholarly field. Moreover, the impact of organizational culture on establishing knowledge-sharing routines needs further observation, along with the impact of emerging technologies on interactions associated with knowledge sharing in virtual teams.

Author details

Samane Sadeghian* and Mohammad Ghaffari Feyzabadi
Department of Management, Faculty of Economic and Administrative Sciences, Ferdowsi University of Mashhad, Mashhad, Iran

*Address all correspondence to: ssadeghian@um.ac.ir

References

[80] Iqbal S, Litvaj I, Drbúl M, Rasheed M. Improving quality of human resources through HRM practices and knowledge sharing. Administrative Sciences. 2023;**13**(10):224

[81] Islam T, Zahra I, Rehman SU, Jamil S. How knowledge sharing encourages innovative work behavior through occupational self-efficacy? The moderating role of entrepreneurial leadership. Global Knowledge, Memory and Communication. 2024;**73**(1/2):67-83

[82] Friedrich J, Becker M, Kramer F, Wirth M, Schneider M. Incentive design and gamification for knowledge management. Journal of Business Research. 2020;**106**:341-352

[83] Sadeghian S, Kafashpoor A, Lagzian M. Assessing impact of organizational culture and organizational structure on organizational effectiveness through knowledge management case study: Mashhad's science and technology park. International Journal of Management Sciences and Business Research. 10 Dec 2013;**2**(12):24-31

[84] Kafashpoor A, Shakoori N, Sadeghian S. Linking organizational culture, structure, leadership style, strategy, and organizational effectiveness: Mediating role of knowledge management. Advanced Research in Economic and Management Sciences. 12 Jul 2013;**10**(3):158-172

[85] Fatemi SZ, Sadeghian S, Ganji SFG, Johnson LW. Do different genders' knowledge sharing behaviors drive different innovative behavior? The moderating effect of social capital. European Journal of Innovation Management. 2022;**25**(2):592-606

[86] Arsawan IWE, Koval V, Rajiani I, Rustiarini NW, Supartha WG, Suryantini NPS. Leveraging knowledge sharing and innovation culture into SMEs sustainable competitive advantage. International Journal of Productivity and Performance Management. 2022;**71**(2):405-428

[87] Singh SK, Gupta S, Busso D, Kamboj S. Top management knowledge value, knowledge sharing practices, open innovation and organizational performance. Journal of Business Research. 2021;**1**(128):788-798

[88] Asrar-ul-Haq M, Anwar S. A systematic review of knowledge management and knowledge sharing: Trends, issues, and challenges. Cogent Business and Management. 31 Dec 2016;**3**(1):1127744

[89] Asbari M, Purba JT, Hariandja ES, Sudibjo N. The mediating role of dynamic leadership towards the relationship between knowledge-sharing behaviour and innovation performance in higher education. International Journal of Learning, Teaching and Educational Research. 2023;**22**(11):466-485

[90] Jarrahi MH, Askay D, Eshraghi A, Smith P. Artificial intelligence and knowledge management: A partnership between human and AI. Business Horizons. 2023;**66**(1):87-99

[91] de Antunes HJG, Pinheiro PG. Linking knowledge management, organizational learning and memory. Journal of Innovation and Knowledge. 2020;**5**(2):140-149

[92] Kim SL, Kim M, Yun S. Knowledge sharing, abusive supervision, and support. Group & Organization Management. 2015;**40**(5):599-624

[93] Yan Y, Guan J. Social capital, exploitative and exploratory innovations: The mediating roles of ego-network dynamics. Technological Forecasting and Social Change. 2018;**126**:244-258

[94] Zhao L, Detlor B. Towards a contingency model of knowledge sharing: Interaction between social capital and social exchange theories. Knowledge Management Research and Practice. 2023;**21**(1):197-209

[95] Swanson E, Kim S, Lee SM, Yang JJ, Lee YK. The effect of leader competencies on knowledge sharing and job performance: Social capital theory. Journal of Hospitality and Tourism Management. 2020;**1**(42):88-96

[96] Wang N, Wang L, Ma Z, Wang S. From knowledge seeking to knowledge contribution: A social capital perspective on knowledge sharing behaviors in online Q&A communities. Technological Forecasting and Social Change. 2022;**182**:121864

[97] Blau PM. Exchange and Power in Social Life. NewYork: Routledge; 2017

[98] Ahmad R, Nawaz MR, Ishaq MI, Khan MM, Ashraf HA. Social exchange theory: Systematic review and future directions. Frontiers in Psychology. 2023;**12**:13

[99] Li J. Knowledge sharing in virtual communities: A social exchange theory perspective. Journal of Industrial Engineering and Management (JIEM). 2015;**8**(1):170-183

[100] McLarnon MJWR, Gellatly IA, Richards D, Arazy O. Knowledge sharing processes and the role of attachment patterns. Journal of Knowledge Management. 2023;**27**(5):1343-1365

[101] Kaba A, Eletter S, Ramaiah CK, El Refae GA. Demographic differences in attitude, subjective norms, behavioral intention, and knowledge sharing behavior: An empirical study of non-academic staff from India and the UAE. VINE Journal of Information and Knowledge Management Systems. 2025;**55**(2):470-491

[102] Xu L, Li Z. Factors affecting the knowledge sharing Behaviors of university teachers: An empirical study in China. International Journal of Information and Education Technology. 2022;**12**(1):36-42

[103] Ajzen I. The theory of planned behavior: Frequently asked questions. Human Behavior and Emerging Technologies. 2020;**2**(4):314-324

[104] Ayala NF, Paslauski CA, Ghezzi A, Frank AG. Knowledge sharing dynamics in service suppliers' involvement for servitization of manufacturing companies. International Journal of Production Economics. 2017;**1**(193):538-553

[105] Chaudhary A, Islam T, Ali HF, Jamil S. Can paternalistic leaders enhance knowledge sharing? The roles of organizational commitment and Islamic work ethics. Global Knowledge, Memory and Communication. 2023;**72**(1/2):98-118

[106] Lei H, Gui L, Le PB. Linking transformational leadership and frugal innovation: The mediating role of tacit and explicit knowledge sharing. Journal of Knowledge Management. 2021;**25**(7):1832-1852

[107] López-Cabarcos MÁ, Srinivasan S, Vázquez-Rodríguez P. The role of product innovation and customer centricity in transforming tacit and explicit knowledge into profitability. Journal of Knowledge Management. 2020;**24**(5):1037-1057

[108] Cyr S, Choo CW. The individual and social dynamics of knowledge sharing: An exploratory study. Journal of Documentation. 2010;**66**(6):824-846

[109] Castellani P, Rossato C, Giaretta E, Davide R. Tacit knowledge sharing in knowledge-intensive firms: The perceptions of team members and team leaders. Review of Managerial Science. 2021;**15**(1):125-155

[110] Asher D, Popper M. Eliciting tacit knowledge in professions based on interpersonal interactions. The Learning Organization. 2021;**28**(6):523-537

[111] de Bem MA, Secinaro S, Calandra D, Lanzalonga F. Knowledge management and digital transformation for industry 4.0: A structured literature review. Knowledge Management Research and Practice. 2022;**20**(2):320-338

[112] Liao LF. Knowledge-sharing in R&D departments: A social power and social exchange theory perspective. The International Journal of Human Resource Management. 2008;**19**(10):1881-1895

[113] Lee Y, Tao W, Li JYQ, Sun R. Enhancing employees' knowledge sharing through diversity-oriented leadership and strategic internal communication during the COVID-19 outbreak. Journal of Knowledge Management. 2021;**25**(6):1526-1549

[114] Huang Y, Ma Z, Meng Y. High-performance work systems and employee engagement: Empirical evidence from China. Asia-Pacific Journal of Human Resources. 2018;**56**(3):341-359

[115] Kang YJ, Lee JY, Kim HW. A psychological empowerment approach to online knowledge sharing. Computers in Human Behavior. 2017;**74**:175-187

[116] Xiao J, Bao Y, Wang J, Yu H, Ma Z, Jing L. Knowledge sharing in R&D teams: An evolutionary game model. Sustainability. 2021;**13**(12):6664

[117] Wang N, Yin J, Ma Z, Liao M. The influence mechanism of rewards on knowledge sharing behaviors in virtual communities. Journal of Knowledge Management. 2022;**26**(3):485-505

[118] Zhang X, Chen Z, Vogel D, Yuan M, Guo C. Knowledge-sharing reward dynamics in knowledge management systems: Game theory-based empirical validation. Human Factors and Ergonomics In Manufacturing. 2010;**20**(2):103-122

[119] Oubrich M, Hakmaoui A, Benhayoun L, Solberg Söilen K, Abdulkader B. Impacts of leadership style, organizational design and HRM practices on knowledge hiding: The indirect roles of organizational justice and competitive work environment. Journal of Business Research. 2021;**1**(137):488-499

[120] Chowdhury S, Dey P, Joel-Edgar S, Bhattacharya S, Rodriguez-Espindola O, Abadie A, et al. Unlocking the value of artificial intelligence in human resource management through AI capability framework. Human Resource Management Review. 2023 Mar;**33**(1):100899

[121] Abukhait RM, Bani-Melhem S, Zeffane R. Empowerment, knowledge sharing and innovative behaviours: Exploring gender differences. International Journal of Innovation Management. 2019;**23**(01):1950006

[122] Eagly AH, Wood W. Social role theory. In: Handbook of Theories of Social Psychology. United Kingdom: SAGE Publications Ltd; 2011. pp. 458-476

[123] Diekman AB, Eagly AH. Stereotypes as dynamic constructs: Women and

men of the past, present, and future. Personality and Social Psychology Bulletin. 2000;**26**(10):1171-1188

[124] Andreeva T, Zappa P. Whose lips are sealed? Gender differences in knowledge hiding at work. Journal of Occupational and Organizational Psychology. 2023;**96**(4):828-855

[125] Bourdieu P. The forms of capital. In: Richardson JG, editor. Handbook of Theory and Research for the Sociology of Education. New York: Greenwood Press; 1985. pp. 241-258

[126] Yin J, Ma Z, Yu H, Jia M, Liao G. Transformational leadership and employee knowledge sharing: Explore the mediating roles of psychological safety and team efficacy. Journal of Knowledge Management. 2020;**24**(2):150-171

Chapter 7

Environmental Challenges in SMEs through KM Prism

Albena Vutsova and Martina Arabadzhieva

Abstract

The aim of this chapter is to explore the level of knowledge management (KM) in SMEs within the context of environmental challenges, with a focus on Bulgaria. In today's dynamic economic environment, KM plays a crucial role in ensuring sustainable development and competitiveness, both for corporations and SMEs. Green accents in KM addresses community priorities by integrating environmental considerations into business processes. Ecological KM systems can embed management-level decisions into standard business practices, enabling practical innovations in industrial ecology. This chapter examines the procedures implemented in Bulgarian SMEs and the role of leadership in KM, including the integration of green aspects. The study reveals that some companies are already leveraging ecological problem-solving, thereby creating a strategic resource for their business.

Keywords: knowledge management, ecology, SMEs, environment, ecosystem, green practices

1. Introduction

According Karl Wiig Knowledge Management (KM) is the systematic, explicit, and deliberate construction, renewal, and application of knowledge to maximize an enterprise's knowledge-related effectiveness and the return on its knowledge assets in the European environment [1]. Knowledge Management includes all the tools and methods to collect and manage knowledge related to a company, and eliminate redundancies and knowledge gaps, which can be created when documentation remains separate between company departments. Steffen Raub [2] gives the following definition of KM—"... the set of models and concepts that focus on the strategic importance of knowledge as an organizational resource, as well as the techniques and tools for consciously structuring the processes in the organization related to the development of knowledge"; some researchers argue that knowledge management is a collective effort in which knowledge is used as a key element for the organization, enhancing its sustainability. This is valid both for small and large organizations. Small enterprises often operate with limited resources but are more flexible and innovative. Large companies, on the other hand, possess scale, finances, and better-structured knowledge management systems. Current trends influence all organizations and collaboration between SMEs and corporations can lead to more effective sharing of knowledge, technologies, and best practices. Additionally, small businesses are often part of

 IntechOpen

the supply chains of large companies. The demands of large enterprises for sustainability, digitalization, and innovation could encourage small businesses to adopt new approaches, including knowledge management and SMEs can serve as a bridgehead for piloting new technologies and offering rapid feedback on their effectiveness. Knowledge management practices help organizations adapt to change, enhance sustainability, and maintain a competitive edge, fostering trust and reliability among stakeholders. Knowledge is essential for organizational success, aiding in acquiring, sharing, and using information to improve customer satisfaction and competitiveness. KM process is key to designing new products, managing operations, and achieving sustainable goals. KM is applied differently across companies, depending on their understanding of the process, mission, and strategic approach. This variation could explain the differing paces of competitiveness development, which is particularly evident in small businesses that must operate in a highly dynamic environment.

Modern economies rely on innovative ideas from human intellectual capital, driving sustainability and profitability [3]. Due to the significant reduction in the availability and quality of natural resources, many organizations are transitioning toward eco-friendly practices. Achieving this goal, however, also requires effectively utilizing green knowledge. Knowledge management is a complex process that largely depends on the size of the organization. In multinational companies or large corporate structures, the process is regulated and operates through teams of experts. In medium-sized or small enterprises, however, a specialized approach is required, along with an awareness of the importance of this process and its effective implementation [4]. Applying KM is specifically crucial for small and medium enterprises (SMEs) as well. According to Durst and Evardssonn [5] point out that in SMEs the errors or bad decisions would have more serious consequences compared to bigger companies, the role of the leader is very important as often there is one person managing the firm and KM is very often informal as knowledge is kept in the heads of the employees and there is not enough structure around formally retaining this knowledge in a documented way. From further investigation of the topic the authors Durst et al. [6] conclude that KM becomes even more critical for SMEs in coping with newly arising challenges. The focus on innovation for environmental sustainability has become increasingly significant for corporate decision-makers in recent years [7]. Knowledge management involves processes that organize and leverage a firm's collective knowledge to promote sustainability and adapt to evolving environmental changes [8]. KM process also contributes to green innovation, leading to eco-friendly products, green working places and enhancing corporate social performance. Ultimately, knowledge resources are crucial for sustainable innovation [9]. Environmental knowledge is a critical intangible asset for organizations in today's competitive landscape, encompassing awareness and concern for ecological issues as well as accumulated data and knowledge resources. While its link to organizational performance has been explored, an important topic remains how environmental knowledge and knowledge management processes influence each other over time [10]. KM in small and SMEs is often less researched, as the focus of studies traditionally leans toward large corporations. In big companies, attention is usually directed toward intellectual property protection, technological innovations, and complex knowledge management systems. They also respond more quickly to environmental aspects. In contrast, SMEs often rely on informal and improvised approaches, leaving a gap in academic literature regarding their specific needs and challenges in this area. Given its importance and the necessity for robust research on KM in SMEs [6], this chapter explores how Bulgarian SMEs implement knowledge management practices, with a particular emphasis on integrating environmental knowledge.

2. Theoretical background

The modern global economy is extremely dynamic and changing, with high migration of labor resources, global competition, and constant changes in the business environment and financial situation, including temporary restrictive regimes. Daniel Bell views knowledge as a sociological factor and attempts to forecast societal development through the lens of knowledge. According to him, knowledge is a set of systematized facts and ideas through which conclusions or experimental results are logically justified. These are communicated *via* an appropriate medium and in a specific format. Edith Penrose emphasizes the importance of knowledge for an organization, which she defines as a combination of administrative structure and resources—both human and material. Knowledge is a key role and become an important resource of top quality and competitive advantages. As a result, the modern business organization cannot compete effectively in the market without the availability of highly qualified managers and employees. Vital to the competitiveness of individuals and organizations is to continuously learn and adapt quickly and adequately to changes in their environment; organization's culture also plays a significant role in shaping how performance is achieved [6]. The acquisition of new knowledge, as well as retention and effective use of the available, becomes an essential factor for the development of organizations. That is why knowledge management is considered a major challenge for modern organizations [11]. KM is a critical driver of business growth, particularly in dynamic and unpredictable environments. By generating and utilizing knowledge effectively, firms can avoid failure and enhance profitability, hence improving their performance. The ISO 30401 Knowledge Management Standard is a specific instrument that provides a comprehensive framework for organizations to establish, implement, maintain, and enhance effective knowledge management systems. Organizations thrive by transforming knowledge into sustainable strategic advantages [12]. The use of knowledge has been shown to significantly impact both financial and non-financial performance. These circumstances stimulate companies to pay attention to the most important resource – knowledge. Friedrich Hayek reveals the importance of knowledge for the development of the entrepreneur and his market success. The market transforms the accumulated knowledge into practical skills, and profit serves as an indicator of the efficiency of the process. The generation, storage and management of this specific production factor has proven to be key to the success and improved performance of business organizations [13].

Three main KM goals can be distinguished: normative, operational, and strategic: normative goals are aimed at the vision of the organization and have an impact on its structuring, culture, and policy; strategic goals are the long-term intentions of the organization regarding future development; operational goals which concern specific management processes—what knowledge is needed for the successful implementation of each individual working process, what skills individual workers must possess and what training they must undergo.

To the extent that modern concepts of knowledge management are explicitly linked to the enhancement of innovation, sustainability, and informed decision-making, this process can be correlated with or viewed as inherently connected to data management. Data, in and of itself, does not constitute knowledge but can easily be transformed into it through analytical actions. Data can be considered the foundation for knowledge, and the process of managing data can be analyzed to determine how it should be handled to achieve specific objectives, particularly in a competitive environment. KM practices related to data management would have a significant influence on an organization's performance. Characteristics, such as being flexible and disposing of adaptive capacity, can make decision-making in SMEs shorter and faster, which can help them to be far more attuned to survival in a world that is subject to increasing number of significant economic shocks or crises as SMEs are used to dealing with uncertainty Durst et al. [6]. As SMEs become more knowledge-intensive, knowledge has become a key factor driving their long-term success. Managing knowledge is essential for SMEs, as it enables them to effectively leverage their most valuable resource [14]. Research indicates that the implementation of KM is predominantly associated with large companies, followed by SMEs [15]. SMEs face unique knowledge KM challenges that differ significantly from those encountered by corporations.

The vital role of SMEs in driving economic growth is extensively studied and acknowledged in academic circles. Over 99% of European businesses are SMEs, employing more than 85 million citizens across the continent. These businesses are key drivers of innovation and entrepreneurship, with the ideas and solutions of 24.3 million entrepreneurs playing a vital role in fostering a sustainable and digital economy. The highest concentration of SMEs in Europe can be found across various key sectors, mainly architecture and engineering; automotive; chemicals; construction; electronic communications networks and services; energy; food and beverages; hotels and accommodation; industrial machinery; pharma; fashion; public transport; waste management [16]. Unlike large firms, KM practices cannot be directly transferred to SMEs due to their distinct characteristics, such as limited resources, informality, and greater flexibility. Existing research highlights that many SMEs lack a strategic approach to KM and instead focus on operational-level solutions. Furthermore, the heterogeneity within SMEs—ranging from micro to medium-sized enterprises—suggests that a single KM approach cannot effectively address the needs of all SMEs [6].

Miklosik et al. [15] support previous findings that the communication of KM-related values to stakeholders and the public is closely linked to company size. It is essential for organizations to convey their commitment to fostering a knowledge-sharing culture and actively promoting knowledge exchange and transfer. This research confirms significant differences in how large companies and SMEs communicate KM-related topics with the general public. While a few exceptions exist, SMEs generally do not include information about knowledge generation, sharing, or KM in the online resources accessible via their websites. However, this does not necessarily mean that SMEs have neglected KM. The lack of information may stem from their focus on core business operations and growth during specific stages of the company lifecycle [15] or from trying to keep their competitive advantages within the organization to ensure enhanced performance.

KM plays a critical role in helping SMEs address challenges like limited qualified human resources by enhancing strategic participation and streamlining operations. KM fosters knowledge growth, enabling firms to explore long-term opportunities, refine strategies, and improve sustainability. Through processes such as capturing, storing, sharing knowledge, and generating ideas, KM links updated information to enhance performance, prevent mistakes, and promote eco-innovation for sustainable SME operations [16]. For SMEs, knowledge management differs from that of large organizations. It is most valuable when SMEs can apply knowledge in a practical and accessible way to achieve strategic goals like higher profits or improved efficiency. Since knowledge is created, shared, and applied by people, SMEs must focus on managing knowledge in a human-centered way, relying more on the tacit knowledge of employees than on complex databases or advanced technologies [14].

KM has gained significant traction in recent years, becoming a key component in strategy development, and operational efficiency as well as enhancing customer satisfaction [12]. Leveraging environmental knowledge can positively influence public perception. Such knowledge benefits both companies and customers, leading to mutually advantageous outcomes, according to Martínez-Martínez et al. [10] and their research in the hospitality industry. A KM approach should encompass not only explicit knowledge, which is pre-defined based on a company's strategy but also tacit components. In dynamic client relationships, flexibility and the ability to learn from experience are crucial. This is where a trial-and-error approach becomes valuable, allowing KM practices to adapt to changing market needs and contingent situations. Although emergent by nature, companies should find ways to cultivate KM practices through daily business activities, helping employees grow and refine them. Executives play a critical role in developing the competencies needed to identify emerging KM needs and integrate them into the organization's established processes [17]. Hermawati and Gunawan [18] claim that SMEs must adapt to external changes by fostering knowledge through continuous learning. This highlights that learning plays a crucial role in all dynamic capability processes, enabling businesses to effectively navigate and thrive in a rapidly evolving environment.

To improve sustainability performance, companies must inbuild sustainability into their overall vision and understand how to incorporate it effectively. This includes turning broad sustainability goals into specific practices for different areas of operation and then measuring progress through key performance indicators. Knowledge plays a crucial role in this process, as organizations need to transform tacit knowledge, such as beliefs and mental models, into explicit knowledge to foster innovation. By understanding the impact of intangible assets on knowledge management, SMEs can enhance their ability to thrive in a knowledge-driven economy and achieve sustainable growth, especially in countries in Eastern Europe [19].

KM serves as an innovation strategy that helps organizations implement sustainability initiatives, building awareness and incorporating sustainable practices into operations. KM processes, such as discovering, capturing, sharing, and applying knowledge, drive creativity and innovation, facilitating the transformation of strategies and operations. Employees are essential in creating and selecting relevant knowledge for sustainable practices, and by fostering commitment, organizations can support knowledge capture, allowing tacit and explicit knowledge to interact and lead to innovation. Sharing knowledge ensures that valuable insights are not lost, supporting continuous improvement and driving sustainable development [20]. In short, research indicates that implementing KM practices can significantly enhance the performance of SMEs.

As environmental challenges escalate, the importance of sustainable practices is gaining widespread recognition among businesses and individuals. Green knowledge management has become a key strategy, combining ecological awareness with informed decision-making. This approach transforms how organizations handle knowledge, information, and innovation, driving sustainability and promoting environmental responsibility. Effective KM systems improve organizational performance, and in response to growing ecological challenges, forward-thinking companies are expanding KM to address environmental concerns [12]. Green innovations enhance sustainability and provide SMEs with a competitive edge. Key knowledge management dimensions—acquisition, dissemination, and responsiveness—play a critical role in fostering green innovation, as highlighted by Polas et al. [7] and Khan et al. [12]. These practices support corporate sustainability goals by addressing organizational adaptability and maturity in a dynamic environment.

To meet market demands, companies must be creative and innovative, offering high-quality products in the most efficient way. Adopting sustainability practices can also improve a firm's reputation, leading to increased sales and better financial performance. Therefore, SMEs can leverage sustainability as a growth strategy. As customers become more aware of the negative impacts of industry activities, they are likely to expect more sustainable practices from businesses [20], including SMEs.

KM is essential for implementing green innovations, with top SME managers who prioritize environmental awareness more likely to leverage government incentives, explore market opportunities, and invest in green technologies [7]. Proper KM fosters collaboration and drives environmental initiatives, although many firms struggle to fully understand and implement effective green innovation practices. While creating environmental knowledge is essential for competitiveness, it alone cannot sustain an advantage. Its development relies on previously established environmental knowledge and the implementation of a knowledge management program, which helps individuals refine their focus on key organizational and customer issues, enabling better use of prior knowledge [10].

The research of Alfarizi and Sari [21] concludes that green knowledge management has a significant positive impact on the performance of micro and SMEs in the culinary sector in Indonesia. The authors confirm that it enables these businesses to adopt environmentally friendly practices, innovate, meet tax requirements, incorporate corporate social responsibility, and enhance their digital capabilities. By integrating these elements, enterprises can reduce waste, conserve resources, and promote sustainability while improving their efficiency and competitiveness. This emphasizes the vital role of green knowledge management in fostering sustainable development within the industry. It impacts SMEs in environmental, economic, social, and strategic dimensions, including fostering partnerships and collaborations with like-minded businesses to share resources and information [22] thus having positive influence on their performance.

The role of leadership in connection to KM is of profound significance. The values of the leader have direct impact on the applied practices in the firm and on the organizational culture, especially considering smaller companies and the attitude toward knowledge sharing and applying. Firmansyah et al. [23] prove that transformational leadership and KM have positive influence on organizational learning and organizational performance. Leaders can leverage data to gain deeper insights into which intangible resources are most critical for SMEs to navigate competitive and turbulent times, which suggest that combining intangible resources with strategic knowledge management initiatives is essential for optimizing the use of limited resources and respecting sustainable practices.

With regard to organizational culture, it creates an interaction environment through the value derived from knowledge is defined. Organizational culture determines how knowledge will be used in a certain situation. This is achieved by the rules, expectations and punishments defined, which guide social interactions between individuals and groups. Based on the rules, the team adopts a way of thinking about what is acceptable for the organization. For example, organizations in which it is not accepted to share lessons learned between different departments or between participants in different projects, even if technology allows it to be done. In this way, the organization loses additional value derived from knowledge [4].

In terms of KM processes and tools in SMEs there are various analyses. However, cloud computing is increasingly recognized as a valuable tool to support an organization's overall KM efforts, facilitating efficient collaboration, information sharing, and data storage across teams and departments [24]. The transition toward a circular economy for European SMEs is a key focus on the European agenda. With the transition to a market economy, many non-eco-friendly production facilities were shut down, and in their place, small businesses, particularly in the service sector, emerged. This shift has made it somewhat easier to absorb and adapt to environmental aspects. The environmental impact of SMEs is a critical theme that is gaining prominence and being increasingly integrated into the economic development of both industrial and service sectors. SMEs are a key pillar in driving the transition from a linear to a circular economic model. However, findings reveal several major barriers hindering this shift, one of which is knowledge [16].

To put the research in context analyzing environmental challenges in Bulgarian SMEs through the lens of knowledge management is relevant as it reflects issues faced by SMEs in other economies undergoing growth and structural changes. SMEs play a significant role in Bulgaria's non-financial business economy, which is very service oriented. In recent years, there has been a growing interest in innovative and sustainable activities, particularly in fields such as information technology, green technologies, and industrial production. Most Bulgarian SMEs are micro-enterprises (with up to 10 employees), which represent a significant share of the country's economy. Small enterprises (with up to 50 employees) and medium-sized enterprises (with up to 250 employees) also play an important role, particularly in manufacturing and export-oriented sectors. The life cycle of Bulgarian SMEs varies, with the average market duration being relatively short—between 5 and 10 years. In 2023, four NACE sectors experienced a decline in employment: mining and quarrying, water supply, sewerage, waste management, and remediation activities; transportation and storage; and administrative and support services [25]. However, historically, more than half of the SMEs in Bulgaria have been interested in ecological practices [26]. While there is research acknowledging that green knowledge management has a significant direct effect on corporate environmental performance [27], there is considerably less for SMEs.

In Bulgaria, SMEs contributed to 75.7% of total employment and 65.3% of the value added to the economy in recent years. They are of great importance for the growth and competitiveness of the European and Bulgarian economies. SMEs are a source of innovative solutions in response to the challenges related to the green economy and the efficient use of resources. The SME strategy 2021–2027 is based on three pillars, and the first pillar concerns sustainable development. Achieving these aims needs proper KM.

Key factors for the competitiveness of SMEs are access to markets, access to finance, the use of ICT solutions and digitalization of processes, the availability of qualified personnel, and the efficient, environmentally friendly use of resources. Some of the factors for the creation and growth of SMEs are related to the availability of information and knowledge, as well as the use of innovative technologies at the global and local levels. By implementing KM in an adequate way, SMEs are able to focus their efforts on adapting green innovations from the EU, especially by providing support systems for innovation and technology. An effective way to improve access to them is to participate in value chain associations, including clusters of enterprises, cooperatives, and production associations.

A review of the literature reveals that while there are numerous studies on KM, the majority focus on corporations, with significantly fewer addressing SMEs. The latter is particularly important since SMEs form the backbone of transition economies. Even fewer studies examine KM at a national level in Eastern Europe, including the role of leadership in implementing these approaches. In this context, green KM practices adopted by SMEs remain largely underexplored.

The aim of this study is to analyze the extent to which SMEs in Bulgaria have adopted KM practices, with a specific focus on the integration of environmental knowledge management. The research seeks to investigate whether these SMEs utilize KM to enhance sustainability and improve overall operational performance as a whole and in the context of environmental challenges.

To address this research gap to a certain extent, we have formulated two key research questions for analysis:

Does the implementation of KM practices in Bulgarian SMEs enhance organizational performance?

Do SMEs in Bulgaria address environmental challenges by integrating green practices into their KM processes?

By exploring how KM can drive sustainability in Bulgaria, this research also offers valuable insights and strategies applicable to SMEs in other regions navigating the green transition.

3. Methods

A mixed approach was adopted – qualitative and quantitative techniques in order to assess the impact of KM, with particular emphasis on its environmental dimension, in SMEs. A descriptive-analytical research method was applied to identify the main characteristics and the role of KM. This study applies a set of approaches – review of research works and national and European documents and statements; a qualitative research methodology was employed, including in-depth interviews with representatives from SMEs in Bulgaria, to gain insights into KM practices of SMEs, particularly in relation to environmental issues and challenges. The range of respondents, subject to in-depth interviews, is a mix of companies in the high-tech and consulting services, generic ones, and those in the manufacturing sector. They have been selected from targeted business associations and on the basis of preliminary elaborated criteria. The main criteria focus on any type of application related to KM, whether the enterprises provide relevant training, and whether they adhere to ecological standards. The share of interviewed companies in the service sector is higher due to the fact that they address the defined criteria. In addition, the national economy is more strongly oriented toward the service sector than toward those in manufacturing.

The data collected from these interviews was analyzed to conduct a comparative study across the various sectors mentioned above. Key aspects of the study included assessing whether SMEs are familiar with the concept of KM and whether they actively apply KM strategies in their operations. It also explored the most common KM practices incorporated into business processes and whether there is a conscious effort to focus on environmental concerns. The study further investigated the attitudes and perspectives of business leaders toward KM and environmental issues, analyzing their leadership approach to fostering a culture of sustainability. Additionally, it examined the transfer of knowledge within these organizations, exploring how knowledge flows between employees and departments and how this affects the implementation of sustainable practices. By analyzing these elements, the study aimed to offer a comprehensive understanding of how SMEs in Bulgaria approach knowledge management and environmental sustainability, with a particular focus on practices and the challenges they face in integrating environmental considerations into their business strategies. Some of the respondents successfully apply data management as well *via* different tools.

4. Results

In-depth interviews were conducted with 14 SMEs in Bulgaria, representing various sectors such as high-tech and consulting services, manufacturing, construction, and tourism. The majority of these companies operate in the high-tech and consulting services sector. All interviewed firms demonstrated awareness of and engagement with knowledge management (KM), applying it in different ways. While a small percentage of the companies implement KM informally, the rest undertake more structured and targeted KM activities.

All respondents recognize KM as a source of competitive advantage and a driver of organizational efficiency, particularly in today's rapidly changing business environment. KM practices are applied at multiple levels—individual, team, and organizational. Although none of the companies have a standalone KM strategy, key strategic elements are integrated into their missions and visions. Only one company reported the existence of a regulatory framework for KM, while for the others, KM remains a voluntary activity (**Figure 1**).

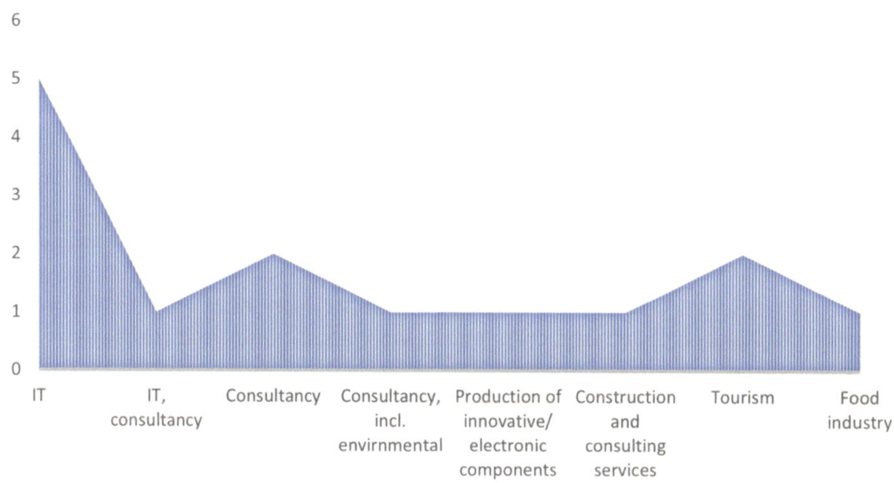

Figure 1.
Propensity for adopting green practices by sector.

To identify key knowledge, companies employ a wide range of traditional methods. The most common approaches include training (internal and/or through external training providers), sharing best practices among employees *via* various channels, and, in certain cases, utilizing external sources. Significant emphasis is placed on feedback from customers or cluster structures, which often leads to the redesign of existing practices. Mentorship is applied by a smaller proportion of firms—approximately one-quarter—though many respondents regard it as a beneficial practice.

Over 50% of respondents noted that their companies participate in various events that contribute to improving the KM process. Frequently, companies draw on information from previously successful projects and exchange knowledge with partner organizations.

In terms of KM focus, efforts are directed toward the dissemination of pre-selected information, enriched with context to enhance its utility. Most companies, particularly in the high-tech services sector, are hesitant to establish networks for sharing certain types of knowledge, likely due to concerns related to potential intellectual property rights issues. Knowledge transfer in these companies often follows a horizontal principle. One-third of the firms view the development of new knowledge as essential. All technological and consulting firms incorporate data management principles as part of their KM practices.

Knowledge sharing among all respondents occurs through targeted meetings, online consultations, and other channels, with no reported barriers to knowledge transfer within the companies. Leadership actively encourages knowledge sharing by organizing targeted events and fostering an open culture of professional exchange. Two-thirds of respondents confirmed the existence of specialized KM training programs in their organizations, while one-quarter reported having mentorship programs. Nearly half of the firms' managers identified KM as a critical factor in improving their overall business performance. All of the above confirms that SMEs value highly knowledge and KM and expect the latter to have a positive impact on their organizational performance, which confirms that KM practices are expected to improve organizational performance regarding the first research question.

All interviewed company managers acknowledge the importance of KM, even though it is not always formalized. They actively promote KM processes and report no barriers to its implementation. Most managers contribute to creating an environment conducive to knowledge sharing and targeted exchanges. The engagement of the leaders demonstrates this approach.

Based on the responses, an attempt was made to analyze the peer effect. Over 80% of the companies have teams whose leadership is comparable in terms of age range, professional experience, and cultural characteristics. A comparison among these companies revealed tendencies such as adherence to environmental regulations and practices, responsiveness to new trends, and subsequent employee training. This trend could reflect generational perspectives that influence the acceptance or rejection of specific policies (**Figure 2**).

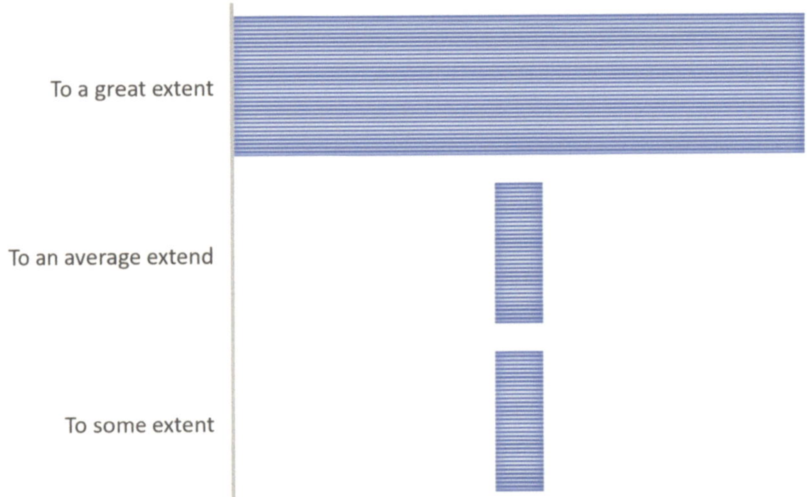

Figure 2.
Degree of KM Implementation.

SMEs often operate in highly competitive sectors where knowledge and information can be decisive assets. KM enables these companies to stand out from competitors by leveraging specific expertise and know-how. It also helps them deliver products and services that meet the rapidly changing needs of markets and customers. Operating in such a competitive environment, SMEs—particularly those in the consulting and ICT sectors—tend to have a well-established ability to adapt quickly. This agility is further facilitated by their lack of rigid organizational structures, making it easier for them to respond effectively to change. In addition to answering the first research question, it might be added that KM appears more crucial for enterprises in more competitive sectors.

Half of the interviewed companies implement some type of green practices, although only two are specifically focused on activities with a clear emphasis on „environmental protection". The broader implementation of green practices, in the wider sense of the term, is an inherent part of knowledge management in the environmental domain. This includes employee training, mentorship, and the sharing of specific knowledge (**Figure 3**).

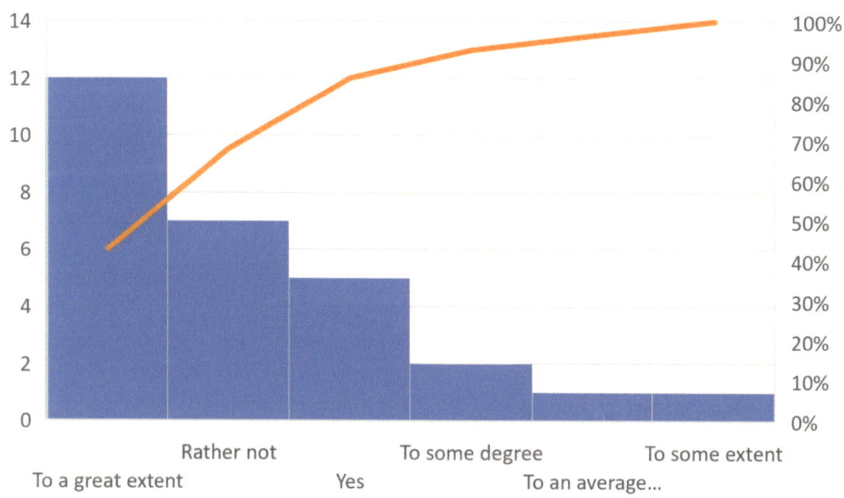

Figure 3.
Implementation of KM, including environmental aspects.

SMEs in Bulgaria are open to adopting green economy practices, which addresses the second research question. On the one hand, at the start of the transition to a market economy, many state-owned enterprises were shut down due to their highly polluting activities. This created space for the emergence of smaller, more agile companies, which were naturally less reliant on environmentally harmful processes. As a result, these new SMEs were more inclined toward sustainable practices from the outset. On the other hand, the orientation toward green policies may also stem from the availability of financial support through national and European funding instruments, which encourage sustainable development. Additionally, adopting environmentally friendly practices helps SMEs improve their public image, making them more attractive to customers, partners, and investors who value sustainability.

Some SMEs already apply ecological standards.

The majority of respondents, with the exception of one, did not specifically highlight a connection between environmental knowledge management and training outcomes. Five companies expressed a strong interest in developing activities related to green innovations, which are, to some extent, accompanied by training processes (**Figure 4**).

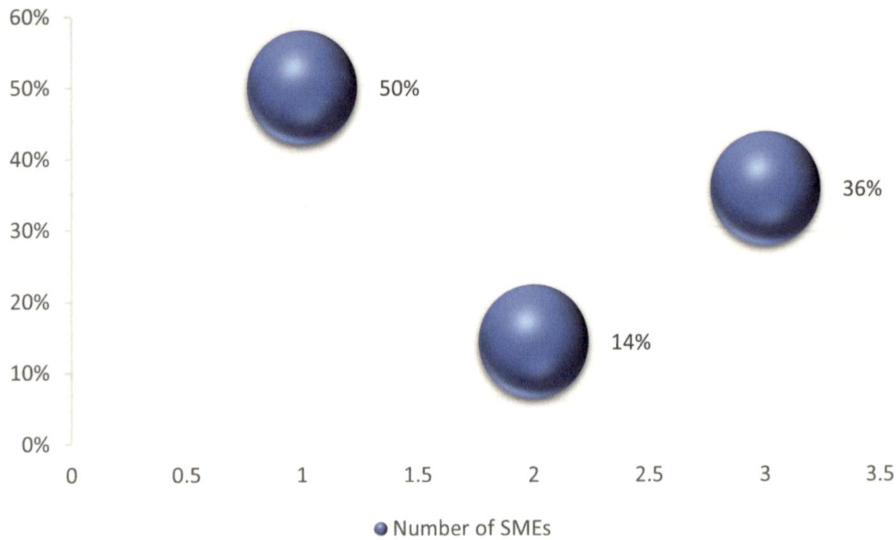

Figure 4.
Percentage of companies utilizing KM in environmental aspects.

Two-thirds of the interviewees are engaged in addressing environmental issues across various fields. Three companies have a noticeable influence in their respective areas of operation, which is further supported by the KM process. SMEs in Bulgaria recognize the importance of green KM and adherence to environmental practices, with a significant number adopting various approaches to integrate sustainability into their operations.

5. Discussion

Based on the conducted interviews, it was found that only some companies use specialized tools for KM, such as Customer Relationship Management (CRM) systems. However, all of them use centralized document storage and platforms for sharing ideas and practices, typically through cloud services. Explicit knowledge is documented, published, and communicated to employees, while tacit knowledge is shared through training sessions, Q&A meetings, and professional forums. When identifying key competencies required to perform activities, knowledge gaps can be pinpointed, and measures are taken to address these issues. While most surveyed enterprises do not report significant barriers to KM or to the sharing of knowledge and practices related to the environment, this may partly stem from a lack of awareness of such activities or untapped opportunities. Bulgarian SMEs are engaging in various KM practices realizing their effect on the overall organizational performance. In almost all of the studied cases leaders strongly support the application of KM, in particular, in highly competitive sectors.

Given the highly dynamic global and regional environmental landscape, often changing for the worse, adapting KM to green production and practices is particularly necessary. Tracking knowledge obsolescence and updating knowledge remains relevant for all companies, regardless of their size, which is shown through the activities of Bulgarian SMEs as well. The redesign of applicable KM practices is most effective when incorporating feedback systems.

The new generation of leaders highly values training programs related to environmental knowledge management offered by universities through relevant programs. KM can help organizations optimize resources and minimize environmental impact by applying ecological principles in industrial processes. Integrating this knowledge into business practices through effective KM methods enhances smaller enterprises' sustainability and competitiveness, at least in a portion of the SMEs in Bulgaria.

Based on the practices in the studied enterprises in order to integrate the knowledge in different processes companies can take a variety of actions, for example:

Facilitating the sharing of innovative ideas and good environmental practices.

Building training and development systems that promote eco-friendly behavior across different organizational levels.

Implementing sustainable strategies into business processes.

Establishing environmentally focused clusters.

Creating networks of stakeholders who share "green practices".

Such integration can help all types of Bulgarian enterprises meet global sustainability requirements while simultaneously improving efficiency and social responsibility.

Leadership and a relevant KM culture are key for the studied SMEs to successfully address environmental challenges. Leaders play a crucial role in setting sustainable goals and implementing KM strategies focused on achieving environmental outcomes. By fostering a culture of collaboration, continuous learning, and innovation, these SMEs ensure the effective sharing and application of environmental knowledge within the organization. Furthermore, leaders can encourage employees to actively contribute to sustainability efforts by promoting transparency and accountability for environmental initiatives. Through these actions, SMEs can build resilient and adaptable businesses capable of meeting the new challenges of environmental responsibility.

Alongside expressed expectations for economic benefits from adopting "green" business practices and positive attitude toward "green activities", SMEs in Bulgaria face some challenges and difficulties in transitioning to sustainable operations. These challenges include: changing corporate culture and understanding the essence of "green" business; the technical complexity, administrative and financial burdens, associated with implementing environmental protection initiatives; leveraging the country's scientific potential for the adoption of "green" innovations; managing and motivating employees in this direction; low awareness among consumers and the public; and effectively communicating "green" initiatives.

To address these challenges, a combination of measures is needed. These should include education on the principles of "green" business management and technologies, systematic efforts to raise awareness about the benefits of transitioning to sustainable practices within companies, and the introduction of targeted financial incentives – direct and indirect – at the national level. Such measures aim to reduce the difficulties faced by SMEs in implementing and developing green technologies [28].

6. Conclusion

KM is a steady element of the majority of national SMEs. They demonstrate a clear interest in knowledge acquisition and knowledge management as a basis of key competencies and further competitiveness.

KM enhances productivity, minimizes knowledge gaps, and fosters environmental innovation, supporting SMEs in adopting more sustainable practices. SMEs are increasingly engaged in the KM process, recognizing its importance for their efficiency and competitiveness. By integrating sustainable practices, SMEs become more flexible and capable of adapting to new market demands and identifying new market niches. Additionally, these enterprises are becoming more aware of the need for green production and innovation, actively accumulating the necessary knowledge and preparing the required human resources.

Knowledge sharing is a core activity for SMEs. Since they operate with smaller production volumes and workforce sizes, they are compelled to be more agile and open to new ideas and initiatives. SMEs utilize diverse communication channels and adopt a culture of openness toward sustainability and green innovation more rapidly. Their specific characteristics, including a lack of rigidity, allow them to respond quickly to emerging trends.

Leaders in SMEs play a pivotal role in implementing these processes. They actively contribute to creating an environment where knowledge-sharing and sustainable practices can be adopted and further developed.

Measuring sustainable development within an environmental context positively impacts business performance by enabling systematic monitoring of progress and results from implemented sustainable practices. By applying KM approaches, SMEs not only increase their productivity and minimize risks but also foster environmental innovations that promote more sustainable and efficient production methods.

KM, including its green dimension, is increasingly recognized as a strategic resource for SMEs. It serves as a cornerstone for driving innovation, enhancing competitiveness, and ensuring long-term sustainability. Green KM, in particular, helps SMEs integrate environmentally friendly practices into their operations, aligning business goals with ecological responsibility. Moreover, effective KM facilitates organizational and process development by improving decision-making, fostering collaboration, and enabling the efficient use of resources. In addition, it catalyzes them to raise their adaptability to the fast-changing economic media and to implement sustained practices.

Future research in the field of KM, with a focus on environmental sustainability, could benefit from exploring the specific dynamics of micro-enterprises in the smart industry by applying a similar approach as the current study. Another potential area of interest is studying the influence of small and medium-sized subsidiaries applying KM practices on their parent companies or across SME networks.

Acknowledgements

This work is supported by the TWIN4ECO project (# BG-RRP-2.005-0001), financed by the European Union – NextGeneration EU.

Author details

Albena Vutsova and Martina Arabadzhieva*
Sofia University, "St. Kl. Ohridski", Sofia, Bulgaria

*Address all correspondence to: m.arabadzhieva@feb.uni-sofia.bg

References

[127] Wiig KM. Knowledge management: Where did it come from and where will it go? Expert Systems with Applications. 1997;**13**(1):1-14

[128] Raub S, Rüling CC. The knowledge management tussle—Speech communities and rhetorical strategies in the development of knowledge management. Journal of Information Technology. 2001;**16**(2):113-130

[129] Ilieva V. Economic effects of the introduction and implementation of European ESG standards for corporate sustainability reporting. ISA. 2024;**30**(2):61-71

[130] Galabova L. Knowledge Management Intellectual Capital [Internet]. 2022. Available from: https://arrow.tudublin.ie/eutpressbooks/1

[131] Durst S, Edvardsson IR. Knowledge management in SMEs: A literature review. Journal of Knowledge Management. 2012;**16**(6):879-903

[132] Durst S, Edvardsson IR, Foli S. Knowledge management in SMEs: A follow-up literature review. Journal of Knowledge Management. 2023;**27**(11):25-58

[133] Polas MRH, Tabash MI, Bhattacharjee A, Dávila GA. Knowledge management practices and green innovation in SMES: The role of environmental awareness towards environmental sustainability. International Journal of Organizational Analysis. 2021;**31**(5):1601-1622

[134] Fakhar Manesh M, Pellegrini MM, Marzi G, Dabic M. Knowledge management in the fourth industrial revolution: Mapping the literature and scoping future avenues. IEEE Transactions on Engineering Management. 2021;**68**(1):289-300

[135] Shahzad M, Qu Y, Zafar AU, Rehman SU, Islam T. Exploring the influence of knowledge management process on corporate sustainable performance through green innovation. Journal of Knowledge Management. 2020;**24**(9):2079-2106

[136] Martínez-Martínez A, Cegarra-Navarro JG, García-Pérez A. Environmental knowledge management: A long-term enabler of tourism development. Tourism Management. 2015;**50**:281-291

[137] Gourova E, Antonova A, Nikolov R. Knowledge Management. 2012. Available from: https://www.academia.edu/25220854/%D0%A3%D0%BF%D1%80%D0%B0%D0%B2%D0%BB%D0%B5%D0%BD%D0%B8%D0%B5_%D0%BD%D0%B0_%D0%B7%D0%BD%D0%B0%D0%BD%D0%B8%D1%8F

[138] Khan AN, Mehmood K, Kwan HK. Green knowledge management: A key driver of green technology innovation and sustainable performance in the construction organizations. Journal of Innovation and Knowledge [Internet]. 2024;**9**(1). Available from: http://www.elsevier.es/en-revista-journal-innovation-knowledge-376-articulo-green-knowledge-management-a-key-S2444569X23001506

[139] Mitov E. Management of Organizational Knowledge. 1st ed. Sofia: Zvezdi; 2017

[140] Manville G, Karakas F, Polkinghorne M, Petford N. Supporting open innovation with the use of a

balanced scorecard approach: A study on deep smarts and effective knowledge transfer to SMEs. Production Planning & Control. 2019;**30**(10-12):842-853

[141] Miklosik A, Evans N, Hasprova M, Lipianska J. Reflection of embedded knowledge culture in communications of Australian companies. Knowledge Management Research & Practice. 2019;**17**(2):172-181

[142] Marino A, Pariso P. The transition towards to the circular economy: European SMEs' trajectories. Entrepreneurship and Sustainability Issues. 2021;**8**(4):431-455

[143] Bolisani E, Scarso E, Giuman L. Knowledge management in client–supplier relationship: Emergent vs deliberate approach in small KIBS. Knowledge Management Research & Practice. 2016;**14**(2):178-185

[144] Hermawati A, Gunawan E. The implementation of dynamic capabilities for small and medium-sized enterprises in creating innovation. VINE Journal of Information and Knowledge Management Systems. 2021;**51**(1):92-108

[145] Petrov V, Ćelić Đ, Uzelac Z, Drašković Z. Three pillars of knowledge management in SMEs: Evidence from Serbia. The International Entrepreneurship and Management Journal. 2020;**16**(2):417-438

[146] López-Torres GC, Garza-Reyes JA, Maldonado-Guzmán G, Kumar V, Rocha-Lona L, Cherrafi A. Knowledge management for sustainability in operations. Production Planning & Control. 2019;**30**(10-12):813-826

[147] Alfarizi M, Sari RK. Interconnection of green knowledge management and sustainable business capabilities: An investigation of the culinary MSME sector in the food waste emergency zone of Indonesia. IOP Conference Series: Earth and Environmental Science. 2024;**1324**(1):012072. DOI: 10.1088/1755-1315/1324/1/012072

[148] Shah R, Hussain RY, Irshad H. Green knowledge management for SMEs with an emphasis on human resource. In: Iqbal S, Khalid K, Nur AC, editors. Advances in Human Resources Management and Organizational Development [Internet]. IGI Global; 2024. pp. 1-21. Available from: https://services.igi-global.com/resolvedoi/resolve.aspx?doi=10.4018/979-8-3693-0972-8.ch001

[149] Firmansyah A, Chen MH, IWR J, Arwani M, Kistyanto A. The role of transformational leadership and knowledge management and learning organization on vocational schools performance during digital era. Frontiers in Psychology. 2022;**13**. Available from: https://www.frontiersin.org/journals/psychology/articles/10.3389/fpsyg.2022.895341/full

[150] Saratchandra M, Shrestha A. The role of cloud computing in knowledge management for small and medium enterprises: A systematic literature review. Journal of Knowledge Management. 2022;**26**(10):2668-2698

[151] SME Performance Review 2024—Bulgaria Country Sheet [Internet]. European Commission; 2024. Available from: https://ec.europa.eu/docsroom/documents/60556

[152] CITYBUILD.BG [Internet]. 59% of Small and Medium Businesses are Interested in Environmental Practices. 2014. Available from: https://citybuild.bg/news/malkiia-sreden-biznes-interesuva

[153] Sahoo S, Kumar A, Upadhyay A. How do green knowledge management

and green technology innovation impact corporate environmental performance? Understanding the role of green knowledge acquisition. Business Strategy and the Environment. 2023;**32**(1):551-569

[154] Vasileva E, Hristova-Pesheva Y, Ivanova D. Възможности и предизвикателства пред МСП за "зелено" управление [Vazmozhnosti i predizvikatelstva pred MSP za "zeleno" upravlenie]. Vol. 5. 2018. Available from: https://unwe-research-papers.org/bg/journalissues/article/10032